The 13th IAAF World Athletics Championships

Daegu, Korea 27 August - 4 September 2011

Complete Results & Athletes Reference

Silverthorn Press

Simon Barclay

2011 edition
© 2011 by Simon Barclay. All rights reserved

ISBN 978-1-4709-4779-8

World Athletics Championships 2011 - Daegu

Contents   Page

World Athletics Championships

Championship	Year	Dates	Host Nation	Countries	Athletes
1st	1983	7 - 14 August	Helsinki, Finland	153	1355
2nd	1987	28 August - 6 September	Rome, Italy	159	1451
3rd	1991	23 August - 1 September	Tokyo, Japan	167	1517
4th	1993	13 - 22 August	Stuttgart, Germany	187	1689
5th	1995	5 - 13 August	Gothenburg, Sweden	191	1804
6th	1997	1 - 10 August	Athens, Greece	198	1882
7th	1999	20 - 29 August	Seville, Spain	201	1821
8th	2001	3 - 12 August	Edmonton, Canada	189	1677
9th	2003	23 - 31 August	Paris, France	198	1679
10th	2005	6 - 14 August	Helsinki, Finland	191	1688
11th	2007	25 August - 2 September	Osaka, Japan	197	1800
12th	2009	15 - 23 August	Berlin, Germany	202	1984
13th	2011	27 August - 4 September	Daegu, South Korea	202	1848

Records at the start of the Championships - MEN

Event	World Record	Mark	Year	Championship Record	Mark	Year
100m	Usain Bolt (Jamaica)	9.58	2009	Usain Bolt (Jamaica)	9.58	2009
200m	Usain Bolt (Jamaica)	19.19	2009	Usain Bolt (Jamaica)	19.19	2009
400m	Michael Johnson (United States)	43.18	1999	Michael Johnson (United States)	43.18	1999
800m	David Rudisha (Kenya)	1:41.01	2010	Billy Konchellah (Kenya)	1:43.06	1987
1500m	Hicham El Guerrouj (Morocco)	3:26.00	1998	Hicham El Guerrouj (Morocco)	3:27.65	1999
5000m	Kenenisa Bekele (Ethiopia)	12:37.35	2004	Eliud Kipchoge (Ethiopia)	12.52.79	2003
10000m	Kenenisa Bekele (Ethiopia)	26:17.53	2005	Kenenisa Bekele (Ethiopia)	26:46.31	2009
Marathon	Haile Gebrselassie (Ethiopia)	2:03:38	2008	Abel Kirui (Kenya)	2:06.54	2009
3000m Steeplechase	Saif Saaeed Shaheen (Qatar)	7:53.63	2004	Ezekiel Kemboi (Kenya)	8:00.43	2009
110m Hurdles	Dayron Robles (Cuba)	12.87	2008	Colin Jackson (Great Britain)	12.91	1993
400m Hurdles	Kevin Young (United States)	46.78	1992	Kevin Young (United States)	47.18	1993
High Jump	Javier Sotomayor (Cuba)	2.45	1993	Javier Sotomayor (Cuba)	2.40	1993
Pole Vault	Sergey Bubka (Ukraine)	6.14	1994	Dmitri Markov (Australia)	6.05	2001
Long Jump	Mike Powell (United States)	8.95	1991	Mike Powell (United States)	8.95	1991
Triple Jump	Jonathan Edwards (Great Britain)	18.29	1995	Jonathan Edwards (Great Britain)	18.29	1995
Shot Put	Randy Barnes (United States)	23.12	1990	Werner Günthör (Switzerland)	22.23	1987
Discus	Jürgen Schult (East Germany)	74.08	1986	Virgilijus Alekna (Lithuania)	70.17	2005
Hammer	Yuriy Sedykh (Soviet Union)	86.74	1986	Ivan Tsikhan (Belarus)	83.89	2005
Javelin	Jan Železný (Czech Republic)	98.48	1996	Jan Železný (Czech Republic)	92.80	2001
Decathlon	Roman Šebrle (Czech Republic)	9026	2001	Tomáš Dvořák (Czech Republic)	8902	2001
20km Walk	Vladimir Kanaykin (Russia)	1:17:16	2007	Jefferson Pérez (Ecuador)	1:17:21	2003
50km Walk	Denis Nizhegorodov (Russia)	3:34:14	2008	Robert Korzeniowski (Poland)	3:36:03	2003
4x100 Relay	Jamaica	37.10	2008	Jamaica	37.31	2009
4x400 Relay	United States	2:54.29	1993	United States	2:54.29	1993

Records at the start of the Championships - WOMEN

Event	World Record	Mark	Year	Championship Record	Mark	Year
100m	Florence Griffith Joyner (United States)	10.49	1988	Marion Jones (United States)	10.70	1999
200m	Florence Griffith Joyner (United States)	21.34	1988	Silke Gladisch-Möller (East Germany)	21.74	1987
400m	Marita Koch (East Germany)	47.60	1985	Jarmila Kratochvílová (Czechoslovakia)	47.99	1983
800m	Jarmila Kratochvílová (Czechoslovakia)	1:53.28	1983	Jarmila Kratochvílová (Czechoslovakia)	1:54.68	1983
1500m	Qu Yunxia (China)	3:50.46	1993	Tatyana Tomashova (Russia)	3:58.52	2003
5000m	Tirunesh Dibaba (Ethiopia)	14:11.15	2008	Tirunesh Dibaba (Ethiopia)	14:38.59	2005
10000m	Wang Junxia (China)	29:31.78	1993	Berhane Adere (Ethiopia)	30:04.18	2003
Marathon	Paula Radcliffe (Great Britain)	2:15:25	2003	Paula Radcliffe (Great Britain)	2:20:57	2005
3000m Steeplechase	Gulnara Samitova-Galkina (Russia)	8:58.81	2008	Yekaterina Volkova (Russia)	9:06.57	2007
110m/100m Hurdles	Yordanka Donkova (Bulgaria)	12.21	1988	Ginka Zagorcheva (Bulgaria)	12.34	1987
400m Hurdles	Yuliya Pechonkina (Russia)	52.34	2003	Melaine Walker (Jamaica)	52.42	2009
High Jump	Stefka Kostadinova (Bulgaria)	2.09	1987	Stefka Kostadinova (Bulgaria)	2.09	1987
Pole Vault	Yelena Isinbayeva (Russia)	5.06	2009	Yelena Isinbayeva (Russia)	5.01	2005
Long Jump	Galina Chistyakova (Soviet Union)	7.52	1988	Jackie Joyner-Kersee (United States)	7.36	1987
Triple Jump	Inessa Kravets (Ukraine)	15.50	1995	Inessa Kravets (Ukraine)	15.50	1995
Shot Put	Natalya Lisovskaya (Soviet Union)	22.63	1987	Natalya Lisovskaya (Soviet Union)	21.24	1987
Discus	Gabriele Reinsch (East Germany)	76.80	1988	Martina Hellmann (East Germany)	71.62	1987
Hammer	Betty Heidler (Germany)	79.42	2009	Anita Włodarczyk (Poland)	77.96	2009
Javelin	Barbora Špotáková (Czech Republic)	72.28	2008	Osleidys Menéndez (Cuba)	71.70	2005
Heptathlon	Jackie Joyner-Kersee (United States)	7291	1988	Jackie Joyner-Kersee (United States)	7128	1987
20km Walk	Vera Sokolova (Russia)	1:25:08	2011	Olimpiada Ivanova (Russia)	1:25:41	2005
4x100 Relay	East Germany	41.37	1985	United States	41.47	1997
4x400 Relay	Soviet Union	3:15.17	1988	United States	3:16.71	1993

Gold Medal Performances in each Championships

Event (Men)	1983	1987	1991	1993	1995	1997	1999	2001	2003	2005	2007	2009	2011
100m	10.07	9.93	9.86 WR	9.87	9.97	9.86	9.80 CR	9.82	10.07	9.88	9.85	9.58 WR	9.92
200m	20.14	20.16	20.01	19.85 CR	19.79 CR	20.04	19.90	20.04	20.30	20.04	19.76 CR	19.19 WR	19.40
400m	45.05	44.33	44.57	43.65	43.39 CR	44.12	43.18 WR	44.64	44.77	43.93	43.45	44.06	44.60
800m	1:43.65	1:43.06 CR	1:43.99	1:44.71	1:45.08	1:43.38	1:43.30	1:43.70	1:44.81	1:44.24	1:47.09	1:45.29	1:43.91
1500m	3:41.59	3:36.80	3:32.84 CR	3:34.24	3:33.73	3:35.83	3:27.65 CR	3:30.68	3:31.77	3:37.88	3:34.77	3:35.93	3:35.69
5000m	13:28.53	13:26.44	13:14.45 CR	13:02.75	13:16.77	13:07.38	12:58.13 CR	13:00.77	12:52.79	13:32.55	13:45.87	13:17.09	13:23.36
10000m	28:01.04	27:38.63 CR	27:38.74	27:46.02	27:12.95 CR	27:24.58	27:57.27	27:53.25	26:49:57 CR	27:08.33	27:05.90	26:46.31 CR	27:13.81
Marathon	2:10:03	2:11:48	2:14:57	2:13:57	2:11:41	2:13:16	2:13:36	2:12:42	2:08:31 CR	2:10:10	2:15:59	2:06:54 CR	2:07:38
3000m Steeplechase	8:15.06	8:08.57	8:12.59	8:06.36 CR	8:04.16 CR	8:05.84	8:11.76	8:15.16	8:04.39	8:13.31	8:13.82	8:00.43 CR	8:14.85
110m Hurdles	13.42	13.21	13.06	12.91 WR	13.00	12.93	13.04	13.04	13.12	13.07	12.95	13.14	13.16
400m Hurdles	47.50	47.46 CR	47.64	47.18	47.98	47.70	47.72	47.49	47.25	47.30	47.61	47.91	48.26
High Jump	2.32	2.38 CR	2.38 CR	2.40	2.37	2.37	2.37	2.36	2.35	2.32	2.35	2.32	2.35
Pole Vault	5.70	5.85 CR	5.95 CR	6.00 CR	5.92	6.01 CR	6.02 CR	6.05 CR	5.90	5.80	5.86	5.90	5.90
Long Jump	8.55	8.67 CR	8.95 WR	8.59	8.70	8.42	8.56	8.40	8.32	8.60	8.57	8.54	8.45
Triple Jump	17.42	17.92 CR	17.78	17.86	18.29 WR	17.85	17.59	17.92	17.72	17.57	17.74	17.73	17.96
Shot Put	21.39	22.23 CR	21.67	21.97	21.47	21.44	21.79	21.87	21.69	21.73	22.04	22.03	21.78
Discus	67.72	68.74 CR	66.20	67.72	68.76 CR	68.54	69.08 CR	69.72 CR	69.69	70.17 CR	68.94	69.43	68.97
Javelin	89.48	83.54 CR	90.82	85.98 CR	89.58	88.40	89.52	92.80 CR	85.44	87.17	90.33	89.59	86.27
Hammer	82.68	83.06 CR	81.70	81.64	81.56	81.78	80.24	83.38 CR	83.05	83.89 CR	83.63	80.24	81.24
Decathlon	8666	8680	8812 CR	8817 CR	8695	8837 CR	8744	8902 CR	8750	8732	8676	8790	8607
20km Walk	1:20:49	1:20:45 CR	1:19:37 CR	1:22:31	1:19:59	1:21:43	1:23:34	1:20:31	1:17:21	1:18:35	1:22:20	1:18:41	1:19:56
50km Walk	3:43:08	3:40:53 CR	3:53:09	3:41:41	3:43:42	3:44:46	3:47:54	3:42:08	3:36:03	3:38:08	3:43:53	3:38:35	3:41:24
4x100 Relay	37.86 WR	37.90	37.50 WR	37.48	38.31	37.86	37.59	38.47	38.06	38.08	37.78	37.31 CR	37.04 WR
4x400 Relay	3:00.79	2:57.29 CR	2:57.53	2:54.29 WR	2:57.32	2:56.65	2:58.91	2:58.19	2:58.96	2:56.91	2:55.56	2:57.86	2:59.31

Event (Women)	1983	1987	1991	1993	1995	1997	1999	2001	2003	2005	2007	2009	2011
100m	10.97	10.90 CR	10.99	10.82 CR	10.85	10.83	10.70 CR	10.82	10.93	10.93	11.01	10.53	10.90
200m	22.13	21.74 CR	22.09	21.98	22.12	22.32	21.77	22.52	22.38	22.16	21.81	22.02	22.22
400m	47.99 WR	49.38	49.13	49.82	49.28	49.77	49.67	49.86	48.89	49.55	49.61	49.00	49.56
800m	1:54.68	1:55.26	1:57.50	1:55.43	1:56.11	1:57.14	1:56.68	1:57.17	1:59.89	1:58.82	1:56.04	1:55.45	1:55.87
1500m	4:00.90	3:58.56 CR	4:02.21	4:00.50	4:02.42	4:04.24	3:59.53	4:00.57	3:58.52 CR	4:00.35	3:58.75	4:03.74	4:05.40
3000m	8:34.62	8:38.73	8:35.82	none	none	none	none	none	none	none	none	none	none
5000m	none	none	none	8:28.71 CR	14:46.47 CR	14:57.68	14:41.82 CR	15:03.39	14:51.72	14:58.59 CR	14:57.91	14:57.97	14:55.36
10000m	none	31:05.85	31:14.31	30:49.30 CR	31:04.99	31:32.92	30:24.56 CR	31:48.81	30:04.18 CR	30:24.02	31:55.41	30:51.24	30:48.98
Marathon	2:28:09	2:25:17	2:29:53	2:30:03	2:25:39*	2:29:48	2:26:59	2:26:01	2:23:55 CR	2:20:57 CR	2:30:37	2:25:15	2:28:43
3000m Steeplechase	none	none	none	none	none	none	none	none	none	9:18.24 CR	9:06.57 CR	9:07.32	9:07.03
100m Hurdles	12.35	12.34 CR	12.59	12.46	12.68	12.50	12.37	12.42	12.53	12.66	12.46	12.51	12.28 CR
400m Hurdles	54.14	53.62 CR	53.11 CR	52.74 WR	52.61 WR	52.97	52.89	53.34	53.22	52.90	53.31	52.42 CR	52.47
High Jump	2.01	2.09 WR	2.05	1.99	2.01	1.99	1.99	2.00	2.06	2.02	2.05	2.04	2.03
Pole Vault	none	none	none	none	none	none	4.60 WR	4.75 CR	4.75	5.01	4.80	4.75	4.85
Long Jump	7.27	7.36 CR	7.32	7.11	6.98	7.05	7.06	7.02	6.99	6.89	7.03	7.10	6.82
Triple Jump	none	none	none	15.09 WR	15.50 WR	15.20	14.88	15.25	15.18	15.11	15.28	14.95	14.94
Shot Put	21.05	21.24 CR	20.83	20.57	21.22	20.71	19.85	20.61	20.63	20.51	20.54	20.44	21.24 CR
Discus	68.94	71.62 CR	71.02	67.40	68.64	66.82	68.14	67.10	67.32	66.56	66.61	65.44	66.52
Javelin	70.82	76.64 CR	68.78	69.18	67.56	68.78	67.09	69.53 CR	66.52	71.70 WR	67.07	67.30	71.99 CR
Hammer	none	none	none	none	none	none	75.20 CR	70.65	73.33	75.10	74.76	77.96 CR	77.13
Heptathlon	6714	7128 CR	6672	6837	6651	6739	6861	6694	7001	6887	7032	6731	6880
10km Walk	none	44:12.00 CR	42:57.00 CR	42:59	42:13.00 CR	42:55.49	none	none	none	none	none	none	none
20km Walk	none	none	none	none	none	none	1:30:50 CR	1:27:48 CR	1:26:52 CR	1:25:41 CR	1:30:09	1:28:09	1:29:42
4x100 Relay	41.76	41.58 CR	41.94	41.49 CR	42.12	41.47 CR	41.92	42.32	41.78	41.78	41.98	42.06	41.56
4x400 Relay	3:19.73	3:18.63 CR	3:18.43	3:16.71 CR	3:22.29	3:20.92	3:21.98	3:20.65	3:22.63	3:20.95	3:18.55	3:17.83	3:18.09

* marathon course was short by 400m.

8

World Records (1)

Event	Mark	Athlete	Country
4x100m Relay (m)	37.04	Nesta Carter; Michael Frater; Yohan Blake; Usain Bolt	Jamaica

Championship Records (3)

Event	Mark	Athlete	Country
Shot Put (w)	21.24	Valerie Adams	New Zealand
Javelin (w)	71.99	Maria Abakumova	Russia
100m Hurdles (w)	12.28	Sally Pearson	Australia

Afghanistan (1)
Albania (1)
Algeria (10)
American Samoa (2)
Angola (2)
Anguilla (2)
Antigua and Barbuda (2)
Argentina (6)
Armenia (2)
Aruba (2)
Australia (41)
Austria (4)
Azerbaijan (1)
Bahamas (17)
Bahrain (11)
Bangladesh (1)
Barbados (4)
Belarus (22)
Belgium (9)
Belize (2)
Benin (2)
Bermuda (1)
Bhutan (1)
Bolivia (2)
Bosnia and Herzegovina (2)
Botswana (3)
Brazil (26)
British Virgin Islands (1)
Brunei (1)
Bulgaria (7)
Burkina Faso (2)
Burundi (2)
Cambodia (1)
Cameroon (2)
Canada (28)
Cape Verde (1)
Cayman Islands (1)
Central African Republic (1)
Chad (2)
Chile (3)
China (54)
Colombia (20)
Comoros (2)
Congo (1)
Democratic Republic of the Congo (2)
Cook Islands (1)
Costa Rica (2)
Côte d'Ivoire (2)
Croatia (6)
Cuba (31)
Cyprus (2)
Czech Republic (21)
Denmark (6)
Djibouti (2)
Dominica (1)
Dominican Republic (4)
Ecuador (5)
Egypt (5)
El Salvador (2)
Eritrea (9)
Estonia (9)
Ethiopia (34)
Federated States of Micronesia (2)
Fiji (1)
Finland (13)
France (39)
French Polynesia (1)
Gabon (2)
Gambia (2)

Germany (65)
Ghana (6)
Gibraltar (1)
Great Britain (59)
Greece (12)
Grenada (3)
Guam (2)
Guatemala (2)
Guinea (2)
Guinea-Bissau (2)
Guyana (1)
Haiti (3)
Honduras (2)
Hong Kong (2)
Hungary (12)
Iceland (2)
India (8)
Indonesia (2)
Iran (7)
Iraq (1)
Ireland (16)
Israel (4)
Italy (30)
Jamaica (45)
Japan (48)
Kazakhstan (14)
Kenya (47)
Kiribati (2)
South Korea (53)
Kuwait (2)
Kyrgyzstan (2)
Laos (2)
Latvia (13)
Lebanon (1)
Lesotho (2)
Liberia (2)
Libya (1)
Lithuania (15)
Macau (1)
Macedonia (1)
Madagascar (1)
Malawi (2)
Malaysia (2)
Maldives (2)
Mali (2)
Malta (2)
Marshall Islands (0)
Mauritania (2)
Mauritius (2)
Mexico (10)
Moldova (3)
Monaco (1)
Mongolia (2)
Montenegro (2)
Morocco (19)
Mozambique (2)
Myanmar (1)
Namibia (2)
Nauru (2)
Nepal (2)
Netherlands (17)
New Zealand (8)
Nicaragua (2)
Niger (2)
Nigeria (15)
Northern Mariana Islands (2)
Norway (13)
Oman (1)
Pakistan (1)

Palau (2)
Palestine (1)
Panama (2)
Papua New Guinea (2)
Paraguay (1)
Peru (5)
Philippines (2)
Poland (37)
Portugal (25)[12]
Puerto Rico (8)
Qatar (4)
Romania (8)
Russia (76)
Rwanda (2)
Saint Kitts and Nevis (4)
Saint Lucia (2)
Saint Vincent and the Grenadines (1)
Samoa (1)
San Marino (2)
São Tomé and Príncipe (2)
Saudi Arabia (8)
Senegal (2)
Serbia (9)
Seychelles (2)
Sierra Leone (2)
Singapore (2)
Slovakia (8)
Slovenia (9)
Solomon Islands (2)
Somalia (1)
South Africa (32)
Spain (43)
Sri Lanka (2)
Sudan (3)
Suriname (2)
Swaziland (2)
Sweden (16)
Switzerland (15)
Syria (1)
Chinese Taipei (7)
Tajikistan (2)
Tanzania (1)
Thailand (6)
Timor-Leste (1)
Togo (1)
Tonga (2)
Trinidad and Tobago (16)
Tunisia (5)
Turkey (20)
Turkmenistan (2)
Tuvalu (2)
Uganda (12)
Ukraine (55)
United Arab Emirates (2)
United States (127)
Uruguay (2)
U.S. Virgin Islands (3)
Uzbekistan (7)
Vanuatu (2)
Venezuela (3)
Vietnam (1)
Yemen (2)
Zambia (3)
Zimbabwe (4)

Medal Table

Rank	Nation	Gold	Silver	Bronze	Total
1	United States	12	8	5	25
2	Russia	9	4	6	19
3	Kenya	7	6	4	17
4	Jamaica	4	4	1	9
5	Germany	3	3	1	7
6	Great Britain	2	4	1	7
7	China	1	2	1	4
8	Australia	1	1	1	3
9	Ethiopia	1	0	4	5
10	Ukraine	1	0	1	2
11	Botswana	1	0	0	1
11	Brazil	1	0	0	1
11	Grenada	1	0	0	1
11	Japan	1	0	0	1
11	New Zealand	1	0	0	1
11	Poland	1	0	0	1
17	South Africa	0	2	2	4
18	Cuba	0	1	3	4
18	France	0	1	3	4
20	Belarus	0	1	1	2
21	Canada	0	1	0	1
21	Croatia	0	1	0	1
21	Czech Republic	0	1	0	1
21	Estonia	0	1	0	1
21	Hungary	0	1	0	1
21	Kazakhstan	0	1	0	1
21	Norway	0	1	0	1
21	Puero Rico	0	1	0	1
21	Sudan	0	1	0	1
21	Tunisia	0	1	0	1
31	Colombia	0	0	2	2
31	St Kitts & Nevis	0	0	2	2
33	Bahamas	0	0	1	1
33	Belgium	0	0	1	1
33	Iran	0	0	1	1
33	Italy	0	0	1	1
33	Latvia	0	0	1	1
33	Slovenia	0	0	1	1
33	Spain	0	0	1	1
33	Trinidad & Tobago	0	0	1	1
33	Zimbabwe	0	0	1	1
	TOTAL	47	47	47	141

Men's 100m

Preliminary Round

Qualification for First Round: first three in each heat plus the next fastest finisher.

Heat 1   27 August 2011

Position	Lane	Athlete	Country		Time
1	2	Abdouraim Haroun	Chad	Q	10.44
2	3	Keiron Rogers	Anguilla	Q	10.55
3	8	Jurgen Themen	Surinam	Q	10.84
4	4	George Pine	Kiribati		11.34
5	7	Kitavanah Kountavong	Laos		11.42
6	5	Joshua Jeremiah	Nauru		11.44
7	1	Okilani Tinilau	Tuvalu		11.58
8	6	Christopher Lima da Costa	São Tomé and Príncipe		11.61

Heat 2   27 August 2011

Position	Lane	Athlete	Country		Time
1	6	Chi Ho Tsui	Hong Kong	Q	10.45
2	4	Fadlin Fadlin	Indonesia	Q	10.70
3	7	Tilak Ram Tharu	Nepal	Q	11.00
4	5	Rodman Teltull	Palau		11.31
5	8	Mohamed Ghassem Ahmed Taled	Mauritania		11.50
6	2	Massoud Azizi	Afghanistan		11.64
7	3	John Howard	Federated States of Micronesia		11.71
	1	Kukyoung Kim	South Korea		DQ

Heat 3   27 August 2011

Position	Lane	Athlete	Country		Time
1	4	Gérard Kobéané	Burundi	Q	10.64
2	2	Geronimo Goeloe	Aruba	Q	10.73
3	6	Foo Ee Yeo	Singapore	Q	10.76
4	7	Delivert Arsene Kimbembe	Congo	q	10.85
5	3	Joseph Andy Lui	Tonga		11.48
6	5	Bledee Jarry	Liberia		11.49
7	1	Ah Chong Sam Chong	Samoa		12.36
8	8	Orrin Ogumoro Pharmin	Northern Mariana Islands		12.60

Heat 4   27 August 2011

Position	Lane	Athlete	Country		Time
1	2	Mohammad Noor Imran A Hadi	Malaysia	Q	10.77
2	1	Dmitrii Ilin	Kyrgyzstan	Q	10.86
3	4	Moudjib Toyb	Comoros	Q	11.07
4	5	Karl Farrugia	Malta		11.21
5	6	Francis Manioru	Solomon Islands		11.28
6	3	Federico Gorrieri	San Marino		11.42
7	7	Sogelau Tuvalu	American Samoa		15.66

Men's 100m (continued)

Qualification for Semi-Finals: first three in each heat plus the next three fastest finishers.

Heat 1   27 August 2011

Position	Lane	Athlete	Country		Time
1	4	Kim Collins	St Kitts & Nevis	Q	10.13
2	1	Trell Kimmons	United States	Q	10.32
3	2	Richard Thompson	Trinidad & Tobago	Q	10.34
4	7	Suwaibou Sanneh	Gambia		10.50
5	3	Ronalds Arajs	Latvia		10.52
6	6	Peter Emelieze	Nigeria		10.58
7	8	Delivert Arsene Kimbembe	Congo		10.94
	5	Adrian Griffith	Bahamas		DQ

Heat 2   27 August 2011

Position	Lane	Athlete	Country		Time
1	2	Walter Dix	United States	Q	10.25
2	1	Harry Aikines-Aryeetey	Great Britain	Q	10.28
3	7	Keston Bledman	Trinidad & Tobago	Q	10.32
4	4	Andrew Hinds	Barbados	q	10.41
5	8	Jason Smyth	Ireland		10.57
6	6	Ogho-Oghene Egwero	Nigeria		10.57
7	3	Geronimo Goeloe	Aruba		10.84
8	5	Fadlin Fadlin	Indonesia		11.10

Heat 3   27 August 2011

Position	Lane	Athlete	Country		Time
1	4	Christophe Lemaître	France	Q	10.14
2	6	Justin Gatlin	United States	Q	10.31
3	7	Churandy Martina	Netherlands	Q	10.32
4	5	Marlon Devonish	Great Britain	q	10.34
5	2	Carlos Jorge	Dominican Republic		10.62
6	1	Gabriel Mvumvure	Zimbabwe		10.63
7	8	Keiron Rogers	Anguilla		10.96
8	3	Dmitrii Ilin	Kyrgyzstan		11.00

Heat 4   27 August 2011

Position	Lane	Athlete	Country		Time
1	4	Yohan Blake	Jamaica	Q	10.12
2	6	Jimmy Vicaut	France	Q	10.25
3	1	Ngonidzashe Makusha	Zimbabwe	Q	10.31
4	5	Justyn Warner	Canada	q	10.33
5	3	Ramon Gittens	Barbados		10.42
6	8	Ben Youssef Meité	Ivory Coast		10.45
7	2	Gérard Kobéané	Burundi		10.59
8	7	Jurgen Themen	Surinam		10.94

Heat 5   27 August 2011

Position	Lane	Athlete	Country		Time
1	3	Nesta Carter	Jamaica	Q	10.26
2	2	Daniel Bailey	Antigua & Barbuda	Q	10.34
3	1	Aziz Ouhadi	Morocco	Q	10.42
4	6	Rytis Sakalauskas	Lithuania		10.42
5	5	Marek Niit	Estonia		10.53
6	4	Aziz Zakari	Ghana		10.55
7	7	Mohammad Noor Imran A Hadi	Malaysia		10.75
8	8	Foo Ee Yeo	Singapore		10.85

Heat 6   27 August 2011

Position	Lane	Athlete	Country		Time
1	4	Usain Bolt	Jamaica	Q	10.10
2	8	Dwain Chambers	Great Britain	Q	10.28
3	7	Ángel David Rodríguez	Spain	Q	10.37
4	3	Simon Magakwe	South Africa		10.53
5	2	Nilson Andrè	Brazil		10.54
6	5	Gerald Phiri	Zambia		10.60
7	6	Abdouraim Haroun	Chad		10.72
8	1	Moudjib Toyb	Comoros		11.12

Heat 7   27 August 2011

Position	Lane	Athlete	Country		Time
1	5	Michael Frater	Jamaica	Q	10.26
2	7	Jaysuma Saidy Ndure	Norway	Q	10.33
3	3	Dariusz Kuc	Poland	Q	10.36
4	1	Reto Schenkel	Switzerland		10.44
5	8	Aaron Armstrong	Trinidad & Tobago		10.48
6	6	Álvaro Gómez	Colombia		10.62
7	2	Chi Ho Tsui	Hong Kong		10.65
8	4	Tilak Ram Tharu	Nepal		11.32

Qualification for Final: first two in each quarter-final plus the next two fastest finishers.

Semi-Final 1   28 August 2011

Position	Lane	Athlete	Country		Time
1	3	Yohan Blake	Jamaica	Q	9.95
2	5	Walter Dix	United States	Q	10.05
3	4	Jimmy Vicault	France	q	10.10
4	8	Daniel Bailey	Antigua & Barbuda	q	10.14
5	7	Keston Bledman	Trinidad & Tobago		10.14
6	1	Andrew Hinds	Barbados		10.32
7	2	Ángel David Rodríguez	Spain		10.49
	6	Dwain Chambers	Great Britain		DQ

Semi-Final 2   28 August 2011

Position	Lane	Athlete	Country		Time
1	3	Usain Bolt	Jamaica	Q	10.05
2	5	Christophe Lemaître	France	Q	10.11
3	7	Richard Thompson	Trinidad & Tobago		10.20
4	6	Trell Kimmons	United States		10.21
5	8	Jaysuma Saidy Ndure	Norway		10.21
6	4	Michael Frater	Jamaica		10.23
7	2	Marlon Devonish	Great Britain		10.25
8	1	Dariusz Kuc	Poland		10.51

Semi-Final 3   28 August 2011

Position	Lane	Athlete	Country		Time
1	5	Kim Collins	St Kitts & Nevis	Q	10.08
2	3	Nesta Carter	Jamaica	Q	10.16
3	4	Harry Aikines-Aryeetey	Great Britain		10.23
4	6	Justin Gatlin	United States		10.23
5	7	Ngonidzashe Makusha	Zimbabwe		10.27
6	8	Churandy Martina	Netherlands		10.29
7	1	Aziz Ouhadi	Morocco		10.45
8	2	Justyn Warner	Canada		10.47

Men's 100m (continued)

FINAL   28 August 2011

Position	Lane	Athlete	Country		Time
GOLD	6	Yohan Blake	Jamaica		9.92
SILVER	4	Walter Dix	United States		10.08
BRONZE	3	Kim Collins	St Kitts & Nevis		10.09
4	8	Christophe Lemaître	France		10.19
5	2	Daniel Bailey	Antigua & Barbuda		10.26
6	1	Jimmy Vicault	France		10.27
7	7	Nesta Carter	Jamaica		10.95
	5	Usain Bolt	Jamaica		DQ

Women's 100m

Preliminary Round

Qualification for First Round: first three in each heat plus the next four fastest finishers.

Heat 1   27 August 2011

Position	Lane	Athlete	Country		Time
1	4	Kaina Martinez	Belize	Q	12.14
2	3	Joanne Pricilla Loutoy	Seychelles	Q	12.29
3	8	Lovelite Detenamo	Nauru	Q	12.63
4	7	Shinelle Proctor	Anguilla		12.89
5	5	Chandra Kala Thapa	Nepal		13.17
6	1	Boudsadee Vongdala	Laos		13.56
7	6	Kabotaake Romeri	Kiribati		13.71
	2	Youlia Camara	Guinea		DQ

Heat 2   27 August 2011

Position	Lane	Athlete	Country		Time
1	1	Delphine Atangana	Cameroon	Q	11.57
2	4	Feta Ahamada	Comoros	Q	12.27
3	2	Diane Borg	Malta	Q	12.29
4	5	Gloria Diogo	São Tomé and Príncipe	q	12.52
5	6	Djénébou Danté	Mali	q	12.62
6	3	Maysa Rejepova	Turkmenistan		13.43
7	7	Mihter Wendolin	Federated States of Micronesia		14.69

Heat 3   27 August 2011

Position	Lane	Athlete	Country		Time
1	6	Phobay Kutu-Akoi	Liberia	Q	11.62
2	3	Vladislava Ovcharenko	Tajikistan	Q	12.26
3	2	Patricia Taea	Cook Islands	Q	12.44
4	5	Pollara Cobb	Guam	q	12.64
5	7	Nafissa Souleymane	Niger		12.74
6	4	Joycelyn Taurikeni	Solomon Islands		13.16
7	1	Rubie Joy Gabriel	Palau		13.48

Heat 4   27 August 2011

Position	Lane	Athlete	Country		Time
1	4	Hye-lim Jung	South Korea	Q	11.90
2	5	Ching-Hsien Liao	Chinese Taipei	Q	11.98
3	6	Alda Paulo	Angola	Q	12.85
4	7	Maguy Safi Makanda	Democratic Republic of Congo		13.05
5	3	Asenate Manoa	Tuvalu		13.92
6	2	Megan West	American Samoa		13.95
7	1	Bonko Camara	Mauritania		14.05

Heat 5   27 August 2011

Position	Lane	Athlete	Country		Time
1	1	Norjannah Hafiszah Jamaludin	Malaysia	Q	12.06
2	4	Anatercia Quive	Mozambique	Q	12.31
3	5	Martina Pretelli	San Marino	Q	12.47
4	7	Ivana Rožhman	FYR Macedonia	q	12.48
5	2	Yvonne Bennett	Northern Mariana Islands		12.78
6	6	Susan Tama	Vanuatu		13.29
7	3	Belinda Talakai	Tonga		13.73

Qualification for Semi-Finals: first three in each heat plus the next three fastest finishers.

Heat 1   28 August 2011

Position	Lane	Athlete	Country		Time
1	3	Carmelita Jeter	United States	Q	11.21
2	5	Sheniqua Ferguson	Bahamas	Q	11.36
3	2	Jeanette Kwakye	Great Britain	Q	11.42
4	1	Nelkis Casabona	Cuba		11.47
5	7	Marta Jeschke	Poland		11.73
6	6	Ching-Hsien Liao	Chinese Taipei		12.16
7	8	Kaina Martinez	Belize		12.18
8	4	Pollara Cobb	Guam		12.55

Heat 2   28 August 2011

Position	Lane	Athlete	Country		Time
1	4	Kerron Stewart	Jamaica	Q	11.13
2	5	Ruddy Zang Milama	Gabon	Q	11.2
3	7	Ezinne Okparaebo	Norway	Q	11.21
4	2	Semoy Hackett	Trinidad & Tobago	q	11.27
5	8	Andreea Ograzeanu	Romania		11.47
6	1	Phobay Kutu-Akoi	Liberia		11.61
7	3	Joanne Pricilla Loutoy	Seychelles		12.35
8	6	Ivana Rožhman	FYR Macedonia		12.44

Heat 3   28 August 2011

Position	Lane	Athlete	Country		Time
1	3	Ivet Lalova	Bulgaria	Q	11.10
2	2	Oludamola Osayomi	Nigeria	Q	11.15
3	1	Michelle-Lee Ahye	Trinidad & Tobago	Q	11.20
4	4	Laura Turner	Great Britain		11.45
5	7	Guzel Khubbieva	Uzbekistan		11.46
6	6	Yomara Hinestroza	Colombia		11.57
7	5	Martina Pretelli	San Marino		12.28
8	8	Patricia Taea	Cook Islands		12.63

Women's 100m (continued)

Heat 4 28 August 2011

Position	Lane	Athlete	Country		Time
1	5	Kelly-Ann Baptiste	Trinidad & Tobago	Q	11.27
2	3	Chisato Fukushima	Japan	Q	11.35
3	7	Rosângela Santos	Brazil	Q	11.38
4	8	Mikele Barber	United States		11.40
5	1	Anyika Onuora	Great Britain		11.41
6	2	Delphine Atangana	Cameroon		11.56
7	6	Anatercia Quive	Mozambique		12.40
8	4	Alda Paulo	Angola		13.02

Heat 5 28 August 2011

Position	Lane	Athlete	Country		Time
1	8	Blessing Okagbare	Nigeria	Q	11.10
2	6	Shelly-Ann Fraser - Pryce	Jamaica	Q	11.13
3	4	Ana Claudia Silva	Brazil	Q	11.27
4	2	Inna Eftimova	Bulgaria		11.36
5	5	Olga Bludova	Kazakhstan		11.63
6	1	Diane Borg	Malta		12.22
7	7	Lovelite Detenamo	Nauru		12.51
	3	Natasha Mayers	St Vincent & the Grenadines		DNS

Heat 6 28 August 2011

Position	Lane	Athlete	Country		Time
1	2	Myriam Soumaré	France	Q	11.12
2	5	Marshevet Myers	United States	Q	11.16
3	1	Olesya Povh	Ukraine	Q	11.26
4	3	Jura Levy	Jamaica	q	11.34
5	8	Leena Günther	Germany		11.36
6	4	Hye-lim Jung	South Korea		11.88
7	6	Feta Ahamada	Comoros		12.22
8	7	Gloria Diogo	São Tomé and Príncipe		12.46

Heat 7 28 August 2011

Position	Lane	Athlete	Country		Time
1	1	Veronica Campbell-Brown	Jamaica	Q	11.19
2	6	Véronique Mang	France	Q	11.2
3	8	Aleksandra Fedoriva	Russia	Q	11.28
4	3	Yasmin Kwadwo	Germany	q	11.29
5	4	Nataliya Pohrebnyak	Ukraine		11.34
6	5	Norjannah Hafiszah Jamaludin	Malaysia		11.74
7	2	Vladislava Ovcharenko	Tajikistan		12.24
8	7	Djénébou Danté	Mali		12.32

Women's 100m (continued)

Qualification for Final: first two in each quarter-final plus the next two fastest finishers.

Semi-Final 1   29 August 2011

Position	Lane	Athlete	Country		Time
1	6	Kerron Stewart	Jamaica	Q	11.26
2	5	Marshevet Myers	United States	Q	11.38
3	3	Myriam Soumaré	France		11.47
4	8	Ezinne Okparaebo	Norway		11.48
5	7	Michelle-Lee Ahye	Trinidad & Tobago		11.48
6	2	Jeanette Kwakye	Great Britain		11.48
7	1	Yasmin Kwadwo	Germany		11.54
8	4	Oludamola Osayomi	Nigeria		11.58

Semi-Final 2   29 August 2011

Position	Lane	Athlete	Country		Time
1	3	Shelly-Ann Fraser - Pryce	Jamaica	Q	11.03
2	6	Veronica Campbell-Brown	Jamaica	Q	11.06
3	5	Blessing Okagbare	Nigeria	q	11.22
4	2	Semoy Hackett	Trinidad & Tobago		11.35
5	4	Ruddy Zang Milama	Gabon		11.43
6	8	Olesya Povh	Ukraine		11.48
7	7	Sheniqua Ferguson	Bahamas		11.59
8	1	Rosângela Santos	Brazil		11.61

Semi-Final 3   29 August 2011

Position	Lane	Athlete	Country		Time
1	6	Carmelita Jeter	United States	Q	11.02
2	3	Kelly-Ann Baptiste	Trinidad & Tobago	Q	11.05
3	4	Ivet Lalova	Bulgaria	q	11.23
4	5	Véronique Mang	France		11.44
5	1	Jura Levy	Jamaica		11.53
6	2	Aleksandra Fedoriva	Russia		11.54
7	7	Ana Claudia Silva	Brazil		11.55
8	8	Chisato Fukushima	Japan		11.59

FINAL   29 August 2011

Position	Lane	Athlete	Country	Time
GOLD	4	Carmelita Jeter	United States	10.90
SILVER	8	Veronica Campbell-Brown	Jamaica	10.97
BRONZE	5	Kelly-Ann Baptiste	Trinidad & Tobago	10.98
4	3	Shelly-Ann Fraser - Pryce	Jamaica	10.99
5	2	Blessing Okagbare	Nigeria	11.12
6	6	Kerron Stewart	Jamaica	11.15
7	1	Ivet Lalova	Bulgaria	11.27
8	7	Marshevet Myers	United States	11.33

Men's 200m

Qualification for semi-finals: first three in each heat plus the next three fastest finishers.

Heat 1   02 September 2011

Position	Lane	Athlete	Country		Time
1	5	Walter Dix	United States	Q	20.42
2	7	Amr Ibrahim Mostafa Seoud	Egypt	Q	20.44
3	6	Kim Collins	St Kitts & Nevis	Q	20.52
4	2	Femi Ogunode	Qatar	q	20.54
5	8	Marc Schneeberger	Switzerland		20.81
6	3	Sebastian Ernst	Germany		20.95
7	4	Sibusiso Matsenjwa	Swaziland		21.29
8	1	Roudy Monrose	Haiti		22.18

Heat 2   02 September 2011

Position	Lane	Athlete	Country		Time
1	7	Usain Bolt	Jamaica	Q	20.30
2	1	Michael Mathieu	Bahamas	Q	20.46
3	2	Pavel Maslák	Czech Republic	Q	20.63
4	6	Christian Malcolm	Great Britain	q	20.66
5	3	Churandy Martina	Netherlands	q	20.70
6	4	Bryan Barnett	Canada		20.75
7	5	Emmanuel Callender	Trinidad & Tobago		20.97

Heat 3   02 September 2011

Position	Lane	Athlete	Country		Time
1	7	Jaysuma Saidy Ndure	Norway	Q	20.65
2	4	Darvis Patton	United States	Q	20.8
3	1	Jonathan Åstrand	Finland	Q	20.87
4	2	Paul Hession	Ireland		21.02
5	6	Brijesh Lawrence	St Kitts & Nevis		21.16
6	8	Rolando Palacios	Honduras		21.22
7	5	Yuichi Kobayashi	Japan		21.27
8	3	Khalilur Rahman	Bangladesh		23.53

Heat 4   02 September 2011

Position	Lane	Athlete	Country		Time
1	5	Christophe Lemaître	France	Q	20.51
2	2	Shinji Takahira	Japan	Q	20.87
3	1	Mosito Lehata	Lesotho	Q	21.03
4	7	Marvin Anderson	Jamaica		21.09
5	4	Lebogang Moeng	South Africa		21.09
6	3	Alex Wilson	Switzerland		21.25
7	8	Leeroy Henriette	Seychelles		21.83
8	6	Brendan Christian	Antigua & Barbuda		DNS

Heat 5   02 September 2011

Position	Lane	Athlete	Country		Time
1	3	Nickel Ashmeade	Jamaica	Q	20.47
2	7	Sandro Viana	Brazil	Q	20.62
3	6	Hitoshi Saito	Japan	Q	20.80
4	2	James Ellington	Great Britain		20.82
5	1	Jeremy Dodson	United States		20.92
6	5	Gabriel Mvumvure	Zimbabwe		21.11
7	4	Calvin Dascent	US Virgin Islands		21.15

Men's 200m (continued)

Heat 6   02 September 2011

Position	Lane	Athlete	Country		Time
1	5	Alonso Edward	Panama	Q	20.55
2	3	Bruno de Barros	Brazil	Q	20.63
3	2	Reto Schenkel	Switzerland	Q	20.77
4	6	Jared Connaughton	Canada		20.83
5	1	Ben Youssef Meité	Ivory Coast		20.97
6	8	Thuso Mpuang	South Africa		21.07
7	4	Omar Jouma Bilal Al-Salfa	United Arab Emirates		21.45
8	7	Luka Rakic	Montenegro		22.73

Heat 7   02 September 2011

Position	Lane	Athlete	Country		Time
1	6	Rondel Sorrillo	Trinidad & Tobago	Q	20.68
2	4	Mario Forsythe	Jamaica	Q	20.68
3	7	Michael Herrera	Cuba	Q	20.76
4	5	Daniel Grueso	Colombia		20.87
5	3	Marek Niit	Estonia		20.90
6	1	Nilson Andrè	Brazil		20.93
7	8	Arnaldo Abrantes	Portugal		21.10
8	2	Holder da Silva	Guinea-Bissau		21.82

Qualification for Final: first two in each semi-final plus the next two fastest finishers.

Semi-Final 1   02 September 2011

Position	Lane	Athlete	Country		Time
1	5	Christophe Lemaître	France	Q	20.17
2	3	Nickel Ashmeade	Jamaica	Q	20.32
3	2	Femi Ogunode	Qatar		20.58
4	8	Kim Collins	St Kitts & Nevis		20.64
5	7	Pavel Maslák	Czech Republic		20.87
	4	Sandro Viana	Brazil		DQ
	6	Michael Mathieu	Bahamas		DNF
	1	Mosito Lehata	Lesotho		DNS

Semi-Final 2   02 September 2011

Position	Lane	Athlete	Country		Time
1	6	Usain Bolt	Jamaica	Q	20.31
2	4	Jaysuma Saidy Ndure	Norway	Q	20.5
3	5	Bruno de Barros	Brazil	q	20.54
4	3	Rondel Sorrillo	Trinidad & Tobago	q	20.56
5	7	Darvis Patton	United States		20.72
6	2	Hitoshi Saito	Japan		21.17
7	8	Reto Schenkel	Switzerland		21.18
	1	Churandy Martina	Netherlands		DNS

Men's 200m (continued)

Semi-Final 3   02 September 2011

Position	Lane	Athlete	Country		Time
1	3	Walter Dix	United States	Q	20.37
2	5	Alonso Edward	Panama	Q	20.52
3	4	Mario Forsythe	Jamaica		20.63
4	7	Michael Herrera	Cuba		20.75
5	2	Christian Malcolm	Great Britain		20.88
6	8	Shinji Takahira	Japan		20.90
7	1	Jonathan Åstrand	Finland		21.03
8	6	Amr Ibrahim Mostafa Seoud	Egypt		21.15

FINAL   03 September 2011

Position	Lane	Athlete	Country	Time
GOLD	3	Usain Bolt	Jamaica	19.40
SILVER	4	Walter Dix	United States	19.70
BRONZE	6	Christophe Lemaître	France	19.80
4	8	Jaysuma Saidy Ndure	Norway	19.95
5	5	Nickel Ashmeade	Jamaica	20.29
6	2	Bruno de Barros	Brazil	20.31
7	1	Rondel Sorrillo	Trinidad & Tobago	20.34
8	7	Alonso Edward	Panama	DNF

Women's 200m

Qualification for semi-finals: first four in each heat plus the next four fastest finishers.

Heat 1   01 September 2011

Position	Lane	Athlete	Country		Time
1	4	Myriam Soumaré	France	Q	22.71
2	2	Kerron Stewart	Jamaica	Q	22.83
3	7	Yulia Gushchina	Russia	Q	22.88
4	3	Nivea Smith	Bahamas	Q	23.09
5	6	Chisato Fukushima	Japan	q	23.25
6	8	Jeneba Tarmoh	United States		23.60
7	1	Seyha Chan	Cambodia		26.34
8	5	Ramona van der Vloot	Surinam		DNS

Heat 2   01 September 2011

Position	Lane	Athlete	Country		Time
1	7	Carmelita Jeter	United States	Q	22.68
2	3	Sherone Simpson	Jamaica	Q	22.94
3	6	Elizabeta Savlinis	Russia	Q	23.09
4	5	Elyzaveta Bryzgina	Ukraine	Q	23.70
5	1	Vanda Gomes	Brazil		23.70
6	2	Viktoriya Zyabkina	Kazakhstan		24.09
7	4	Mary Jane Vincent	Mauritius		25.20
8	8	Blessing Okagbare	Nigeria		DNS

Women's 200m (continued)

Heat 3   01 September 2011

Position	Lane	Athlete	Country		Time
1	4	Dafne Schippers	Netherlands	Q	22.69
2	8	Allyson Felix	United States	Q	22.71
3	5	Ana Claudia Silva	Brazil	Q	22.96
4	1	Janelle Redhead	Grenada	Q	23.11
5	3	Allison Peter	US Virgin Islands	q	23.17
6	7	Endurance Abinuwa	Nigeria		23.53
7	6	Phumlile Ndzinisa	Swaziland		24.15
8	2	Afa Ismail	Maldives		26.48

Heat 4   01 September 2011

Position	Lane	Athlete	Country		Time
1	6	Shalonda Solomon	United States	Q	22.69
2	8	Mariya Ryemyen	Ukraine	Q	22.77
3	4	Kai Selvon	Trinidad & Tobago	Q	22.89
4	2	Anthonique Strachan	Bahamas	Q	23.20
5	3	Nelkis Casabona	Cuba	q	23.21
6	7	Anna Kielbasinska	Poland		23.34
7	1	Kimberly Hyacinthe	Canada		23.83
8	5	Hinikissia Albertine Ndikert	Chad		24.81

Heat 5   01 September 2011

Position	Lane	Athlete	Country		Time
1	8	Veronica Campbell-Brown	Jamaica	Q	22.46
2	4	Ivet Lalova	Bulgaria	Q	22.62
3	2	Debbie Ferguson-McKenzie	Bahamas	Q	22.86
4	3	Hrystyna Stuy	Ukraine	Q	22.92
5	5	Anyika Onuora	Great Britain	q	22.93
6	1	Moa Hjelmer	Sweden		23.31
7	7	Maryam Toosi	Iran		24.17
8	6	Fanny Shonobi	Gambia		25.55

Qualification for Final: first two in each semi-final plus the next two fastest finishers.

Semi-Final 1   01 September 2011

Position	Lane	Athlete	Country		Time
1	6	Carmelita Jeter	United States	Q	22.47
2	4	Sherone Simpson	Jamaica	Q	22.88
3	3	Mariya Ryemyen	Ukraine		22.94
4	7	Ana Claudia Silva	Brazil		22.97
5	5	Myriam Soumaré	France		23.02
6	8	Nivea Smith	Bahamas		23.06
7	2	Nelkis Casabona	Cuba		23.32
8	1	Chisato Fukushima	Japan		23.52

Semi-Final 2   01 September 2011

Position	Lane	Athlete	Country		Time
1	6	Shalonda Solomon	United States	Q	22.46
2	3	Kerron Stewart	Jamaica	Q	22.77
3	8	Hrystyna Stuy	Ukraine	q	22.79
4	5	Debbie Ferguson-McKenzie	Bahamas	q	22.85
5	4	Dafne Schippers	Netherlands		22.92
6	7	Elizabeta Savlinis	Russia		23.04
7	2	Anyika Onuora	Great Britain		23.08
8	1	Allison Peter	US Virgin Islands		23.56

Women's 200m (continued)

Semi-Final 3   01 September 2011

Position	Lane	Athlete	Country		Time
1	4	Veronica Campbell-Brown	Jamaica	Q	22.53
2	6	Allyson Felix	United States	Q	22.67
3	5	Ivet Lalova	Bulgaria		23.03
4	7	Kai Selvon	Trinidad & Tobago		23.11
5	3	Yulia Gushchina	Russia		23.26
6	8	Janelle Redhead	Grenada		23.57
7	2	Anthonique Strachan	Bahamas		23.85
	1	Elyzaveta Bryzgina	Ukraine		DNF

FINAL   02 September 2011

Position	Lane	Athlete	Country	Time
GOLD	5	Veronica Campbell-Brown	Jamaica	22.22
SILVER	4	Carmelita Jeter	United States	22.37
BRONZE	3	Allyson Felix	United States	22.42
4	6	Shalonda Solomon	United States	22.61
5	8	Kerron Stewart	Jamaica	22.70
6	1	Debbie Ferguson-McKenzie	Bahamas	22.96
7	2	Hrystyna Stuy	Ukraine	23.02
8	7	Sherone Simpson	Jamaica	23.17

Men's 400m

Qualification for semi-finals: first four in each heat plus the next four fastest finishers.

Heat 1   28 August 2011

Position	Lane	Athlete	Country		Time
1	3	Rondell Bartholomew	Grenada	Q	44.82
2	1	Renny Quow	Trinidad & Tobago	Q	44.84
3	4	Greg Nixon	United States	Q	45.16
4	5	Tabarie Henry	US Virgin Islands	Q	45.22
5	2	Riker Hylton	Jamaica	q	45.54
6	6	Mathieu Gnanligo	Benin		47.01
7	7	Nelson Stone	Papua New Guinea		47.86
8	8	Kerfalla Camara	Guinea		49.74

Heat 2   28 August 2011

Position	Lane	Athlete	Country		Time
1	7	Jermaine Gonzales	Jamaica	Q	45.12
2	5	Jamaal Torrance	United States	Q	45.44
3	6	Marcin Marciniszyn	Poland	Q	45.51
4	2	Demetrius Pinder	Bahamas	Q	45.53
5	1	Erison Hurtault	Dominica	q	46.10
6	4	Nicolau Palanca	Angola		49.37
7	8	Ak. Hafiy Tajuddin Rositi	Brunei		50.12

Heat 3   28 August 2011

Position	Lane	Athlete	Country		Time
1	7	LaShawn Merritt	United States	Q	44.35
2	2	Kévin Borlée	Belgium	Q	44.77
3	3	Rabah Yousif	Sudan	Q	45.20
4	4	Yuzo Kanemaru	Japan	Q	45.51
5	5	Pavel Trenikhin	Russia	q	45.55
6	1	Arnold Sorina	Vanuatu		48.76
	8	Gary Kikaya	Democratic Republic of Congo		DNS
	6	Arismendy Peguero	Dominican Republic		DNS

Heat 4   28 August 2011

Position	Lane	Athlete	Country		Time
1	7	Kirani James	Grenada	Q	45.12
2	8	Jonathan Borlée	Belgium	Q	45.16
3	3	Ramon Miller	Bahamas	Q	45.31
4	2	William Collazo	Cuba	Q	45.89
5	4	Bonggo Park	South Korea		46.42
6	6	Pako Seribe	Botswana		46.97
7	5	Augusto Stanley	Paraguay		47.31
8	1	Bahaa Al Farra	Palestine		49.04

Heat 5   28 August 2011

Position	Lane	Athlete	Country		Time
1	2	Chris Brown	Bahamas	Q	45.29
2	3	Martyn Rooney	Great Britain	Q	45.30
3	8	Oscar Pistorius	South Africa	Q	45.39
4	7	Femi Ogunode	Qatar	Q	45.42
5	1	Nery Brenes	Costa Rica	q	45.47
6	6	Tony McQuay	United States		46.76
7	4	Ahmed Mohamed Al-Merjabi	Oman		47.99
	5	Abdou Razack Rabo Samma	Niger		DQ

Men's 400m (continued)

Qualification for Final: first two in each semi-final plus the next two fastest finishers.

Semi-Final 1   29 August 2011

Position	Lane	Athlete	Country		Time	
1	6	LaShawn Merritt	United States	Q	44.76	Q
2	3	Kévin Borlée	Belgium	Q	45.02	Q
3	4	Rabah Yousif	Sudan		45.43	
4	5	Renny Quow	Trinidad & Tobago		45.72	
5	7	Ramon Miller	Bahamas		45.88	
6	8	Yuzo Kanemaru	Japan		46.11	
7	1	William Collazo	Cuba		46.13	
8	2	Erison Hurtault	Dominica		46.41	

Semi-Final 2   29 August 2011

Position	Lane	Athlete	Country		Time	
1	4	Kirani James	Grenada	Q	45.20	Q
2	7	Tabarie Henry	US Virgin Islands	Q	45.53	Q
3	3	Chris Brown	Bahamas		45.54	
4	6	Jamaal Torrance	United States		45.73	
5	2	Nery Brenes	Costa Rica		45.93	
6	8	Marcin Marciniszyn	Poland		45.94	
7	5	Martyn Rooney	Great Britain		46.09	
8	1	Riker Hylton	Jamaica		46.99	

Semi-Final 3   29 August 2011

Position	Lane	Athlete	Country		Time
1	5	Jermaine Gonzales	Jamaica	Q	44.99
2	3	Jonathan Borlée	Belgium	Q	45.14
3	4	Rondell Bartholomew	Grenada	q	45.17
4	8	Femi Ogunode	Qatar	q	45.41
5	6	Greg Nixon	United States		45.51
6	2	Pavel Trenikhin	Russia		45.68
7	1	Demetrius Pinder	Bahamas		45.87
8	7	Oscar Pistorius	South Africa		46.19

FINAL   30 August 2011

Position	Lane	Athlete	Country	Time
GOLD	5	Kirani James	Grenada	44.60
SILVER	4	LaShawn Merritt	United States	44.63
BRONZE	6	Kévin Borlée	Belgium	44.90
4	3	Jermaine Gonzales	Jamaica	44.99
5	8	Jonathan Borlée	Belgium	45.07
6	2	Rondell Bartholomew	Grenada	45.45
7	7	Tabarie Henry	US Virgin Islands	45.55
8	1	Femi Ogunode	Qatar	45.55

Women's 400m

Qualification for semi-finals: first four in each heat plus the next four fastest finishers.

Heat 1   27 August 2011

Position	Lane	Athlete	Country		Time
1	8	Novlene Williams-Mills	Jamaica	Q	51.30
2	5	Allyson Felix	United States	Q	51.45
3	7	Joanne Cuddihy	Ireland	Q	51.82
4	3	Marta Milani	Italy	Q	51.94
5	1	Geisa Aparecida Coutinho	Brazil	q	52.15
6	2	Pinar Saka	Turkey		53.59
7	6	Graciela Martins	Guinea-Bissau		58.22
8	4	Sandrine Thiébaud-Kangni	Togo		59.68

Heat 2   27 August 2011

Position	Lane	Athlete	Country		Time
1	3	Antonina Yefremova	Ukraine	Q	51.35
2	7	Anastasiya Kapachinskaya	Russia	Q	51.43
3	5	Ndeye Fatou Soumah	Senegal	Q	52.23
4	6	Jessica Beard	United States	Q	52.40
5	4	Aliann Pompey	Guyana		53.59
6	1	Tjipekapora Herunga	Namibia		54.08
7	2	Alaa Hikmat Al-Qaysi	Iraq		55.62

Heat 3   27 August 2011

Position	Lane	Athlete	Country		Time
1	8	Rosemarie Whyte	Jamaica	Q	51.38
2	3	Antonina Krivoshapka	Russia	Q	51.52
3	4	Nataliya Pyhyda	Ukraine	Q	51.67
4	6	Fantu Magiso	Ethiopia	Q	52.23
5	1	Racheal Nachula	Zambia	q	53.49
6	7	Daisurami Bonne	Cuba		53.69
7	2	Evodie-Lydie Saramandji	Central African Republic		1:05.10
	5	Christine Ohuruogu	Great Britain		DQ

Heat 4   27 August 2011

Position	Lane	Athlete	Country		Time
1	2	Amantle Montsho	Botswana	Q	50.95
2	3	Francena McCorory	United States	Q	52.18
3	5	Lee McConnell	Great Britain	Q	52.75
4	1	Maris Mägi	Estonia	Q	52.93
5	4	Norma González	Colombia	q	53.35
6	7	Aymeé Martínez	Cuba		53.67
7	6	Ambwene Simukonda	Malawi		54.81

Heat 5   27 August 2011

Position	Lane	Athlete	Country		Time
1	5	Sanya Richards-Ross	United States	Q	51.37
2	3	Shericka Williams	Jamaica	Q	51.66
3	6	Moa Hjelmer	Sweden	Q	52.26
4	2	Denisa Rosolová	Czech Republic	Q	52.51
5	1	Nicola Sanders	Great Britain	q	52.65
6	4	Kseniya Karandyuk	Ukraine		54.10
7	7	Betty Burua	Papua New Guinea		56.98

Women's 400m (continued)

Qualification for Final: first two in each semi-final plus the next two fastest finishers.

Semi-Final 1   28 August 2011

Position	Lane	Athlete	Country		Time
1	3	Allyson Felix	United States	Q	50.36
2	6	Novlene Williams-Mills	Jamaica	Q	50.48
3	4	Antonina Krivoshapka	Russia	q	50.55
4	5	Nataliya Pyhyda	Ukraine		51.61
5	7	Moa Hjelmer	Sweden		52.35
6	1	Nicola Sanders	Great Britain		52.47
7	2	Maris Mägi	Estonia		53.27
8	8	Fantu Magiso	Ethiopia		53.41

Semi-Final 2   28 August 2011

Position	Lane	Athlete	Country		Time
1	6	Francena McCorory	United States	Q	50.24 Q
2	5	Shericka Williams	Jamaica	Q	50.46 Q
3	4	Sanya Richards-Ross	United States	q	50.66 q
4	3	Antonina Yefremova	Ukraine		50.88
5	7	Marta Milani	Italy		51.86
6	2	Geisa Aparecida Coutinho	Brazil		51.87
7	8	Lee McConnell	Great Britain		51.97
8	1	Norma González	Colombia		52.29

Semi-Final 3   28 August 2011

Position	Lane	Athlete	Country		Time
1	4	Amantle Montsho	Botswana	Q	50.13
2	5	Anastasiya Kapachinskaya	Russia	Q	50.41
3	3	Rosemarie Whyte	Jamaica		50.90
4	8	Jessica Beard	United States		51.27
5	7	Ndeye Fatou Soumah	Senegal		52.10
6	1	Denisa Rosolová	Czech Republic		52.53
7	2	Racheal Nachula	Zambia		53.30
	6	Joanne Cuddihy	Ireland		DQ

FINAL   29 August 2011

Position	Lane	Athlete	Country	Time
GOLD	4	Amantle Montsho	Botswana	49.56
SILVER	3	Allyson Felix	United States	49.59
BRONZE	6	Anastasiya Kapachinskaya	Russia	50.24
4	5	Francena McCorory	United States	50.45
5	2	Antonina Krivoshapka	Russia	50.66
6	7	Shericka Williams	Jamaica	50.79
7	1	Sanya Richards-Ross	United States	51.32
8	8	Novlene Williams-Mills	Jamaica	52.89

Men's 800m

Qualification for semi-finals: first three in each heat plus the next six fastest finishers.

Heat 1   27 August 2011

Position	Lane	Athlete	Country		Time
1	4	Nick Symmonds	United States	Q	1:46.54
2	6	Andreas Bube	Denmark	Q	1:46.64
3	5	Kevin López	Spain	Q	1:46.79
4	1	Mouhcine El Amine	Morocco		1:46.98
5	7	Andrew Ellerton	Canada		1:47.47
6	2	Moise Joseph	Haiti		1:48.17
7	3	Zaw Win Thet	Myanmar		1:58.36

Heat 2   27 August 2011

Position	Lane	Athlete	Country		Time
1	7	Yuriy Borzakovskiy	Russia	Q	1:46.14
2	1	Jackson Mumbwa Kivuva	Kenya	Q	1:46.57
3	5	Antonio Manuel Reina	Spain	Q	1:46.66
4	6	Prince Mumba	Zambia	q	1:46.73
5	4	Michael Rimmer	Great Britain		1:47.11
6	3	Masato Yokota	Japan		1:47.60
7	2	Shifaz Mohamed	Maldives		2:01.05

Heat 3   27 August 2011

Position	Lane	Athlete	Country		Time
1	4	Abubaker Kaki	Sudan	Q	1:44.83
2	5	Mohammed Aman	Ethiopia	Q	1:45.17
3	2	Alfred Kirwa Yego	Kenya	Q	1:45.50
4	1	Luis Alberto Marco	Spain	q	1:46.19
5	7	Moussa Camara	Mali	q	1:46.38
6	6	Ashot Hayrapetyan	Armenia		1:50.09
7	3	Fernando da Silva	Brazil		1:51.58

Heat 4   27 August 2011

Position	Lane	Athlete	Country		Time
1	6	David Lekuta Rudisha	Kenya	Q	1:46.29
2	1	Marcin Lewandowski	Poland	Q	1:46.73
3	2	Bram Som	Netherlands	Q	1:46.79
4	4	Mahfoud Brahimi	Algeria		1:46.94
5	7	Charles Jock	United States		1:47.95
6	5	Brice Etes	Monaco		1:48.22
7	3	Edgar Cortez	Nicaragua		1:49.10

Heat 5   27 August 2011

Position	Lane	Athlete	Country		Time
1	5	Kleberson Davide	Brazil	Q	1:46.06
2	7	Andrew Osagie	Great Britain	Q	1:46.08
3	1	Adam Kszczot	Poland	Q	1:46.16
4	4	Sajad Moradi	Iran	q	1:46.39
5	3	Mohammad Al-Azemi	Kuwait	q	1:46.64
6	8	Julius Mutekanga	Uganda		1:47.54
7	6	Farhan Ahmad	Pakistan		1:50.14
	2	Thomas Vandy	Sierra Leone		DNS

Men's 800m (continued)

Heat 6   27 August 2011

Position	Lane	Athlete	Country		Time
1	4	Rafith Rodríguez	Colombia	Q	1:48.26
2	3	Tamás Kazi	Hungary	Q	1:48.29
3	1	Khadevis Robinson	United States	Q	1:48.41
4	6	Daniel Nghipandulwa	Namibia		1:48.79
5	2	Lutmar Paes	Brazil		1:48.97
6	7	Ismail Ahmed Ismail	Sudan		1:52.33
7	8	Derek Mandell	Guam		1:57.11
8	5	Richard Blagg	Gibraltar		1:59.34

Qualification for Final: first two in each quarter-final plus the next two fastest finishers.

Semi-Final 1   28 August 2011

Position	Lane	Athlete	Country		Time
1	7	Mohammed Aman	Ethiopia	Q	1:44.57
2	5	Marcin Lewandowski	Poland	Q	1:44.60
3	6	Abubaker Kaki	Sudan	q	1:44.62
4	3	Alfred Kirwa Yego	Kenya	q	1:44.82
5	4	Khadevis Robinson	United States		1:45.27
6	1	Andreas Bube	Denmark		1:45.48
7	2	Sajad Moradi	Iran		1:46.17
8	8	Antonio Manuel Reina	Spain		1:48.45

Semi-Final 2   28 August 2011

Position	Lane	Athlete	Country		Time
1	6	Nick Symmonds	United States	Q	1:45.73
2	4	Yuriy Borzakovskiy	Russia	Q	1:45.73
3	5	Jackson Mumbwa Kivuva	Kenya		1:45.97
4	7	Andrew Osagie	Great Britain		1:46.12
5	2	Tamás Kazi	Hungary		1:46.53
6	8	Bram Som	Netherlands		1:46.69
7	3	Kevin López	Spain		1:46.86
8	1	Prince Mumba	Zambia		1:47.06

Semi-Final 3   28 August 2011

Position	Lane	Athlete	Country		Time
1	4	David Lekuta Rudisha	Kenya	Q	1:44.20
2	3	Adam Kszczot	Poland	Q	1:44.81
3	6	Kleberson Davide	Brazil		1:45.06
4	5	Rafith Rodríguez	Colombia		1:46.41
5	8	Mahfoud Brahimi	Algeria		1:46.79
6	1	Luis Alberto Marco	Spain		1:47.45
7	2	Moussa Camara	Mali		1:48.15
	7	Mohammad Al-Azemi	Kuwait		DNF

FINAL   30 August 2011

Position	Lane	Athlete	Country	Time
GOLD	6	David Lekuta Rudisha	Kenya	1:43.91
SILVER	4	Abubaker Kaki	Sudan	1:44.41
BRONZE	5	Yuriy Borzakovskiy	Russia	1:44.49
4	2	Marcin Lewandowski	Poland	1:44.80
5	3	Nick Symmonds	United States	1:45.12
6	7	Adam Kszczot	Poland	1:45.25
7	8	Alfred Kirwa Yego	Kenya	1:45.83
8	1	Mohammed Aman	Ethiopia	1:45.93

Women's 800m

Qualification for semi-finals: first four in each heat plus the next four fastest finishers.

Heat 1   01 September 2011

Position	Lane	Athlete	Country		Time
1	7	Jennifer Meadows	Great Britain	Q	2:01.11
2	5	Maggie Vessey	United States	Q	2:01.32
3	4	Rosibel García	Colombia	Q	2:01.33
4	2	Eunice Jepkoech Sum	Kenya	Q	2:01.37
5	6	Yuliya Rusanova	Russia	q	2:01.38
6	3	Egle Balciūnaité	Lithuania		2:02.88
7	1	Yvonne Hak	Netherlands		2:03.05

Heat 2   01 September 2011

Position	Lane	Athlete	Country		Time
1	4	Kenia Sinclair	Jamaica	Q	2:01.66
2	8	Halima Hachlaf	Morocco	Q	2:01.80
3	3	Yuliya Krevsun	Ukraine	Q	2:01.88
4	2	Maryna Arzamasava	Belarus	Q	2:01.97
5	7	Fantu Magiso	Ethiopia	q	2:02.58
6	5	Merve Aydin	Turkey		2:04.88
7	6	Yeon-jung Huh	South Korea		2:08.05
8	1	Zourah Ali	Djibouti		2:36.36

Heat 3   01 September 2011

Position	Lane	Athlete	Country		Time
1	2	Janeth Jepkosgei Busienei	Kenya	Q	1:59.36
2	5	Ekaterina Kostetskaya	Russia	Q	1:59.61
3	4	Alysia Johnson Montano	United States	Q	1:59.62
4	7	Marilyn Okoro	Great Britain	Q	1:59.74
5	1	Luiza Gega	Albania		2:03.21
6	6	Margarita Matsko	Kazakhstan		2:04.24
	3	Tetiana Petlyuk	Ukraine		DNF

Heat 4   01 September 2011

Position	Lane	Athlete	Country		Time
1	3	Mariya Savinova	Russia	Q	2:01.01
2	4	Caster Semenya	South Africa	Q	2:01.01
3	5	Cherono Koech	Kenya	Q	2:01.03
4	6	Alice Schmidt	United States	q	2:01.11
5	1	Emma Jackson	Great Britain	q	2:01.17
6	2	Tintu Luka	India	q	2:01.89
7	7	Truong Thanh Hang	Vietnam		2:03.52

Heat 5   01 September 2011

Position	Lane	Athlete	Country		Time
1	6	Annet Negesa	Uganda	Q	2:02.75
2	1	Zahra Bouras	Algeria	Q	2:02.77
3	3	Lucia Klocová	Slovakia	Q	2:02.81
4	7	Liliya Lobanova	Ukraine	Q	2:02.84
5	2	Nikki Hamblin	New Zealand		2:02.87
6	4	Lemlem Bereket	Canada		2:03.62
7	5	Sviatlana Usovich	Belarus		2:05.62

Women's 800m (continued)

Qualification for Final: first two in each quarter-final plus the next two fastest finishers.

Semi-Final 1   02 September 2011

Position	Lane	Athlete	Country		Time
1	3	Yuliya Rusanova	Russia	Q	1:58.73
2	4	Maggie Vessey	United States	Q	1:58.98
3	6	Jennifer Meadows	Great Britain		1:59.07
4	8	Eunice Jepkoech Sum	Kenya		1:59.94
5	2	Rosibel García	Colombia		2:00.79
6	1	Annet Negesa	Uganda		2:01.51
7	7	Maryna Arzamasava	Belarus		2:02.13
	5	Halima Hachlaf	Morocco		DNF

Semi-Final 2   02 September 2011

Position	Lane	Athlete	Country		Time
1	3	Mariya Savinova	Russia	Q	1:58.45
2	5	Janeth Jepkosgei Busienei	Kenya	Q	1:58.50
3	4	Alysia Johnson Montano	United States	q	1:58.67
4	6	Liliya Lobanova	Ukraine		1:59.38
5	2	Emma Jackson	Great Britain		1:59.77
6	1	Tintu Luka	India		2:00.95
7	8	Lucia Klocová	Slovakia		2:01.85
8	7	Zahra Bouras	Algeria		2:12.08

Semi-Final 3   02 September 2011

Position	Lane	Athlete	Country		Time
1	4	Caster Semenya	South Africa	Q	1:58.07
2	3	Ekaterina Kostetskaya	Russia	Q	1:58.64
3	5	Kenia Sinclair	Jamaica	q	1:58.93
4	1	Fantu Magiso	Ethiopia		1:59.17
5	6	Alice Schmidt	United States		2:01.16
6	2	Cherono Koech	Kenya		2:01.48
7	7	Marilyn Okoro	Great Britain		2:01.54
8	8	Yuliya Krevsun	Ukraine		2:05.37

FINAL   04 September 2011

Position	Lane	Athlete	Country	Time
GOLD	6	Mariya Savinova	Russia	1:55.87
SILVER	5	Caster Semenya	South Africa	1:56.35
BRONZE	1	Janeth Jepkosgei Busienei	Kenya	1:57.42
4	7	Alysia Johnson Montano	United States	1:57.48
5	4	Ekaterina Kostetskaya	Russia	1:57.82
6	2	Maggie Vessey	United States	1:58.50
7	8	Kenia Sinclair	Jamaica	1:58.66
8	3	Yuliya Rusanova	Russia	1:59.74

Men's 1500m

Qualification for semi-finals: first six in each heat plus the next six fastest finishers.

Heat 1   30 August 2011

Position	Athlete	Country		Time
1	Daniel Kipchirchir Komen	Kenya	Q	3:38.54
2	Nicholas Willis	New Zealand	Q	3:39.24
3	Yoann Kowal	France	Q	3:39.33
4	Diego Ruiz	Spain	Q	3:39.33
5	Mohamed Moustaoui	Morocco	Q	3:39.35
6	Matthew Centrowitz	United States	Q	3:39.46
7	Chaminda Indika Wijekoon	Sri Lanka	q	3:39.61
8	Ryan Gregson	Australia	q	3:40.01
9	Zebene Alemayehu	Ethiopia	q	3:41.08
10	James Shane	Great Britain		3:41.17
11	Sang-Min Sin	South Korea		3:55.02
	Mohammed Shaween	Saudi Arabia		DNF

Heat 2   30 August 2011

Position	Athlete	Country		Time
1	Asbel Kiprop	Kenya	Q	3:41.22
2	Mekonnen Gebremedhin	Ethiopia	Q	3:41.28
3	Abdalaati Iguider	Morocco	Q	3:41.41
4	Manuel Olmedo	Spain	Q	3:41.78
5	Tarek Boukensa	Algeria	Q	3:41.87
6	Eduar Villanueva	Venezuela	Q	3:41.89
7	Jeffrey Riseley	Australia		3:42.22
8	Andrew Wheating	United States		3:42.68
9	Dmitrijs Jurkevics	Latvia		3:42.69
10	Jeroen D'Hoedt	Belgium		3:45.54
11	Charles Delys	French Polynesia		3:51.36
12	Mehdi Baala	France		4:13.10
13	Ribeiro Pinto de Carvalho	East Timor		4:30.56

Heat 3   30 August 2011

Position	Athlete	Country		Time
1	Amine Laalou	Morocco	Q	3:39.86
2	Deresse Mekonnen	Ethiopia	Q	3:40.08
3	Silas Kiplagat	Kenya	Q	3:40.13
4	Taoufik Makhloufi	Algeria	Q	3:40.15
5	Yusuf Saad Kamel	Brunei	Q	3:40.27
6	Ciaran O'Lionaird	Ireland	Q	3:40.41
7	Juan Carlos Higuero	Spain	q	3:40.71
8	Leonel Manzano	United States	q	3:40.77
9	Geoffrey Martinson	Canada	q	3:40.98
10	Andreas Vojta	Austria		3:41.34
11	Hamza Driouch	Qatar		3:42.09
12	Nabil Mohammed Al-Garbi	Yemen		3:50.17
13	Florian Carvalho	France		3:53.88

Men's 1500m (continued)

Qualification for Final: first five in each semi-final plus the next two fastest finishers.

Semi-Final 1   01 September 2011

Position	Athlete	Country		Time
1	Matthew Centrowitz	United States	Q	3:46.66
2	Mekonnen Gebremedhin	Ethiopia	Q	3:46.71
3	Silas Kiplagat	Kenya	Q	3:46.75
4	Mehdi Baala	France	Q	3:46.87
5	Abdalaati Iguider	Morocco	Q	3:46.89
6	Yusuf Saad Kamel	Brunei		3:47.18
7	Amine Laalou	Morocco		3:47.65
8	Ryan Gregson	Australia		3:47.89
9	Geoffrey Martinson	Canada		3:48.83
10	Diego Ruiz	Spain		3:49.26
11	Taoufik Makhloufi	Algeria		3:50.86
12	Zebene Alemayehu	Ethiopia		3:51.19

Semi-Final 2   01 September 2011

Position	Athlete	Country		Time
1	Asbel Kiprop	Kenya	Q	3:36.75
2	Tarek Boukensa	Algeria	Q	3:36.84
3	Mohamed Moustaoui	Morocco	Q	3:36.87
4	Manuel Olmedo	Spain	Q	3:36.91
5	Eduar Villanueva	Venezuela	Q	3:36.96
6	Ciaran O'Lionaird	Ireland	q	3:36.96
7	Nicholas Willis	New Zealand	q	3:37.39
8	Yoann Kowal	France		3:37.44
9	Daniel Kipchirchir Komen	Kenya		3:37.58
10	Juan Carlos Higuero	Spain		3:37.92
11	Deresse Mekonnen	Ethiopia		3:44.65
12	Chaminda Indika Wijekoon	Sri Lanka		3:44.81
13	Leonel Manzano	United States		3:47.98

FINAL   03 September 2011

Position	Athlete	Country	Time
GOLD	Asbel Kiprop	Kenya	3:35.69
SILVER	Silas Kiplagat	Kenya	3:35.92
BRONZE	Matthew Centrowitz	United States	3:36.08
4	Manuel Olmedo	Spain	3:36.33
5	Abdalaati Iguider	Morocco	3:36.56
6	Mohamed Moustaoui	Morocco	3:36.80
7	Mekonnen Gebremedhin	Ethiopia	3:36.81
8	Eduar Villanueva	Venezuela	3:37.31
9	Mehdi Baala	France	3:37.46
10	Ciaran O'Lionaird	Ireland	3:37.81
11	Tarek Boukensa	Algeria	3:38.05
12	Nicholas Willis	New Zealand	3:38.69

Women's 1500m

Qualification for semi-finals: first six in each heat plus the next six fastest finishers.

Heat 1   28 August 2011

Position	Athlete	Country		Time
1	Hannah England	Great Britain	Q	4:13.45
2	Mimi Belete	Brunei	Q	4:13.50
3	Siham Hilali	Morocco	Q	4:13.59
4	Natalya Evdokimova	Russia	Q	4:14.36
5	Nancy Jebet Langat	Kenya	Q	4:14.37
6	Shannon Rowbury	United States	Q	4:14.43
7	Kalkidan Gezahegne	Ethiopia	q	4:14.45
8	Isabel Macías	Spain		4:14.75
9	Anzhelika Shevchenko	Ukraine		4:16.22
10	Tandiwe Nyathi	Zimbabwe		4:32.79
11	Nikki Hamblin	New Zealand		4:36.70

Heat 2   28 August 2011

Position	Athlete	Country		Time
1	Tugba Karakaya	Turkey	Q	4:10.38
2	Btissam Lakhouad	Morocco	Q	4:10.71
3	Viola Jelagat Kibiwot	Kenya	Q	4:10.74
4	Natalia Rodríguez	Spain	Q	4:10.76
5	Jennifer Simpson	United States	Q	4:10.84
6	Nataliya Tobias	Ukraine	Q	4:10.99
7	Olesya Syreva	Russia	q	4:11.24
8	Natallia Kareiva	Belarus		4:12.03
9	Genzeb Shumi	Brunei		4:12.32
10	Meskerem Assefa	Ethiopia		4:12.43
11	Lisa Dobriskey	Great Britain		4:12.70
12	Gladys Landaverde	El Salvador		4:28.50

Heat 3   28 August 2011

Position	Athlete	Country		Time
1	Maryam Yusuf Jamal	Brunei	Q	4:07.04
2	Nuria Fernández	Spain	Q	4:07.29
3	Morgan Uceny	United States	Q	4:07.43
4	Hellen Onsando Obiri	Kenya	Q	4:07.59
5	Ekaterina Martynova	Russia	Q	4:07.76
6	Gelete Burka	Ethiopia	Q	4:07.91
7	Asli Cakir	Turkey	q	4:08.05
8	Ingvill Måkestad Bovim	Norway	q	4:08.26
9	Kaila McKnight	Australia		4:08.74
10	Renata Plis	Poland		4:08.83
11	Anna Mishchenko	Ukraine		4:09.02
12	Malika Akkaoui	Morocco		4:14.79

Women's 1500m (continued)

Qualification for Final: first five in each semi-final plus the next two fastest finishers.

Semi-Final 1   30 August 2011

Position	Athlete	Country		Time
1	Tugba Karakaya	Turkey	Q	4:08.58
2	Hellen Onsando Obiri	Kenya	Q	4:08.93
3	Kalkidan Gezahegne	Ethiopia	Q	4:08.96
4	Maryam Yusuf Jamal	Brunei	Q	4:08.96
5	Morgan Uceny	United States	Q	4:09.03
6	Nuria Fernández	Spain		4:09.53
7	Siham Hilali	Morocco		4:09.64
8	Anna Mishchenko	Ukraine		4:09.78
9	Olesya Syreva	Russia		4:09.83
10	Kaila McKnight	Australia		4:10.83
11	Renata Plis	Poland		4:11.12
12	Shannon Rowbury	United States		4:11.49
13	Natalya Evdokimova	Russia		4:11.70

Semi-Final 2   30 August 2011

Position	Athlete	Country		Time
1	Natalia Rodríguez	Spain	Q	4:07.88
2	Jennifer Simpson	United States	Q	4:07.90
3	Nataliya Tobias	Ukraine	Q	4:07.99
4	Ingvill Måkestad Bovim	Norway	Q	4:08.03
5	Btissam Lakhouad	Morocco	Q	4:08.10
6	Hannah England	Great Britain	q	4:08.31
7	Mimi Belete	Brunei	q	4:08.42
8	Viola Jelagat Kibiwot	Kenya		4:08.64
9	Ekaterina Martynova	Russia		4:08.67
10	Asli Cakir	Turkey		4:11.54
11	Nancy Jebet Langat	Kenya		4:12.92
	Gelete Burka	Ethiopia		DNF

FINAL   01 September 2011

Position	Athlete		Country	Time
GOLD	Jennifer Simpson	USA	United States	4:05.40
SILVER	Hannah England	GBR	Great Britain	4:05.68
BRONZE	Natalia Rodríguez	ESP	Spain	4:05.87
4	Btissam Lakhouad	MAR	Morocco	4:06.18
5	Kalkidan Gezahegne	ETH	Ethiopia	4:06.42
6	Ingvill Måkestad Bovim	NOR	Norway	4:06.85
7	Mimi Belete	BRN	Brunei	4:07.60
8	Tugba Karakaya	TUR	Turkey	4:08.14
9	Nataliya Tobias	UKR	Ukraine	4:08.68
10	Morgan Uceny	USA	United States	4:19.71
11	Hellen Onsando Obiri	KEN	Kenya	4:20.23
12	Maryam Yusuf Jamal	BRN	Brunei	4:22.67

Men's 5000m

Qualification for final: first five in each heat plus the next five fastest finishers.

Heat 1   01 September 2011

Position	Athlete	Country		Time
1	Bernard Lagat	United States	Q	13:33.90
2	Thomas Pkemei Longosiwa	Kenya	Q	13:34.46
3	Dejen Gebremeskel	Ethiopia	Q	13:34.48
4	Isiah Kiplangat Koech	Kenya	Q	13:34.54
5	Galen Rupp	United States	Q	13:34.91
6	Hussain Jamaan Alhamdah	Saudi Arabia	q	13:35.47
7	Bilisuma Shugi	Brunei	q	13:35.86
8	Daniele Meucci	Italy	q	13:39.90
9	Javier Carriqueo	Argentina		13:47.51
10	Collis Birmingham	Australia		13:47.88
11	Mumin Gala	Djibouti		13:48.19
12	Rui Silva	Portugal		13:50.16
13	Craig Mottram	Australia		13:56.60
14	Moses Kibet	Uganda		14:05.15
15	Goitom Kifle	Eritrea		14:06.42
16	Abdishakur Nageye Abdulle	Somalia		15:13.64
	Mounir Miout	Algeria		DNF
	Francisco Javier Alves	Spain		DNF
	Kenenisa Bekele	Ethiopia		DNS
	Adrian Blincoe	New Zealand		DNS

Heat 2   01 September 2011

Position	Athlete	Country		Time
1	Imane Merga	Ethiopia	Q	13:37.96
2	Mohamed Farah	Great Britain	Q	13:38.03
3	Abera Kuma	Ethiopia	Q	13:38.41
4	Eliud Kipchoge	Kenya	Q	13:39.02
5	Alistair Ian Cragg	Ireland	Q	13:39.36
6	Amanuel Mesel	Eritrea	q	13:39.97
7	Jesús España	Spain	q	13:40.38
8	Abraham Kiplimo	Uganda		13:44.09
9	Andrew Bumbalough	United States		13:44.38
10	Elroy Gelant	South Africa		13:48.33
11	Ben St.Lawrence	Australia		13:51.64
12	Jake Robertson	New Zealand		13:53.57
13	Geofrey Kusuro	Uganda		13:54.58
14	Dejene Regassa	Brunei		13:56.83
15	Sylvain Rukundo	Rwanda		15:58.92
16	Rabah Aboud	Algeria		14:00.34
17	Gérard Gahungu	Burundi		14:09.15
18	Kazuya Watanabe	Japan		14:20.62
19	Seung-Ho Baek	South Korea		15:01.37
20	Christian Ngningba	Gabon		18:44.06
	Abdullah Abdulaziz Aljoud	Saudi Arabia		DNF

Men's 5000m (continued)

FINAL 04 September 2011

Position	Athlete	Country	Time
GOLD	Mohamed Farah	Great Britain	13:23.36
SILVER	Bernard Lagat	United States	13:23.64
BRONZE	Dejen Gebremeskel	Ethiopia	13:23.92
4	Isiah Kiplangat Koech	Kenya	13:24.95
5	Abera Kuma	Ethiopia	13:25.50
6	Thomas Pkemei Longosiwa	Kenya	13:26.73
7	Eliud Kipchoge	Kenya	13:27.27
8	Bilisuma Shugi	Brunei	13:27.67
9	Galen Rupp	United States	13:28.64
10	Daniele Meucci	Italy	13:29.11
11	Amanuel Mesel	Eritrea	13:33.99
12	Jesús España	Spain	13:33.99
13	Hussain Jamaan Alhamdah	Saudi Arabia	13:34.83
14	Alistair Ian Cragg	Ireland	13:45.33
15	Jake Robertson	New Zealand	14:03.09
	Imane Merga	Ethiopia	DQ

Women's 5000m

Qualification for final: first five in each heat plus the next five fastest finishers.

Heat 1   30 August 2011

Position	Athlete	Country		Time
1	Meseret Defar	Ethiopia	Q	15:19.46
2	Mercy Cherono	Kenya	Q	15:20.01
3	Sylvia Jebiwott Kibet	Kenya	Q	15:20.08
4	Sentayehu Ejigu	Ethiopia	Q	15:20.13
5	Yelena Zadorozhnaya	Russia	Q	15:23.90
6	Amy Hastings	United States	q	15:29.49
7	Hitomi Niiya	Japan	q	15:31.09
8	Helen Clitheroe	Great Britain	q	15:37.73
9	Kayo Sugihara	Japan		15:41.78
10	Alia Saeed Mohammed	United Arab Emirates		16:10.37
11	Pauline Niyongere	Burundi		17:23.56
	Sabina Fischer	Switzerland		DNS

Heat 2   30 August 2011

Position	Athlete	Country		Time
1	Genzebe Dibaba	Ethiopia	Q	15:33.06
2	Tejitu Daba	Brunei	Q	15:33.67
3	Linet Chepkwemoi Masai	Kenya	Q	15:33.99
4	Lauren Fleshman	United States	Q	15:34.04
5	Vivian Jepkemoi Cheruiyot	Kenya	Q	15:34.80
6	Zakia Mrisho	Tanzania	q	15:35.37
7	Elizaveta Grechishnikova	Russia	q	15:35.64
8	Megumi Kinukawa	Japan		15:38.23
9	Alemitu Bekele	Turkey		15:38.25
10	Molly Huddle	United States		15:42.00
11	Viktoriia Poliudina	Kyrgyzstan		16:32.68

FINAL   02 September 2011

Position	Athlete	Country	Time
GOLD	Vivian Jepkemoi Cheruiyot	Kenya	14:55.36
SILVER	Sylvia Jebiwott Kibet	Kenya	14:56.21
BRONZE	Meseret Defar	Ethiopia	14:56.94
4	Sentayehu Ejigu	Ethiopia	14:59.99
5	Mercy Cherono	Kenya	15:00.23
6	Linet Chepkwemoi Masai	Kenya	15:01.01
7	Lauren Fleshman	United States	15:09.25
8	Genzebe Dibaba	Ethiopia	15:09.35
9	Tejitu Daba	Brunei	15:14.62
10	Yelena Zadorozhnaya	Russia	15:15.48
11	Zakia Mrisho	Tanzania	15:18.81
12	Helen Clitheroe	Great Britain	15:21.22
13	Hitomi Niiya	Japan	15:41.67
14	Elizaveta Grechishnikova	Russia	15:45.61
15	Amy Hastings	United States	15:56.06

Men's 10000m

FINAL   28 August 2011

Position	Athlete	Country	Time
1	Ibrahim Jeilan	Ethiopia	27:13.81
2	Mohamed Farah	Great Britain	27:14.07
3	Imane Merga	Ethiopia	27:19.14
4	Zersenay Tadese	Eritrea	27:22.57
5	Martin Irungu Mathathi	Kenya	27:23.87
6	Peter Cheruiyot Kirui	Kenya	27:25.63
7	Galen Rupp	United States	27:26.84
8	Sileshi Sihine	Ethiopia	27:34.11
9	Paul Kipngetich Tanui	Kenya	27:54.03
10	Matthew Tegenkamp	United States	28:41.62
11	Rui Silva	Portugal	28:48.62
12	Daniele Meucci	Italy	28:50.28
13	Stephen Mokoka	South Africa	28:51.97
14	Scott Bauhs	United States	29:03.92
15	Yuki Sato	Japan	29:04.15
16	Juan Carlos Romero	Mexico	29:38.38
	Ali Hasan Mahbood	Brunei	DNF
	Bayron Piedra	Ecuador	DNF
	Kenenisa Bekele	Ethiopia	DNF
	Teklemariam Medhin	Eritrea	DNS

Women's 10000m

FINAL   27 August 2011

Position	Athlete	Country	Time
1	Vivian Jepkemoi Cheruiyot	Kenya	30:48.98
2	Sally Kipyego	Kenya	30:50.04
3	Linet Chepkwemoi Masai	Kenya	30:53.59
4	Priscah Jepleting Cherono	Kenya	30:56.43
5	Meselech Melkamu	Ethiopia	30:56.55
6	Shitaye Eshete	Brunei	31:21.57
7	Shalane Flanagan	United States	31:25.57
8	Ana Dulce Félix	Portugal	31:37.03
9	Jennifer Rhines	United States	31:47.59
10	Jessica Augusto	Portugal	32:06.68
11	Tigist Kiros	Ethiopia	32:11.37
12	Christelle Daunay	France	32:22.20
13	Kara Goucher	United States	32:29.58
14	Hikari Yoshimoto	Japan	32:32.22
15	Kayo Sugihara	Japan	32:53.89
16	Krisztina Papp	Hungary	32:56.02
17	Megumi Kinukawa	Japan	34:08.37
	Meseret Defar	Ethiopia	DNF
	Eloise Wellings	Australia	DNS

Men's Marathon

FINAL   04 September 2011

Position	Athlete	Country	Time
GOLD	Abel Kirui	Kenya	2:07:38
SILVER	Vincent Kipruto	Kenya	2:10:06
BRONZE	Feyisa Lilesa	Ethiopia	2:10:32
4	Abderrahime Bouramdane	Morocco	2:10:55
5	David Barmasai Tumo	Kenya	2:11:39
6	Eliud Kiptanui	Kenya	2:11:50
7	Hiroyuki Horibata	Japan	2:11:52
8	Ruggero Pertile	Italy	2:11:57
9	Stephen Kiprotich	Uganda	2:12:57
10	Kentaro Nakamoto	Japan	2:13:10
11	Rachid Kisri	Morocco	2:13:24
12	Eshetu Wendimu	Ethiopia	2:13:37
13	Marius Ionescu	Romania	2:15:32
14	Guojian Dong	China	2:15:45
15	David Webb	Great Britain	2:15:48
16	Cuthbert Nyasango	Zimbabwe	2:15:56
17	Beraki Beyene	Eritrea	2:16:03
18	Yuki Kawauchi	Japan	2:16:11
19	Aleksey Sokolov	Russia	2:16:23
20	Ser-Od Bat-Ochir	Mongolia	2:16:41
21	Aleksey Sokolov	Russia	2:16:48
22	Lee Merrien	Great Britain	2:16:59
23	Jin-hyeok Jeong	South Korea	2:17:04
24	Zicheng Li	China	2:17:35
25	José Manuel Martínez	Spain	2:17:44
26	Rafael Iglesias	Spain	2:17:45
27	Ahmed Baday	Morocco	2:17:59
28	Myongseung Lee	South Korea	2:18:05
29	Yoshinori Oda	Japan	2:18:05
30	Pablo Villalobos	Spain	2:18:12
31	Mike Morgan	United States	2:18:30
32	Urige Buta	Norway	2:20:16
33	Shiwei Wu	China	2:21:12
34	Jesper Faurschou	Denmark	2:21:15
35	Junhyeon Hwang	South Korea	2:21:54
36	Mike Tebulo	Malawi	2:22:45
37	Mike Sayenko	United States	2:22:49
38	Yukihiro Kitaoka	Japan	2:23:11
39	Jeff Eggleston	United States	2:23:33
40	Jun-Suk Hwang	South Korea	2:23:47
41	Nicholas Arciniaga	United States	2:24:06
42	Anton Kosmac	Slovenia	2:24:16
43	Samuel Goitom	Eritrea	2:25:42
44	Min Kim	South Korea	2:27:20
45	Sergio Reyes	United States	2:29:15
46	Coolboy Ngamole	South Africa	2:30:01
47	Bekir Karayel	Turkey	2:33:20
48	Ruben Sanca	Cape Verde	2:34:40
49	Jhon Lennon Casallo	Peru	2:36:43
50	Modike Lucky Mohale	South Africa	2:38:22
51	Sangay Wangchuk	Bhutan	2:38:33
	Jeff Hunt	Australia	DNF
	Khalid Kamal Yaseen	Brunei	DNF
	Yared Asmerom	Eritrea	DNF
	Yonas Kifle	Eritrea	DNF
	Michael Tesfay	Eritrea	DNF
	Chala Dechase	Ethiopia	DNF

Men's Marathon (continued)

Position	Athlete	Country	Time
	Gebregziabher Gebremariam	Ethiopia	DNF
	Bazu Worku	Ethiopia	DNF
	Zohar Zemiro	Israel	DNF
	Benjamin Kolum Kiptoo	Kenya	DNF
	Ali Mabrouk El Zaidi	Libya	DNF
	Adil Ennani	Morocco	DNF
	Abderrahim Goumri	Morocco	DNF
	David Ngakane	South Africa	DNF
	Daniel Kipkorir Chepyegon	Uganda	DNF
	Nicholas Kiprono	Uganda	DNF

Women's Marathon

FINAL 27 August 2011

Position	Athlete	Country	Time
GOLD	Edna Ngeringwony Kiplagat	Kenya	2:28:43
SILVER	Priscah Jeptoo	Kenya	2:29:00
BRONZE	Sharon Jemutai Cherop	Kenya	2:29:14
4	Bezunesh Bekele	Ethiopia	2:29:21
5	Yukiko Akaba	Japan	2:29:35
6	Xiaolin Zhu	China	2:29:58
7	Isabellah Andersson	Sweden	2:30:13
8	Jiali Wang	China	2:30:25
9	Marisa Barros	Portugal	2:30:29
10	Remi Nakazato	Japan	2:30:52
11	Rong Chen	China	2:31:11
12	Aberu Kebede	Ethiopia	2:31:22
13	Irene Jerotich Kosgei	Kenya	2:31:29
14	Atsede Baysa	Ethiopia	2:31:37
15	Tetyana Gamera-Shmyrko	Ukraine	2:31:58
16	Chaofeng Jia	China	2:31:58
17	Tera Moody	United States	2:32:04
18	Yoshimi Ozaki	Japan	2:32:31
19	Azusa Nojiri	Japan	2:33:42
20	Lishan Dula	Brunei	2:33:47
21	Olena Burkovska	Ukraine	2:34:21
22	Mai Ito	Japan	2:35:16
23	Margarita Plaksina	Russia	2:35:39
24	Susan Partridge	Great Britain	2:35:57
25	Diana Lobacevske	Lithuania	2:36:05
26	Xuequin Wang	China	2:36:10
27	Lisa Christina Stublic	Croatia	2:37:05
28	Sung-eun Kim	South Korea	2:37:05
29	Caroline Rotich	Kenya	2:37:07
30	Kathy Newberry	United States	2:37:28
31	René Kalmer	South Africa	2:38:16
32	Alisa McKaig	United States	2:38:23
33	Tetyana Holovchenko	Ukraine	2:39:25
34	Sook-Jung Lee	South Korea	2:40:23
35	Yun-hee Chung	South Korea	2:42:28
36	Bahar Dogan	Turkey	2:42:56
37	Annerien van Schalkwyk	South Africa	2:43:59
38	Colleen De Reuck	United States	2:44:35
39	Luvsanlundeg Otgonbayar	Mongolia	2:45:58
40	Zoila Gómez	United States	2:46:44
41	Judith Toribio	Peru	2:47:21
42	Alyson Dixon	Great Britain	2:50:51
43	Jun-Sook Park	South Korea	3:03:35
44	Bo-ra Choi	South Korea	3:10:06
45	Moleboheng Mafata	Lesotho	3:28:30
46	Shariska Winterdal	Aruba	3:49:49
	Dire Tune	Ethiopia	DQ
	Lucia Kimani	Bosnia & Herzegovina	DNF
	Alessandra Aguilar	Spain	DNF
	Aselefech Mergia	Ethiopia	DNF
	Jemena Misayauri	Peru	DNF
	Epiphanie Nyirabarame	Rwanda	DNF
	Yuliya Ruban	Ukraine	DNF
	Kateryna Stetsenko	Ukraine	DNF
	Tanith Maxwell	South Africa	DNS

Men's 3000m Steeplechase

Qualification for Final: first four in each heat plus the next three fastest finishers.

Heat 1   29 August 2011

Position	Athlete	Country		Time
1	Jacob Araptany	Uganda	Q	8:18.57
2	Mahiedine Mekhissi-Benabbad	France	Q	8:23.71
3	Richard Kipkemboi Mateelong	Kenya	Q	8:23.76
4	Ion Luchianov	Moldova	Q	8:23.88
5	Víctor García	Spain		8:28.97
6	Amor Ben Yahia	Tunisia		8:30.02
7	Abubaker Ali Kamal	Qatar		8:30.37
8	Andrey Farnosov	Russia		8:34.44
9	Alex Genest	Canada		8:36.67
10	Steffen Uliczka	Germany		8:37.35
11	Abdelkader Hachlaf	Morocco		8:46.14
12	William Nelson	United States		8:51.20

Heat 2   29 August 2011

Position	Athlete	Country		Time
1	Ezekiel Kemboi	Kenya	Q	8:10.93
2	Ruben Ramolefi	South Africa	Q	8:11.50
3	Hamid Ezzine	Morocco	Q	8:11.81
4	Nahom Mesfin	Ethiopia	Q	8:12.04
5	Bouabdellah Tahri	France	q	8:13.22
6	Ali Ahmed Al-Amri	Saudi Arabia		8:26.75
7	Simon Ayeko	Uganda		8:29.02
8	Jukka Keskisalo	Finland		8:31.52
9	Daniel Huling	United States		8:34.70
10	Tomás Tajadura	Spain		8:36.23
11	Bjørnar Ustad Kristensen	Norway		8:39.85
12	Lukasz Parszczynski	Poland		8:44.09

Heat 3   29 August 2011

Position	Athlete	Country		Time
1	Benjamin Kiplagat	Uganda	Q	8:19.96
2	Roba Gari	Ethiopia	Q	8:20.28
3	Brimin Kiprop Kipruto	Kenya	Q	8:21.89
4	Alberto Paulo	Portugal	Q	8:22.41
5	Abraham Kipkirong Chirchir	Kenya	q	8:23.09
6	Vincent Zouaoui-Dandrieux	France	q	8:23.79
7	Ángel Mullera	Spain		8:31.83
8	Youcef Abdi	Australia		8:38.42
9	Ben Bruce	United States		8:39.96
10	Matthew Hughes	Canada		8:58.52
	Mario Bazán	Peru		DNF

Men's 3000m Steeplechase (continued)

FINAL   01 September 2011

Position	Athlete	Country		Time
GOLD	Ezekiel Kemboi	Kenya		8:14.85
SILVER	Brimin Kiprop Kipruto	Kenya		8:16.05
BRONZE	Mahiedine Mekhissi-Benabbad	France		8:16.09
4	Bouabdellah Tahri	France		8:17.56
5	Roba Gari	Ethiopia		8:18.37
6	Jacob Araptany	Uganda		8:18.67
7	Richard Kipkemboi Mateelong	Kenya		8:19.31
8	Ion Luchianov	Moldova		8:19.69
9	Hamid Ezzine	Morocco		8:21.97
10	Benjamin Kiplagat	Uganda		8:22.21
11	Nahom Mesfin	Ethiopia		8:25.39
12	Vincent Zouaoui-Dandrieux	France		8:30.39
13	Ruben Ramolefi	South Africa		8:30.47
14	Abraham Kipkirong Chirchir	Kenya		8:33.56
15	Alberto Paulo	Portugal		8:33.84

Women's 3000m Steeplechase

Qualification for final: first four in each heat plus the next three fastest finishers.

Heat 1   27 August 2011

Position	Athlete	Country		Time
1	Binnaz Uslu	Turkey	Q	9:24.06
2	Habiba Ghribi	Tunisia	Q	9:24.56
3	Mercy Wanjiku Njoroge	Kenya	Q	9:24.95
4	Hanane Ouhaddou	Morocco	Q	9:25.96
5	Birtukan Fente	Ethiopia	q	9:28.82
6	Fionnuala Britton	Ireland		9:41.17
7	Bridget Franek	United States		9:43.09
8	Korene Hinds	Jamaica		9:52.11
9	Jana Sussmann	Germany		9:59.53
10	Diana Martín	Spain		10:04.59
11	Ángela Figueroa	Colombia		10:06.00

Heat 2   27 August 2011

Position	Athlete	Country		Time
1	Sofia Assefa	Ethiopia	Q	9:32.48
2	Lydia Chebet Rotich	Kenya	Q	9:36.70
3	Sara Moreira	Portugal	Q	9:36.97
4	Emma Coburn	United States	Q	9:38.42
5	Lyubov Kharlamova	Russia	q	9:40.04
6	Cristina Casandra	Romania		9:51.00
7	Gülcan Mingir	Turkey		10:04.83
8	Minori Hayakari	Japan		10:05.34
9	Salima El Ouali Alami	Morocco		10:07.71
10	Marcela Lustigová	Czech Republic		10:12.54
	Mardrea Hyman	Jamaica		DNF

Women's 3000m Steeplechase (continued)

Heat 3   27 August 2011

Position	Athlete	Country		Time
1	Milcah Chemos Cheywa	Kenya	Q	9:35.61
2	Yuliya Zaripova	Russia	Q	9:35.80
3	Gesa Felicitas Krause	Germany	Q	9:35.83
4	Birtukan Adamu	Ethiopia	Q	9:37.31
5	Barbara Parker	Great Britain	q	9:38.21
6	Beverly Ramos	Puerto Rico		9:45.50
7	Stephanie Garcia	United States		9:53.47
8	Stephanie Reilly	Ireland		9:55.49
9	Sandra Eriksson	Finland		10:03.20
10	Svitlana Shmidt	Ukraine		10:14.16
11	Iríni Kokkinaríou	Greece		10:15.18

FINAL   30 August 2011

Position	Athlete	Country	Time
GOLD	Yuliya Zaripova	Russia	9:07.03
SILVER	Habiba Ghribi	Tunisia	9:11.97
BRONZE	Milcah Chemos Cheywa	Kenya	9:17.16
4	Mercy Wanjiku Njoroge	Kenya	9:17.88
5	Lydia Chebet Rotich	Kenya	9:25.74
6	Sofia Assefa	Ethiopia	9:28.24
7	Binnaz Uslu	Turkey	9:31.06
8	Hanane Ouhaddou	Morocco	9:32.36
9	Gesa Felicitas Krause	Germany	9:32.74
10	Birtukan Fente	Ethiopia	9:36.81
11	Lyubov Kharlamova	Russia	9:44.14
12	Sara Moreira	Portugal	9:47.87
13	Emma Coburn	United States	9:51.40
14	Barbara Parker	Great Britain	9:56.66
15	Birtukan Adamu	Ethiopia	10:05.10

Men's 110m Hurdles

Qualification for semi-finals: first three in each heat plus the next four fastest finishers.

Heat 1   28 August 2011

Position	Lane	Athlete	Country		Time
1	5	Xiang Liu	China	Q	13.20
2	1	Andrew Turner	Great Britain	Q	13.32
3	4	Willi Mathiszik	Germany	Q	13.53
4	8	Richard Phillips	Jamaica	q	13.53
5	6	Ryan Brathwaite	Barbados		13.57
6	3	Sergey Shubenkov	Russia		13.70
7	2	Andreas Kundert	Switzerland		13.87
8	7	Ahmad Hazer	Lebanon		14.42

Heat 2   28 August 2011

Position	Lane	Athlete	Country		Time
1	3	Jason Richardson	United States	Q	13.19
2	5	Dwight Thomas	Jamaica	Q	13.31
3	2	Ronald Forbes	Cayman Islands	Q	13.54
4	1	Konstadínos Douvalídis	Greece		13.59
5	8	Lawrence Clarke	Great Britain		13.65
6	6	Alexander John	Germany		13.68
7	4	Dominik Bochenek	Poland		13.96
8	7	Balázs Baji	Hungary		14.06

Heat 3   28 August 2011

Position	Lane	Athlete	Country		Time
1	3	David Oliver	United States	Q	13.27
2	5	Fan Jiang	China	Q	13.47
3	6	Andrew Riley	Jamaica	Q	13.47
4	7	Dimitri Bascou	France	q	13.51
5	1	William Sharman	Great Britain	q	13.52
6	4	Héctor Cotto	Puerto Rico		13.60
7	8	Lehann Fourie	South Africa		13.86
8	2	Kim Fai long	Macau		15.35

Heat 4   28 August 2011

Position	Lane	Athlete	Country		Time
1	2	Aries Merritt	United States	Q	13.36
2	4	Dayron Robles	Cuba	Q	13.42
3	5	Dongpeng Shi	China	Q	13.55
3	3	Paulo Villar	Colombia	q	13.55
5	1	Erik Balnuweit	Germany		13.56
6	7	Emanuele Abate	Italy		13.63
7	8	Othman Hadj Lazib	Algeria		13.63
8	6	Tae-kyong Park	South Korea		13.83

Men's 110m Hurdles (continued)

Qualification for the Final: first three in each semi-final, plus the next two fastest finishers.

Semi-Final 1   29 August 2011

Position	Lane	Athlete	Country		Time
1	4	Xiang Liu	China	Q	13.31
2	5	Dayron Robles	Cuba	Q	13.32
3	3	Aries Merritt	United States	Q	13.32
4	6	Andrew Turner	Great Britain	q	13.44
5	1	Dimitri Bascou	France		13.62
6	7	Paulo Villar	Colombia		13.73
7	2	Richard Phillips	Jamaica		13.76
8	8	Willi Mathiszik	Germany		13.81

Semi-Final 2   29 August 2011

Position	Lane	Athlete	Country		Time
1	3	Jason Richardson	United States	Q	13.11
2	5	David Oliver	United States	Q	13.4
3	2	William Sharman	Great Britain	Q	13.51
4	4	Dwight Thomas	Jamaica	q	13.56
5	1	Dongpeng Shi	China		13.57
6	7	Ronald Forbes	Cayman Islands		13.67
7	6	Fan Jiang	China		13.71
8	8	Andrew Riley	Jamaica		13.75

FINAL   29 August 2011

Position	Lane	Athlete	Country	Time
GOLD	3	Jason Richardson	United States	13.16
SILVER	6	Xiang Liu	China	13.27
BRONZE	1	Andrew Turner	Great Britain	13.44
4	4	David Oliver	United States	13.44
5	8	William Sharman	Great Britain	13.67
5	7	Aries Merritt	United States	13.67
	5	Dayron Robles	Cuba	DQ
	2	Dwight Thomas	Jamaica	DNF

Women's 100m Hurdles

Qualification for semi-finals: first four in each heat plus the next four fastest finishers.

Heat 1 02 September 2011

Position	Lane	Athlete	Country		Time
1	2	Kellie Wells	United States	Q	12.73
2	1	Vonette Dixon	Jamaica	Q	12.82
3	6	Nikkita Holder	Canada	Q	12.90
4	3	Natalya Ivoninskaya	Kazakhstan	Q	12.96
5	4	Nevin Yanit	Turkey	q	13.07
6	8	Sonata Tamošaityte	Lithuania		13.28
7	7	Kierre Beckles	Barbados		13.44
8	5	Dipna Lim Prasad	Singapore		14.40

Heat 2 02 September 2011

Position	Lane	Athlete	Country		Time
1	2	Sally Pearson	Australia	Q	12.53
2	3	Derval O'Rourke	Ireland	Q	13.07
3	1	Brigitte Merlano	Colombia	Q	13.23
4	7	Beate Schrott	Austria	Q	13.25
5	6	Marina Tomic	Slovenia		13.36
6	4	Lavonne Idlette	Dominica		13.39
7	5	Hye-lim Jung	South Korea		13.39

Heat 3 02 September 2011

Position	Lane	Athlete	Country		Time
1	4	Tiffany Porter	Great Britain	Q	12.84
2	1	Lina Flórez	Colombia	Q	12.98
3	2	Tatyana Dektyareva	Russia	Q	13.05
4	5	Lisa Urech	Switzerland	Q	13.16
5	3	Marzia Caravelli	Italy		13.29
6	8	Cindy Billaud	France		13.50
7	7	Dedeh Erawati	Indonesia		13.56
8	6	Jeimy Bernárdez	Honduras		14.45

Heat 4 02 September 2011

Position	Lane	Athlete	Country		Time
1	2	Danielle Carruthers	United States	Q	12.79
2	4	Phylicia George	Canada	Q	12.84
3	3	Lucie Škrobáková	Czech Republic	Q	12.89
4	7	Brigitte Foster-Hylton	Jamaica	Q	12.96
5	8	Cindy Roleder	Germany	q	13.01
6	6	Seun Adigun	Nigeria	q	13.13
7	1	Anne Zagre	Belgium		13.47
8	5	Béatrice Kamboulé	Burkina Faso		13.76

Women's 100m Hurdles (continued)

Heat 5   02 September 2011

Position	Lane	Athlete	Country		Time
1	5	Dawn Harper	United States	Q	12.89 Q
2	6	Perdita Felicien	Canada	Q	12.95 Q
3	1	Yawei Sun	China	Q	13.03 Q
4	3	Sandra Gomis	France	Q	13.07 Q
4	8	Indira Spence	Jamaica	q	13.07 q
6	7	Anastasiya Soprunova	Kazakhstan		13.43
7	2	Pak Yan Poon	Hong Kong		14.04
	4	Demetra Arachovití	Cyprus		DNS

Qualification for the Final: first two in each semi-final, plus the next two fastest finishers.

Semi-Final 1   03 September 2011

Position	Lane	Athlete	Country		Time
1	6	Phylicia George	Canada	Q	12.73
2	4	Kellie Wells	United States	Q	12.79
3	1	Lisa Urech	Switzerland		12.86
4	3	Lina Flórez	Colombia		12.94
5	5	Vonette Dixon	Jamaica		13.00
6	7	Yawei Sun	China		13.19
7	2	Nevin Yanit	Turkey		13.31
8	8	Sandra Gomis	France		13.55

Semi-Final 2   03 September 2011

Position	Lane	Athlete	Country		Time
1	3	Sally Pearson	Australia	Q	12.36
2	5	Dawn Harper	United States	Q	12.74
3	8	Tatyana Dektyareva	Russia	q	12.76
4	4	Perdita Felicien	Canada		12.88
5	1	Indira Spence	Jamaica		12.93
6	7	Natalya Ivoninskaya	Kazakhstan		12.96
7	6	Lucie Škrobáková	Czech Republic		12.98
8	2	Seun Adigun	Nigeria		13.14

Semi-Final 3   03 September 2011

Position	Lane	Athlete	Country		Time
1	6	Tiffany Porter	Great Britain	Q	12.56
2	3	Danielle Carruthers	United States	Q	12.65
3	4	Nikkita Holder	Canada	q	12.84
4	8	Brigitte Foster-Hylton	Jamaica		12.87
5	1	Cindy Roleder	Germany		12.91
6	2	Beate Schrott	Austria		13.02
7	7	Brigitte Merlano	Colombia		13.21
	5	Derval O'Rourke	Ireland		DNS

FINAL   03 September 2011

Position	Lane	Athlete	Country		Time
GOLD	3	Sally Pearson	Australia	CR	12.28
SILVER	6	Danielle Carruthers	United States		12.47
BRONZE	8	Dawn Harper	United States		12.47
4	5	Tiffany Porter	Great Britain		12.63
5	1	Tatyana Dektyareva	Russia		12.82
6	2	Nikkita Holder	Canada		12.93
7	4	Phylicia George	Canada		17.97
	7	Kellie Wells	United States		DNF

Men's 400m Hurdles

Qualification for semi-finals: first four in each heat plus the next four fastest finishers.

Heat 1   29 August 2011

Position	Lane	Athlete	Country		Time
1	2	David Greene	Great Britain	Q	48.52
2	5	Cornel Fredericks	South Africa	Q	48.52
3	4	Georg Fleischhauer	Germany	Q	48.72
4	1	Emir Bekric	Serbia	Q	49.67
5	3	Omar Cisneros	Cuba	q	49.69
6	6	Mahau Suguimati	Brazil	q	49.74

Heat 2   29 August 2011

Position	Lane	Athlete	Country		Time
1	6	Louis van Zyl	South Africa	Q	48.58
2	3	Isa Phillips	Jamaica	Q	48.64
3	4	Felix Sánchez	Dominica	Q	48.74
4	5	Kerron Clement	United States	Q	48.91
5	2	Vincent Kiplangat Kosgei	Kenya	q	49.49
6	7	Jorge Paula	Portugal		49.82
7	1	Jamele Mason	Puerto Rico		49.98

Heat 3   29 August 2011

Position	Lane	Athlete	Country		Time
1	3	Javier Culson	Puerto Rico	Q	48.95
2	2	Angelo Taylor	United States	Q	49.38
3	1	Aleksandr Derevyagin	Russia	Q	49.43
4	7	Andrés Silva	Uruguay	Q	49.48
5	5	Takayuki Kishimoto	Japan	q	49.51
6	6	Zhilong Li	China		50.44
7	4	Seung-yun Lee	South Korea		52.98

Heat 4   29 August 2011

Position	Lane	Athlete	Country		Time
1	5	Bershawn Jackson	United States	Q	49.82
2	2	Jehue Gordon	Trinidad & Tobago	Q	49.90
3	6	Josef Robertson	Jamaica	Q	50.29
4	4	Jack Green	Great Britain	Q	50.39
5	7	Wen Cheng	China		50.51
6	1	Kenneth Medwood	Belize		51.19
7	3	Takatoshi Abe	Japan		51.90

Heat 5   29 August 2011

Position	Lane	Athlete	Country		Time
1	1	Jeshua Anderson	United States	Q	48.81
2	7	Nathan Woodward	Great Britain	Q	49.06
3	5	Stanislav Melnykov	Ukraine	Q	49.24
4	6	Leford Green	Jamaica	Q	49.45
5	2	Kurt Couto	Mozambique		49.86
6	4	Yuta Imazeki	Japan		50.92
7	3	Jean Antonio Vieillesse	Mauritius		51.02

Men's 400m Hurdles (continued)

Qualification for Final: first two in each semi-final plus the next two fastest finishers.

Semi-Final 1   30 August 2011

Position	Lane	Athlete	Country		Time
1	4	Javier Culson	Puerto Rico	Q	48.52
2	3	Cornel Fredericks	South Africa	Q	48.83
3	6	Angelo Taylor	United States	q	48.86
4	5	Jeshua Anderson	United States		49.33
5	2	Jack Green	Great Britain		49.62
6	8	Stanislav Melnykov	Ukraine		49.74
7	1	Takayuki Kishimoto	Japan		50.05
8	7	Josef Robertson	Jamaica		50.39

Semi-Final 2   30 August 2011

Position	Lane	Athlete	Country		Time
1	5	David Greene	Great Britain	Q	48.62
2	4	Felix Sánchez	Dominica	Q	49.01
3	3	Jehue Gordon	Trinidad & Tobago		49.08
4	6	Isa Phillips	Jamaica		49.16
5	7	Andrés Silva	Uruguay		49.63
6	1	Emir Bekric	Serbia		49.94
7	2	Mahau Suguimati	Brazil		50.89
8	8	Kerron Clement	United States		52.11

Semi-Final 3   30 August 2011

Position	Lane	Athlete	Country		Time
1	4	Bershawn Jackson	United States	Q	48.80
2	6	Louis van Zyl	South Africa	Q	49.05
3	7	Aleksandr Derevyagin	Russia	q	49.07
4	8	Leford Green	Jamaica		49.29
5	3	Georg Fleischhauer	Germany		49.36
6	5	Nathan Woodward	Great Britain		49.57
7	2	Vincent Kiplangat Kosgei	Kenya		49.71
8	1	Omar Cisneros	Cuba		50.10

FINAL   01 September 2011

Position	Lane	Athlete	Country	Time
GOLD	6	David Greene	Great Britain	48.26
SILVER	3	Javier Culson	Puerto Rico	48.44
BRONZE	8	Louis van Zyl	South Africa	48.80
4	7	Felix Sánchez	Dominica	48.87
5	4	Cornel Fredericks	South Africa	49.12
6	5	Bershawn Jackson	United States	49.24
7	1	Angelo Taylor	United States	49.31
8	2	Aleksandr Derevyagin	Russia	49.32

Women's 400m Hurdles

Qualification for semi-finals: first four in each heat plus the next four fastest finishers.

Heat 1   29 August 2011

Position	Lane	Athlete	Country		Time
1	3	Kaliese Spencer	Jamaica	Q	54.93
2	6	Anastasiya Rabchenyuk	Ukraine	Q	55.08
3	5	Queen Harrison	United States	Q	55.11
4	7	Lauren Boden	Australia	Q	55.78
5	2	Vera Barbosa	Portugal	q	56.31
6	4	Christine Merrill	Sri Lanka		57.05
7	1	Bimbo Miel Ayedou	Benin		58.80

Heat 2   29 August 2011

Position	Lane	Athlete	Country		Time
1	6	Zuzana Hejnová	Czech Republic	Q	55.12
2	7	Elena Churakova	Russia	Q	55.39
3	2	Elodie Ouédraogo	Belgium	Q	55.40
3	4	Hanna Titimets	Ukraine	Q	55.40
5	1	Sara Petersen	Denmark	q	56.32
6	5	Nikolina Horvat	Croatia	q	56.60
7	3	Hanitrasoa Olga Razanamalala	Madagascar		57.25

Heat 3   29 August 2011

Position	Lane	Athlete	Country		Time
1	4	Lashinda Demus	United States	Q	54.93
2	6	Perri Shakes-Drayton	Great Britain	Q	55.90
3	1	Hanna Yaroshchuk	Ukraine	Q	55.99
4	2	Nickiesha Wilson	Jamaica	Q	56.08
5	5	Jailma de Lima	Brazil		57.21
6	7	Birsen Engin	Turkey		57.22
7	8	Sharolyn Scott	Costa Rica		58.78
8	3	Fatima Sulaiman Dahman	Yemen		1:11.49

Heat 4   29 August 2011

Position	Lane	Athlete	Country		Time
1	4	Vania Stambolova	Bulgaria	Q	55.29
2	6	Ristananna Tracey	Jamaica	Q	55.96
3	1	Eilidh Child	Great Britain	Q	56.18
4	8	Muizat Ajoke Odumosu	Nigeria	Q	56.23
5	2	Nagihan Karadere	Turkey		56.76
6	3	Stine Meland Tomb	Norway		57.51
7	5	Déborah Rodríguez	Uruguay		59.52
8	7	Jessica Aguilera	Nicaragua		1:02.78

Heat 5   29 August 2011

Position	Lane	Athlete	Country		Time
1	7	Melaine Walker	Jamaica	Q	54.86
2	8	Natalya Antyukh	Russia	Q	54.88
3	3	Wenda Theron	South Africa	Q	56.13
4	5	Jasmine Chaney	United States	Q	56.28
5	1	Satomi Kubokura	Japan	q	56.66
6	2	Manuela Gentili	Italy		56.71
7	4	Amailya Sharoyan	Armenia		58.54
8	6	Kyeong-Mi Son	South Korea		1:00.21

Women's 400m Hurdles (continued)

Qualification for Final: first two in each quarter-final plus the next two fastest finishers.

Semi-Final 1   30 August 2011

Position	Lane	Athlete	Country		Time
1	6	Vania Stambolova	Bulgaria	Q	54.72
2	4	Elena Churakova	Russia	Q	55.02
3	3	Kaliese Spencer	Jamaica	q	55.02
4	7	Hanna Yaroshchuk	Ukraine		55.09
5	5	Elodie Ouédraogo	Belgium		55.29
6	8	Eilidh Child	Great Britain		55.89
7	1	Jasmine Chaney	United States		55.97
8	2	Nikolina Horvat	Croatia		57.02

Semi-Final 2   30 August 2011

Position	Lane	Athlete	Country		Time
1	4	Natalya Antyukh	Russia	Q	54.51
2	6	Melaine Walker	Jamaica	Q	54.97
3	5	Anastasiya Rabchenyuk	Ukraine	q	55.06
4	3	Queen Harrison	United States		55.44
5	1	Muizat Ajoke Odumosu	Nigeria		56.41
6	8	Nickiesha Wilson	Jamaica		56.58
7	2	Satomi Kubokura	Japan		56.87
8	7	Wenda Theron	South Africa		57.06

Semi-Final 3   30 August 2011

Position	Lane	Athlete	Country		Time
1	5	Lashinda Demus	United States	Q	53.82
2	6	Zuzana Hejnová	Czech Republic	Q	54.76
3	3	Perri Shakes-Drayton	Great Britain		55.07
4	4	Ristananna Tracey	Jamaica		55.55
5	8	Hanna Titimets	Ukraine		55.82
6	1	Sara Petersen	Denmark		56.49
7	7	Lauren Boden	Australia		56.68
8	2	Vera Barbosa	Portugal		57.70

FINAL   01 September 2011

Position	Lane	Athlete	Country	Time
GOLD	3	Lashinda Demus	United States	52.47
SILVER	8	Melaine Walker	Jamaica	52.73
BRONZE	5	Natalya Antyukh	Russia	53.85
4	2	Kaliese Spencer	Jamaica	54.01
5	1	Anastasiya Rabchenyuk	Ukraine	54.18
6	6	Vania Stambolova	Bulgaria	54.23
7	4	Zuzana Hejnová	Czech Republic	54.23
8	7	Elena Churakova	Russia	55.17

Men's High Jump

Qualification for the Final: Minimum achieved height 2.31m or 12 best qualifiers.

Group A   30 August 2011

Position	Athlete	Country		Height
1	Darvin Edwards	St Lucia	Q	2.31
2	Jesse Williams	United States	Q	2.31
3	Donald Thomas	Bahamas	Q	2.31
4	Jaroslav Bába	Czech Republic	Q	2.31
5	Dmytro Dem'yanyuk	Ukraine	Q	2.31
6	Aleksey Dmitrik	Russia	q	2.28
7	Erik Kynard	United States		2.28
8	Eike Onnen	Germany		2.28
8	Konstadínos Baniótis	Greece		2.28
8	Bohdan Bondarenko	Ukraine		2.28
11	Tom Parsons	Great Britain		2.25
12	Raivydas Stanys	Lithuania		2.25
13	Rožle Prezelj	Slovenia		2.25
14	Majed Aldin Ghazal	Syria		2.21
15	Edgar Rivera	Mexico		2.21
16	Víctor Moya	Cuba		2.21
	Ye-Hwan Yun	South Korea		-

Athlete	2.16	2.21	2.25	2.28	2.31
Darvin Edwards	O	O	XO	O	O
Jesse Williams	-	O	O	O	XO
Donald Thomas	XO	O	XXO	O	XO
Jaroslav Bába	-	O	O	O	XXO
Dmytro Dem'yanyuk	O	XO	O	XO	XXO
Aleksey Dmitrik	O	O	O	O	XXX
Erik Kynard	O	O	XO	O	XXX
Eike Onnen	O	O	XO	XO	XXX
Konstadínos Baniótis	O	XO	O	XO	XXX
Bohdan Bondarenko	O	O	XO	XO	XXX
Tom Parsons	O	XO	XO	XXX	
Raivydas Stanys	O	O	XXO	XXX	
Rožle Prezelj	O	XO	XXO	XXX	
Majed Aldin Ghazal	O	O	XXX		
Edgar Rivera	O	XO	XXX		
Víctor Moya	O	XXO	XXX		
Ye-Hwan Yun	XXX				

Group B 30 August 2011

Position	Athlete	Country		Height
1	Dimítrios Chondrokoúkis	Greece	Q	2.31
2	Mutaz Essa Barshim	Qatar	Q	2.31
3	Ivan Ukhov	Russia	Q	2.31
4	Aleksandr Shustov	Russia	Q	2.31
5	Guowei Zhang	China	Q	2.31
6	Trevor Barry	Bahamas	q	2.28
6	Raul Spank	Germany	q	2.28
8	Viktor Ninov	Bulgaria		2.28
9	Silvano Chesani	Italy		2.25
10	Diego Ferrín	Ecuador		2.21
11	Kabelo Kgosiemang	Botswana		2.21
12	Andriy Protsenko	Ukraine		2.21
13	Martyn Bernard	Great Britain		2.21
14	Dusty Jonas	United States		2.16
15	Osku Torro	Finland		2.16
15	Dmitry Kroyter	Israel		2.16
	Kyriakos Ioannou	Cyprus		DNS

Athlete	2.16	2.21	2.25	2.28	2.31
Dimítrios Chondrokoúkis	O	O	O	O	O
Mutaz Essa Barshim	O	O	O	XO	O
Ivan Ukhov	O	O	XO	XO	O
Aleksandr Shustov	O	O	XO	O	XO
Guowei Zhang	O	O	O	XO	XXO
Trevor Barry	O	O	O	O	XXX
Raul Spank	-	O	O	O	XXX
Viktor Ninov	O	XO	XO	XO	XXX
Silvano Chesani	XO	XXO	XXO	XXX	
Diego Ferrín	O	O	XXX		
Kabelo Kgosiemang	XXO	O	XXX		
Andriy Protsenko	XO	XO	XXX		
Martyn Bernard	XXO	XXO	XXX		
Dusty Jonas	O	XXX			
Osku Torro	XXO	XXX			
Dmitry Kroyter	XXO	XXX			

Men's High Jump (continued)

FINAL   01 September 2011

Position	Athlete	Country	Height
GOLD	Jesse Williams	United States	2.35
SILVER	Aleksey Dmitrik	Russia	2.35
BRONZE	Trevor Barry	Bahamas	2.32
4	Jaroslav Bába	Czech Republic	2.32
5	Dimítrios Chondrokoúkis	Greece	2.32
5	Ivan Ukhov	Russia	2.32
7	Mutaz Essa Barshim	Qatar	2.32
8	Aleksandr Shustov	Russia	2.29
9	Raul Spank	Germany	2.29
10	Guowei Zhang	China	2.25
11	Donald Thomas	Bahamas	2.20
12	Darvin Edwards	St Lucia	2.20
12	Dmytro Dem'yanyuk	Ukraine	2.20

Athlete	2.20	2.25	2.29	2.32	2.35	2.37
Jesse Williams	O	O	O	O	O	XXX
Aleksey Dmitrik	O	O	XO	XO	XO	XXX
Trevor Barry	O	O	-	O	XXX	
Jaroslav Bába	O	O	XXO	O	XXX	
Dimítrios Chondrokoúkis	O	O	O	XXO	XXX	
Ivan Ukhov	O	O	O	XXO	XXX	
Mutaz Essa Barshim	O	XO	XO	XXO	XXX	
Aleksandr Shustov	O	XO	O	XXX		
Raul Spank	O	O	XO	XXX		
Guowei Zhang	XO	O	XXX			
Donald Thomas	O	XXX				
Darvin Edwards	XO	XXX				
Dmytro Dem'yanyuk	XO	XXX				

Women's High Jump

Qualification for the Final: Minimum achieved height 1.95m or 12 best qualifiers.

Group A 01 September 2011

Position	Athlete	Country		Height
1	Anna Chicherova	Russia	Q	1.95
2	Svetlana Shkolina	Russia	Q	1.95
2	Emma Green Tregaro	Sweden	Q	1.95
4	Deirdre Ryan	Ireland	Q	1.95
5	Anna Iljuštšenko	Estonia	Q	1.95
6	Levern Spencer	St Lucia		1.92
7	Melanie Melfort	France		1.92
8	Ruth Beitia	Spain		1.92
9	Vita Styopina	Ukraine		1.92
10	Venelina Veneva-Mateeva	Bulgaria		1.89
11	Tonje Angelsen	Norway		1.85
12	Raffaella Lamera	Italy		1.85
12	Marielys Rojas	Venezula		1.85
14	Inika McPherson	United States		1.80
15	Da-Rye Han	South Korea		1.75

Athlete	1.75	1.80	1.85	1.89	1.92	1.95
Anna Chicherova	-	-	O	O	O	O
Svetlana Shkolina	-	-	O	O	O	XO
Emma Green Tregaro	-	-	O	O	O	XO
Deirdre Ryan	-	O	O	O	XXO	XO
Anna Iljuštšenko	-	XO	O	XO	XO	XXO
Levern Spencer	-	O	O	O	O	XXX
Melanie Melfort	-	O	XO	XO	O	XXX
Ruth Beitia	-	O	O	O	XO	XXX
Vita Styopina	O	O	O	O	XXO	XXX
Venelina Veneva-Mateeva	-	O	XO	O	XXX	
Tonje Angelsen	O	XO	O	XXX		
Raffaella Lamera	-	O	XXO	XXX		
Marielys Rojas	O	O	XXO	XXX		
Inika McPherson	O	O	XXX			
Da-Rye Han	XO	XXX				

Group B 01 September 2011

Position	Athlete	Country		Height
1	Blanka Vlašic	Croatia	Q	1.95
1	Antonietta Di Martino	Italy	Q	1.95
1	Brigetta Barrett	United States	Q	1.95
4	Doreen Amata	Nigeria	Q	1.95
5	Xingjuan Zheng	China	Q	1.95
5	Elena Slesarenko	Russia	Q	1.95
5	Svetlana Radzivil	Uzbekistan	Q	1.95
8	Esthera Petre	Romania		1.92
9	Ebba Jungmark	Sweden		1.92
10	Marina Aitova	Kazakhstan		1.89
10	Oksana Okuneva	Ukraine		1.89
12	Wanida Boonwan	Thailand		1.85
13	Danielle Frenkel	Israel		1.85
14	Marija Vukovic	Montenegro		1.80

Women's High Jump (continued)

Athlete	1.75	1.80	1.85	1.89	1.92	1.95
Blanka Vlašic	-	-	O	O	O	O
Antonietta Di Martino	-	O	O	O	O	O
Brigetta Barrett	O	O	O	O	O	O
Doreen Amata	-	-	O	O	XXO	XO
Xingjuan Zheng	-	O	O	O	O	XXO
Elena Slesarenko	-	O	O	O	O	XXO
Svetlana Radzivil	-	O	O	O	O	XXO
Esthera Petre	O	O	O	XO	O	XXX
Ebba Jungmark	-	O	O	XO	XO	XXX
Marina Aitova	-	O	O	O	XXX	
Oksana Okuneva	-	O	O	O	XXX	
Wanida Boonwan	O	O	O	XXX		
Danielle Frenkel	XO	XXO	O	XXX		
Marija Vukovic	O	XO	XXX			

FINAL   03 September 2011

Position	Athlete	Country	Height
GOLD	Anna Chicherova	Russia	2.03
SILVER	Blanka Vlašic	Croatia	2.03
BRONZE	Antonietta Di Martino	Italy	2.00
4	Elena Slesarenko	Russia	1.97
5	Svetlana Shkolina	Russia	1.97
6	Xingjuan Zheng	China	1.93
6	Deirdre Ryan	Ireland	1.93
8	Doreen Amata	Nigeria	1.93
8	Svetlana Radzivil	Uzbekistan	1.93
10	Brigetta Barrett	United States	1.93
11	Emma Green Tregaro	Sweden	1.89
12	Anna Iljuštšenko	Estonia	1.89

Athlete	1.89	1.93	1.97	2.00	2.03	2.05
Anna Chicherova	O	O	O	O	O	XXX
Blanka Vlašic	O	O	O	XO	XO	XXX
Antonietta Di Martino	O	O	O	XXO	XXX	
Elena Slesarenko	O	XO	O	XXX		
Svetlana Shkolina	O	O	XXO	XXX		
Xingjuan Zheng	XO	O	XXX			
Deirdre Ryan	XO	O	XXX			
Doreen Amata	XO	XO	XXX			
Svetlana Radzivil	XO	XO	XXX			
Brigetta Barrett	O	XXO	XXX			
Emma Green Tregaro	O	XXX				
Anna Iljuštšenko	XO	XXX				

Men's Pole Vault

Qualification for the Final: Minimum achieved height 5.70m or 12 best qualifiers.

Group A   27 August 2011

Position	Athlete	Country		Height
1	Romain Mesnil	France	q	5.65
1	Konstadínos Filippídis	Greece	q	5.65
1	Dmitry Starodubtsev	Russia	q	5.65
4	Fábio Gomes da Silva	Brazil	q	5.65
4	Malte Mohr	Germany	q	5.65
6	Mateusz Didenkow	Poland	q	5.65
7	Daichi Sawano	Japan	q	5.50
7	Pawel Wojciechowski	Poland	q	5.50
9	Alhaji Jeng	SWE		5.50
10	Raphael Holzdeppe	Germany		5.50
11	Mark Hollis	United States		5.35
12	Jere Bergius	Finland		5.35
	Steven Hooker	Australia		-
	Edi Maia	Portugal		-

Athlete	5.20	5.35	5.50	5.60	5.65
Romain Mesnil	-	-	O	-	O
Konstadínos Filippídis	-	O	O	O	O
Dmitry Starodubtsev	-	O	O	O	O
Fábio Gomes da Silva	-	-	O	XO	O
Malte Mohr	-	-	XO	O	O
Mateusz Didenkow	-	O	O	O	XO
Daichi Sawano	-	-	O	XXX	
Pawel Wojciechowski	-	O	O	XXX	
Alhaji Jeng	-	XO	O	XXX	
Raphael Holzdeppe	-	-	XXO	XXX	
Mark Hollis	-	O	XXX		
Jere Bergius	-	XO	-	XXX	
Steven Hooker	-	-	XXX		
Edi Maia	XXX				

Group B   27 August 2011

Position	Athlete	Country		Height
1	Lázaro Borges	Cuba	q	5.65
1	Renaud Lavillenie	France	q	5.65
3	Jeremy Scott	United States	q	5.60
4	Lukasz Michalski	Poland	q	5.60
4	Derek Miles	United States	q	5.60
6	Jan Kudlicka	Czech Republic	q	5.50
6	Steven Lewis	Great Britain	q	5.50
8	Igor Bychkov	Spain	q	5.50
9	Jérôme Clavier	France		5.50
9	Evgeniy Lukyanenko	Russia		5.50
11	Giovanni Lanaro	Mexico		5.50
12	Denys Yurchenko	Ukraine		5.35
13	Karsten Dilla	Germany		5.35
14	Yoo Suk Kim	South Korea		5.20

Men's Pole Vault (continued)

Athlete	5.20	5.35	5.50	5.60	5.65
Lázaro Borges	-	O	O	O	O
Renaud Lavillenie	-	-	O	-	O
Jeremy Scott	-	O	O	O	-
Lukasz Michalski	-	O	XO	O	X-
Derek Miles	-	O	XO	O	-
Jan Kudlicka	-	O	O	XXX	
Steven Lewis	O	O	O	XXX	
Igor Bychkov	O	-	O	X-	XX
Jérôme Clavier	-	O	XO	-	XXX
Evgeniy Lukyanenko	-	O	XO	XXX	
Giovanni Lanaro	-	XO	XXO	XXX	
Denys Yurchenko	-	O	XXX		
Karsten Dilla	-	XO	-	XXX	
Yoo Suk Kim	O	XXX			

FINAL   29 August 2011

Position	Athlete	Country	Height
GOLD	Pawel Wojciechowski	Poland	5.90
SILVER	Lázaro Borges	Cuba	5.90
BRONZE	Renaud Lavillenie	France	5.85
4	Lukasz Michalski	Poland	5.85
5	Malte Mohr	Germany	5.85
6	Konstadínos Filippídis	Greece	5.75
7	Mateusz Didenkow	Poland	5.75
8	Fábio Gomes da Silva	Brazil	5.65
9	Jan Kudlicka	Czech Republic	5.65
9	Steven Lewis	Great Britain	5.65
9	Jeremy Scott	United States	5.65
12	Dmitry Starodubtsev	Russia	5.65
13	Derek Miles	United States	5.65
14	Daichi Sawano	Japan	5.65
	Igor Bychkov	Spain	-
	Romain Mesnil	France	-

Athlete	5.50	5.65	5.75	5.85	5.90	5.95
Pawel Wojciechowski	O	O	O	X-	XO	XXX
Lázaro Borges	O	O	XXO	O	XXO	XXX
Renaud Lavillenie	-	O	O	O	XXX	
Lukasz Michalski	O	O	XO	O	XXX	
Malte Mohr	O	XO	O	XXO	XXX	
Konstadínos Filippídis	O	XO	XO	XXX		
Mateusz Didenkow	XO	XO	XXO	XXX		
Fábio Gomes da Silva	XO	O	XXX			
Jan Kudlicka	O	XO	XXX			
Steven Lewis	O	X	XXX			
Jeremy Scott	O	XO	XXX			
Dmitry Starodubtsev	XO	XO	XXX			
Derek Miles	O	XXO	XXX			
Daichi Sawano	XO	XXO	XXX			
Igor Bychkov	XXX					
Romain Mesnil	-	XXX				

Women's Pole Vault

Qualification for the Final: Minimum achieved height 4.60m or 12 best qualifiers.

Group A   28 August 2011

Position	Athlete	Country		Height
1	Martina Strutz	Germany	q	4.55
2	Jennifer Suhr	United States	q	4.55
3	Silke Spiegelburg	Germany	q	4.55
3	Svetlana Feofanova	Russia	q	4.55
5	Monika Pyrek	Poland	q	4.50
6	Alana Boyd	Australia		4.50
7	Kylie Hutson	United States		4.50
8	Anna Katharina Schmid	Switzerland		4.40
9	Anastasiya Shvedova	Belarus		4.40
10	Tina Šutej	Slovenia		4.40
11	Dailis Caballero	Cuba		4.40
12	Kelsie Hendry	Canada		4.25
13	Maria Eleonor Tavares	Portugal		4.25
13	Malin Dahlström	Sweden		4.25
	Holly Bleasdale	Great Britain		-
	Cathrine Larsåsen	Norway		-
	Sha Wu	China		DNS

Athlete	4.10	4.25	4.40	4.50	4.55
Martina Strutz	-	-	O	O	O
Jennifer Suhr	-	-	-	XXO	O
Silke Spiegelburg	-	-	O	O	XO
Svetlana Feofanova	-	-	O	-	XO
Monika Pyrek	-	O	O	O	XXX
Alana Boyd	O	XO	O	XO	XXX
Kylie Hutson	-	O	O	XXO	XXX
Anna Katharina Schmid	O	O	O	XXX	
Anastasiya Shvedova	-	XO	O	XX	
Tina Šutej	O	O	XO	XXX	
Dailis Caballero	O	XXO	XXO	XXX	
Kelsie Hendry	-	O	XXX		
Maria Eleonor Tavares	O	XO	XXX		
Malin Dahlström	O	XO	XXX		
Holly Bleasdale	-	XXX			
Cathrine Larsåsen	XXX				

Group B   28 August 2011

Position	Athlete	Country		Height
1	Fabiana Murer	Brazil	q	4.55
1	Anna Rogowska	Poland	q	4.55
1	Elena Isinbaeva	Russia	q	4.55
4	Jirina Ptácniková	Czech Republic	q	4.55
5	Yarisley Silva	Cuba	q	4.55
6	Nikoléta Kiriakopoúlou	Greece	q	4.55
7	Kristina Gadschiew	Germany	q	4.50
8	Kate Dennison	Great Britain		4.50
9	Nicole Büchler	Switzerland		4.50
10	Yun-hee Choi	South Korea		4.40
11	Lacy Janson	United States		4.40
12	Anna Giordano Bruno	Italy		4.40
13	Caroline Bonde Holm	Denmark		4.25
13	Jillian Schwartz	Israel		4.25
15	Ling Li	China		4.25
16	Tori Pena	Ireland		4.10
	Ana Pinero	Spain		-
	Minna Nikkanen	Finland		DNS

Athlete	4.10	4.25	4.40	4.50	4.55
Fabiana Murer	-	-	-	-	O
Anna Rogowska	-	-	O	-	O
Elena Isinbaeva	-	-	-	-	O
Jirina Ptácniková	-	O	XO	O	O
Yarisley Silva	-	-	XO	XO	XO
Nikoléta Kiriakopoúlou	-	O	XXO	O	XXO
Kristina Gadschiew	-	-	O	O	XXX
Kate Dennison	-	O	XO	XO	-
Nicole Büchler	O	O	XXO	XXO	XXX
Yun-hee Choi	O	XO	O	XXX	
Lacy Janson	-	XXO	O	XXX	
Anna Giordano Bruno	O	O	XXO	XXX	
Caroline Bonde Holm	O	XO	XXX		
Jillian Schwartz	O	XO	XXX		
Ling Li	O	XXO	XXX		
Tori Pena	O	XXX			
Ana Pinero	-	XXX			

FINAL 30 August 2011

Position	Athlete	Country	Height
GOLD	Fabiana Murer	Brazil	4.85
SILVER	Martina Strutz	Germany	4.80
BRONZE	Svetlana Feofanova	Russia	4.75
4	Jennifer Suhr	United States	4.70
5	Yarisley Silva	Cuba	4.70
6	Elena Isinbaeva	Russia	4.65
7	Jirina Ptácniková	Czech Republic	4.65
8	Nikoléta Kiriakopoúlou	Greece	4.65
9	Silke Spiegelburg	Germany	4.65
10	Kristina Gadschiew	Germany	4.55
10	Monika Pyrek	Poland	4.55
10	Anna Rogowska	Poland	4.55

Athlete	4.30	4.45	4.55	4.65	4.70
Fabiana Murer	-	-	O	O	-
Martina Strutz	-	XO	O	O	O
Svetlana Feofanova	-	O	O	O	-
Jennifer Suhr	-	-	O	-	XO
Yarisley Silva	-	O	O	O	XXO
Elena Isinbaeva	-	-	-	O	-
Jirina Ptácniková	O	O	XO	O	XXX
Nikoléta Kiriakopoúlou	O	-	O	XO	XXX
Silke Spiegelburg	-	XXO	XO	XXO	XXX
Kristina Gadschiew	O	O	O	XXX	
Monika Pyrek	-	O	O	XXX	
Anna Rogowska	-	O	O	-	XXX

Athlete	4.75	4.80	4.85	4.90	4.92
Fabiana Murer	O	XO	O	XX-	X
Martina Strutz	XO	O	X-	XX	
Svetlana Feofanova	O	XXX			
Jennifer Suhr	XXX				
Yarisley Silva	-	XXX			
Elena Isinbaeva	X-	XX			
Jirina Ptácniková					
Nikoléta Kiriakopoúlou					
Silke Spiegelburg					
Kristina Gadschiew					
Monika Pyrek					
Anna Rogowska					

Men's Long Jump

Qualification for the Final: Minimum achieved distance 8.15m or 12 best qualifiers.

Group A   01 September 2011

Position	Athlete	Country	Wind		Distance
1	Dwight Phillips	United States	(-0.2)	Q	8.32
2	Mitchell Watt	Australia	-0.2	Q	8.15
3	Christian Reif	Germany	-0.3	q	8.13
4	Aleksandr Menkov	Russia	(-1.2)	q	8.07
5	Yahya Berrabah	Morocco	-0.1	q	8.05
6	Deokhyeon Kim	South Korea	-0.4	q	8.02
7	Christopher Tomlinson	Great Britain	(-0.5)	q	8.02
8	Marquise Goodwin	United States	(-0.1)		8.02
9	Godfrey Khotso Mokoena	South Africa	(-0.2)		8.00
10	Ignisious Gaisah	Ghana	(-1.0)		7.92
11	Damar Forbes	Jamaica	-0.7		7.91
12	Luis Felipe Méliz	Spain	0.0		7.82
13	Robert Crowther	Australia	(-0.2)		7.74
14	Jorge McFarlane	Peru	-0.1		7.66
15	Michel Tornéus	Sweden	0.0		7.65
16	Salim Sdiri	France	(-1.3)		7.58
	Mohamed Fathalla Difallah	Egypt			-
	Povilas Mykolaitis	Lithuania			-

Athlete	Jump 1	Jump 2	Jump 3
Dwight Phillips	8.32	-	-
Mitchell Watt	6.43	8.15	-
Christian Reif	X	8.13	X
Aleksandr Menkov	8.07	X	-
Yahya Berrabah	X	8.03	8.05
Deokhyeon Kim	7.86	7.99	8.02
Christopher Tomlinson	7.95	7.84	8.02
Marquise Goodwin	7.92	7.78	8.02
Godfrey Khotso Mokoena	X	X	8.00
Ignisious Gaisah	X	7.92	7.78
Damar Forbes	X	X	7.91
Luis Felipe Méliz	7.80	7.69	7.82
Robert Crowther	7.74	7.64	7.67
Jorge McFarlane	X	X	7.66
Michel Tornéus	X	7.62	7.65
Salim Sdiri	7.49	7.58	7.48
Mohamed Fathalla Difallah	X	X	X
Povilas Mykolaitis	X	X	X

Men's Long Jump (continued)

Group B   01 September 2011

Position	Athlete	Country	Wind		Distance
1	Ngonidzashe Makusha	Zimbabwe	(-0.3)	q	8.11
2	Sebastian Bayer	Germany	-1.3	q	8.11
3	Marcos Chuva	Portugal	(-0.4)	q	8.10
4	Will Claye	United States	-0.1	q	8.09
5	Luvo Manyonga	South Africa	(-0.2)	q	8.04
6	Loúis Tsátoumas	Greece	(-0.9)		8.01
7	Greg Rutherford	Great Britain	-1.4		8.00
8	Eusebio Cáceres	Spain	-0.3		7.91
9	Tyrone Smith	Bermuda	(-0.1)		7.91
10	Fabrice Lapierre	Australia	(-1.2)		7.89
11	Irving Saladino	Panama	-0.2		7.84
12	Raymond Higgs	Bahamas	(-0.8)		7.72
13	Ching-Hsuan Lin	Chinese Taipei	-0.4		7.30
14	Kristinn Torfason	Iceland	-0.2		7.17
15	Trevell Quinley	United States	(-2.3)		7.09
16	Xiongfeng Su	China	-1.0		7.03
	Henry Dagmil	Philippines			-
	Stanley Gbagbeke	Nigeria			DNS

Athlete	Jump 1	Jump 2	Jump 3
Ngonidzashe Makusha	8.05	7.83	8.11
Sebastian Bayer	8.11	-	-
Marcos Chuva	X	8.10	X
Will Claye	7.83	7.94	8.09
Luvo Manyonga	7.77	7.72	8.04
Loúis Tsátoumas	8.01	7.89	X
Greg Rutherford	8.00	X	-
Eusebio Cáceres	7.60	7.90	7.91
Tyrone Smith	X	7.79	7.91
Fabrice Lapierre	7.80	7.89	7.76
Irving Saladino	X	X	7.84
Raymond Higgs	X	7.72	X
Ching-Hsuan Lin	7.30	X	X
Kristinn Torfason	5.52	6.25	7.17
Trevell Quinley	7.09	X	X
Xiongfeng Su	7.03	-	-
Henry Dagmil	X	X	X
Stanley Gbagbeke			

Men's Long Jump (continued)

FINAL   02 September 2011

Position	Athlete	Country	Wind	Distance
GOLD	Dwight Phillips	United States	0.0	8.45
SILVER	Mitchell Watt	Australia	-0.4	8.33
BRONZE	Ngonidzashe Makusha	Zimbabwe	-0.3	8.29
4	Yahya Berrabah	Morocco	-0.4	8.23
5	Luvo Manyonga	South Africa	-0.2	8.21
6	Aleksandr Menkov	Russia	0.0	8.19
7	Christian Reif	Germany	-0.6	8.19
8	Sebastian Bayer	Germany	-0.3	8.17
9	Will Claye	United States	-0.1	8.10
10	Marcos Chuva	Portugal	-0.1	8.05
11	Christopher Tomlinson	Great Britain	-0.1	7.87
	Deokhyeon Kim	South Korea		DNS

Athlete	Jump 1	Jump 2	Jump 3	Jump 4	Jump 5	Jump 6
Dwight Phillips	8.31	8.45	X	-	X	X
Mitchell Watt	X	8.33	4.90	7.79	X	8.06
Ngonidzashe Makusha	8.29	8.15	8.14	8.00	8.07	X
Yahya Berrabah	8.03	8.23	X	X	X	X
Luvo Manyonga	8.21	X	7.82	X	X	X
Aleksandr Menkov	7.74	8.19	X	X	8.07	X
Christian Reif	7.90	8.19	X	7.98	X	7.97
Sebastian Bayer	8.17	8.06	8.13	8.04	7.91	8.02
Will Claye	8.08	7.98	8.10			
Marcos Chuva	8.05	X	7.99			
Christopher Tomlinson	7.86	X	7.87			
Deokhyeon Kim						

Women's Long Jump

Qualification for the Final: Minimum achieved distance 6.75m or 12 best qualifiers.

Group A   27 August 2011

Position	Athlete	Country	Wind		Distance
1	Brittney Reese	United States	(-0.3)	Q	6.79
2	Naide Gomes	Portugal	-0.2	Q	6.76
3	Olga Kucherenko	Russia	-0.3	q	6.67
4	Carolina Klüft	Sweden	-0.5	q	6.60
5	Janay DeLoach	United States	(-0.1)	q	6.51
6	Bianca Kappler	Germany	-0.5		6.48
7	Viktoriya Rybalko	Ukraine	-0.2		6.45
8	Veronika Shutkova	Belarus	-0.1		6.45
9	Bianca Stuart	Bahamas	-0.6		6.44
10	Marestella Torres	Philippines	-0.4		6.31
11	Teresa Dobija	Poland	(-0.2)		6.30
12	Lauma Griva	Latvia	-0.2		6.27
13	Keila Costa	Brazil	-0.3		6.26
14	Yuliya Tarasova	Uzbekistan	-0.4		6.26
15	Jovanee Jarrett	Jamaica	-0.3		6.19
16	Ola Sesay	Sierra Leone	-0.3		5.94
17	Enas Gharib	Egypt	-0.2		5.48
	Ivana Španovic	Serbia			DNS

Athlete	Jump 1	Jump 2	Jump 3
Brittney Reese	6.41	X	6.79
Naide Gomes	6.76	-	-
Olga Kucherenko	6.37	6.67	X
Carolina Klüft	6.60	X	6.40
Janay DeLoach	X	6.29	6.51
Bianca Kappler	6.48	6.48	6.32
Viktoriya Rybalko	6.45	X	6.40
Veronika Shutkova	6.45	X	6.29
Bianca Stuart	X	3.96	6.44
Marestella Torres	6.31	6.19	6.22
Teresa Dobija	X	X	6.30
Lauma Griva	6.27	6.16	6.10
Keila Costa	6.09	6.07	6.26
Yuliya Tarasova	X	6.26	X
Jovanee Jarrett	6.19	X	5.75
Ola Sesay	5.64	5.94	5.43
Enas Gharib	5.35	5.48	5.44
Ivana Španovic			

Women's Long Jump (continued)

Group B   27 August 2011

Position	Athlete	Country	Wind		Distance
1	Maurren Higa Maggi	Brazil	-0.1	Q	6.86
2	Nastassia Mironchyk-Ivanova	Belarus	-0.3	Q	6.80
3	Darya Klishina	Russia	0.0	Q	6.77
4	Funmi Jimoh	United States	(-0.4)	q	6.68
5	Ineta Radevica	Latvia	-0.4	q	6.59
6	Mayookha Johny	India	(-0.4)	q	6.53
7	Karin Mey Melis	Turkey	(-0.2)	q	6.52
8	Olga Zaytseva	Russia	-0.1		6.50
9	Blessing Okagbare	Nigeria	-0.3		6.36
10	Irene Pusterla	Switzerland	-0.5		6.34
11	Shara Proctor	Great Britain	(-0.4)		6.34
12	Éloyse Lesueur	France	-0.4		6.22
13	Nina Kolaric	Slovenia	(-0.3)		6.19
14	Soonok Jung	South Korea	(-0.4)		6.18
15	Chantel Malone	British Virgin Islands	(-0.4)		6.12
16	Sostene Moguenara	Germany	(-0.8)		6.02
17	Tori Polk	United States	(-0.3)		5.66
	Concepción Montaner	Spain			-

Athlete	Jump 1	Jump 2	Jump 3
Maurren Higa Maggi	6.55	6.86	-
Nastassia Mironchyk-Ivanova	6.80	-	-
Darya Klishina	6.77	-	-
Funmi Jimoh	6.68	X	6.26
Ineta Radevica	X	6.59	X
Mayookha Johny	6.52	X	6.53
Karin Mey Melis	X	X	6.52
Olga Zaytseva	6.50	X	X
Blessing Okagbare	X	6.36	6.27
Irene Pusterla	6.34	6.22	6.21
Shara Proctor	X	X	6.34
Éloyse Lesueur	X	X	6.22
Nina Kolaric	X	6.19	6.15
Soonok Jung	X	X	6.18
Chantel Malone	5.96	6.12	X
Sostene Moguenara	X	X	6.02
Tori Polk	X	5.66	X
Concepción Montaner	X	X	X

Women's Long Jump (continued)

FINAL　　　　　28 August 2011

Position	Athlete	Country	Wind	Distance
GOLD	Brittney Reese	United States	-0.1	6.82
SILVER	Olga Kucherenko	Russia	0.0	6.77
BRONZE	Ineta Radevica	Latvia	(-0.3)	6.76
4	Nastassia Mironchyk-Ivanova	Belarus	-0.2	6.74
5	Carolina Klüft	Sweden	-0.4	6.56
6	Janay DeLoach	United States	-0.3	6.56
7	Darya Klishina	Russia	-0.1	6.5
8	Karin Mey Melis	Turkey	-0.4	6.44
9	Mayookha Johny	India	(-0.3)	6.37
10	Naide Gomes	Portugal	(-0.2)	6.26
11	Maurren Higa Maggi	Brazil	-0.6	6.17
	Funmi Jimoh	United States		-

Athlete	Jump 1	Jump 2	Jump 3	Jump 4	Jump 5	Jump 6
Brittney Reese	6.82	X	X	X	X	X
Olga Kucherenko	6.48	6.56	6.65	6.77	X	6.77
Ineta Radevica	6.61	6.63	6.66	6.61	X	6.76
Nastassia Mironchyk-Ivanova	X	6.71	6.74	X	X	X
Carolina Klüft	X	6.44	6.56	X	6.37	X
Janay DeLoach	6.32	6.39	X	X	6.32	6.56
Darya Klishina	6.39	6.30	6.49	X	6.50	6.33
Karin Mey Melis	X	6.44	X	X	6.44	6.19
Mayookha Johny	6.37	6.31	6.26			
Naide Gomes	X	6.16	6.26			
Maurren Higa Maggi	X	X	6.17			
Funmi Jimoh	X	X	X			

Men's Triple Jump

Qualification for the Final: Minimum achieved distance 17.10m or 12 best qualifiers.

Group A   02 September 2011

Position	Athlete	Country	Wind		Distance
1	Will Claye	United States	(-0.4)	Q	17.19
2	Phillips Idowu	Great Britain	-0.5	Q	17.17
3	Leevan Sands	Bahamas	-0.4	Q	17.13
4	Benjamin Compaoré	France	-0.1	Q	17.11
5	Christian Taylor	United States	-0.7	q	16.99
6	Sheryf El-Sheryf	Ukraine	-0.4	q	16.81
7	Arnie David Girat	Cuba	-0.2		16.74
8	Fabrizio Schembri	Italy	-0.3		16.71
9	Aleksey Fedorov	Russia	-0.5		16.42
10	Samyr Laine	Haiti	-0.1		16.38
11	Yanxi Li	China	-0.4		16.28
12	Wilbert Walker	Jamaica	-0.2		15.97
	Sief El Islem Temacini	Algeria			-
	Renjith Maheshwary	India			-
	Deokhyeon Kim	South Korea			-
	Tumelo Thagane	South Africa			-

Athlete	Jump 1	Jump 2	Jump 3
Will Claye	X	17.19	
Phillips Idowu	17.17		
Leevan Sands	17.13		
Benjamin Compaoré	17.11		
Christian Taylor	X	16.99	16.81
Sheryf El-Sheryf	16.81	X	16.73
Arnie David Girat	16.74	16.68	16.17
Fabrizio Schembri	16.71	16.28	16.63
Aleksey Fedorov	15.84	16.42	16.26
Samyr Laine	16.38	15.83	16.30
Yanxi Li	15.68	16.28	15.42
Wilbert Walker	15.66	14.50	15.97
Sief El Islem Temacini	X	X	X
Renjith Maheshwary	X	X	X
Deokhyeon Kim	X	X	X
Tumelo Thagane	X	X	X

Group B   02 September 2011

Position	Athlete	Country	Wind		Distance
1	Alexis Copello	Cuba	-0.2	Q	17.31
2	Nelson Évora	Portugal	-0.6	Q	17.20
3	Christian Olsson	Sweden	0.0	Q	17.16
4	Yoandris Betanzos	Cuba	0.0	q	17.01
5	Fabrizio Donato	Italy	(-0.1)	q	16.88
6	Henry Frayne	Australia	-0.2	q	16.83
7	Marian Oprea	Romania	-0.7		16.61
8	Tosin Oke	Nigeria	(-1.2)		16.60
9	Jefferson Sabino	Brazil	(-0.1)		16.51
10	Hugo Mamba-Schlick	Cameroon	(-0.7)		16.15
11	Anders Møller	Denmark	-0.2		16.14
12	Walter Davis	United States	(-0.1)		16.12
13	Yevhen Semenenko	Ukraine	(-0.9)		15.96
14	Maximiliano Díaz	Argentina	0.0		15.91
	Yevgeniy Ektov	Kazakhstan			-

Men's Triple Jump (continued)

Athlete	Jump 1	Jump 2	Jump 3
Alexis Copello	17.06	17.31	
Nelson Évora	17.05	17.20	
Christian Olsson	16.55	17.16	
Yoandris Betanzos	17.01	13.66	-
Fabrizio Donato	16.55	16.70	16.88
Henry Frayne	16.54	16.83	16.64
Marian Oprea	X	16.61	16.19
Tosin Oke	X	16.50	16.60
Jefferson Sabino	16.18	15.91	16.51
Hugo Mamba-Schlick	15.66	15.93	16.15
Anders Møller	16.14	14.07	X
Walter Davis	15.28	13.90	16.12
Yevhen Semenenko	X	15.72	15.96
Maximiliano Díaz	15.91	15.65	X
Yevgeniy Ektov	X	X	X

FINAL   04 September 2011

Position	Athlete	Country	Wind	Distance
GOLD	Christian Taylor	United States	-0.1	17.96
SILVER	Phillips Idowu	Great Britain	0.0	17.77
BRONZE	Will Claye	United States	-0.1	17.50
4	Alexis Copello	Cuba	-0.1	17.47
5	Nelson Évora	Portugal	0.0	17.35
6	Christian Olsson	Sweden	0.0	17.23
7	Leevan Sands	Bahamas	(-0.2)	17.21
8	Benjamin Compaoré	France	-0.2	17.17
9	Henry Frayne	Australia	(-0.1)	16.78
10	Fabrizio Donato	Italy	-0.1	16.77
11	Yoandris Betanzos	Cuba	(-0.1)	16.67
12	Sheryf El-Sheryf	Ukraine	(-0.1)	16.38

Athlete	Jump 1	Jump 2	Jump 3	Jump 4	Jump 5	Jump 6
Christian Taylor	X	17.04	17.40	17.96	-	15.64
Phillips Idowu	17.56	17.38	17.70	17.77	17.48	17.49
Will Claye	X	X	17.50	17.30	-	17.14
Alexis Copello	X	17.19	X	17.36	17.47	16.11
Nelson Évora	17.35	16.80	16.63	16.18	16.57	16.95
Christian Olsson	17.23	16.80	17.22	16.75	-	-
Leevan Sands	16.81	X	17.07	17.12	17.21	16.59
Benjamin Compaoré	X	17.04	17.17	X	16.99	X
Henry Frayne	16.45	16.78	16.60			
Fabrizio Donato	16.77	X	X			
Yoandris Betanzos	14.93	16.22	16.67			
Sheryf El-Sheryf	16.29	X	16.38			

Women's Triple Jump

Qualification for the Final: Minimum achieved distance 14.45m or 12 best qualifiers.

Group A   30 August 2011

Position	Athlete	Country	Wind		Distance
1	Mabel Gay	Cuba	-0.1	Q	14.53
2	Caterine Ibargüen	Colombia	-0.1	Q	14.52
3	Olha Saladuha	Ukraine	-0.5	q	14.40
4	Anna Kuropatkina	Russia	-0.7	q	14.31
5	Natalia Iastrebova	Ukraine	-0.1	q	14.21
6	Keila Costa	Brazil	-0.6	q	14.15
7	Yarianna Martínez	Cuba	(-0.1)		14.07
8	Simona La Mantia	Italy	-0.8		14.06
9	Irina Litvinenko Ektova	Kazakhstan	-0.3		14.01
10	Mayookha Johny	India	-0.2		13.99
11	Níki Panéta	Greece	-0.1		13.97
12	Marija Šestak	Slovenia	-0.3		13.87
13	Valeriya Kanatova	Uzbekistan	0.0		13.86
14	Patricia Mamona	Portugal	-0.8		13.59
15	Yanmei Li	China	-0.3		13.52
16	Hye-kyung Jung	South Korea	-0.2		13.50
17	Amanda Smock	United States	(-0.3)		13.48

Athlete	Jump 1	Jump 2	Jump 3
Mabel Gay	14.21	14.53	
Caterine Ibargüen	14.52		
Olha Saladuha	14.40	14.36	14.35
Anna Kuropatkina	14.05	X	14.31
Natalia Iastrebova	13.94	14.07	14.21
Keila Costa	13.50	14.02	14.15
Yarianna Martínez	14.07	13.92	X
Simona La Mantia	14.06	X	X
Irina Litvinenko Ektova	13.66	13.57	14.01
Mayookha Johny	13.64	13.99	13.79
Níki Panéta	12.87	13.75	13.97
Marija Šestak	X	13.87	X
Valeriya Kanatova	13.86	13.72	13.75
Patricia Mamona	13.48	13.27	13.59
Yanmei Li	X	X	13.52
Hye-kyung Jung	X	11.35	13.50
Amanda Smock	X	13.48	13.37

Women's Triple Jump (continued)

Group B 30 August 2011

Position	Athlete	Country	Wind		Distance
1	Yargeris Savigne	Cuba	-0.4	Q	14.62
2	Yamilé Aldama	Great Britain	-0.7	q	14.35
3	Olga Rypakova	Kazakhstan	0.0	q	14.33
4	Baya Rahouli	Algeria	(-0.1)	q	14.3
5	Dana Veldáková	Slovakia	(-0.2)	q	14.28
6	Biljana Topic	Serbia	-0.1	q	14.21
7	Kimberly Williams	Jamaica	-0.2		14.06
8	Paraskeví Papahrístou	Greece	(-0.1)		14.05
9	Anastasiya Juravleva	Uzbekistan	-0.3		14.00
10	Dailenys Alcántara	Cuba	(-0.8)		13.78
11	Aleksandra Kotlyarova	Uzbekistan	-0.1		13.78
12	Limei Xie	China	-0.3		13.75
13	Andriyana Bânova	Bulgaria	0.0		13.66
14	Anna Jagaciak	Poland	(-0.3)		13.57
15	Ruslana Tsykhotska	Ukraine	-0.3		13.28
16	Sarah Nambawa	Uganda	(-0.1)		13.22
17	Patricia Sarrapio	Spain	-0.2		13.12

Athlete	Jump 1	Jump 2	Jump 3
Yargeris Savigne	14.32	14.40	14.62
Yamilé Aldama	14.35	14.20	X
Olga Rypakova	X	14.33	X
Baya Rahouli	14.30	13.95	X
Dana Veldáková	X	14.28	X
Biljana Topic	14.03	13.93	14.21
Kimberly Williams	13.10	14.06	14.03
Paraskeví Papahrístou	13.71	14.05	X
Anastasiya Juravleva	14.00	13.82	13.79
Dailenys Alcántara	13.66	13.78	X
Aleksandra Kotlyarova	13.49	13.78	X
Limei Xie	13.55	13.74	13.75
Andriyana Bânova	13.34	13.63	13.66
Anna Jagaciak	13.57	13.57	X
Ruslana Tsykhotska	X	X	13.28
Sarah Nambawa	11.65	13.22	13.19
Patricia Sarrapio	X	13.11	13.12

FINAL　　　　　　01 September 2011

Position	Athlete	Country	Wind	Distance
GOLD	Olha Saladuha	Ukraine	-0.2	14.94
SILVER	Olga Rypakova	Kazakhstan	-0.2	14.89
BRONZE	Caterine Ibargüen	Colombia	-0.4	14.84
4	Mabel Gay	Cuba	-0.4	14.67
5	Yamilé Aldama	Great Britain	-0.4	14.50
6	Yargeris Savigne	Cuba	0.0	14.43
7	Anna Kuropatkina	Russia	-0.2	14.23
8	Baya Rahouli	Algeria	-0.2	14.12
9	Natalia Iastrebova	Ukraine	(-0.1)	14.12
10	Biljana Topic	Serbia	0.0	14.03
11	Dana Veldáková	Slovakia	-0.1	13.96
12	Keila Costa	Brazil	0.0	13.72

Athlete	Jump 1	Jump 2	Jump 3	Jump 4	Jump 5	Jump 6
Olha Saladuha	14.94	13.64	14.68	14.65	14.22	14.48
Olga Rypakova	X	14.72	X	X	14.89	14.54
Caterine Ibargüen	14.64	14.67	13.76	14.81	14.84	14.80
Mabel Gay	14.45	14.31	X	14.53	14.67	14.18
Yamilé Aldama	14.50	X	X	X	X	14.33
Yargeris Savigne	14.43	X	X	-	-	-
Anna Kuropatkina	13.89	14.23	X	14.09	X	14.06
Baya Rahouli	13.95	13.79	14.12	X	14.03	13.97
Natalia Iastrebova	13.34	13.89	14.12			
Biljana Topic	14.03	13.84	X			
Dana Veldáková	13.96	X	X			
Keila Costa	13.71	X	13.72			

Men's Shot Put

Qualification for the Final: Minimum achieved distance 20.60m or 12 best qualifiers.

Group A   01 September 2011

Position	Athlete	Country		Distance
1	David Storl	Germany	Q	21.50
2	Andrei Mikhnevich	Belarus	Q	20.79
3	Ryan Whiting	United States	Q	20.77
4	Tomasz Majewski	Poland	Q	20.73
5	Ralf Bartels	Germany	q	20.45
6	Adam Nelson	United States	q	20.23
7	Asmir Kolašinac	Serbia	q	20.14
8	Kim Christensen	Denmark		19.74
9	Jan Marcell	Czech Republic		19.51
10	Germán Lauro	Argentina		19.50
11	Andriy Semenov	Ukraine		19.45
12	Om Prakash Singh	India		19.29
13	Borja Vivas	Spain		18.37
14	In-sung Hwang	South Korea		17.75

Athlete	Throw 1	Throw 2	Throw 3
David Storl	X	21.50	-
Andrei Mikhnevich	20.79	-	-
Ryan Whiting	20.40	20.77	-
Tomasz Majewski	20.73	-	-
Ralf Bartels	20.45	X	20.04
Adam Nelson	20.23	X	X
Asmir Kolašinac	19.58	20.08	20.14
Kim Christensen	19.02	19.40	19.74
Jan Marcell	19.51	X	19.46
Germán Lauro	19.50	19.45	X
Andriy Semenov	X	X	19.45
Om Prakash Singh	19.29	19.06	X
Borja Vivas	18.37	X	18.22
In-sung Hwang	17.75	17.62	X

Group B   01 September 2011

Position	Athlete	Country		Distance
1	Dylan Armstrong	Canada	Q	21.05
2	Reese Hoffa	United States	Q	20.96
3	Christian Cantwell	United States	Q	20.73
4	Marco Fortes	Portugal	q	20.32
5	Carlos Véliz	Cuba	q	20.24
6	Marco Schmidt	Germany		20.06
7	Lajos Kürthy	Hungary		20.02
8	Maksim Sidorov	Russia		19.95
9	Pavel Lyzhyn	Belarus		19.91
10	Hamza Alic	Bosnia & Herzegovina		19.70
11	Ming-Huang Chang	Chinese Taipei		19.60
12	Amin Nikfar	Iran		19.18
13	Milan Jotanovic	Serbia		18.39

Men's Shot Put (continued)

Athlete	Throw 1	Throw 2	Throw 3
Dylan Armstrong	20.52	21.05	-
Reese Hoffa	20.96	-	-
Christian Cantwell	20.55	20.73	-
Marco Fortes	19.83	20.32	20.02
Carlos Véliz	20.24	19.79	X
Marco Schmidt	20.06	19.96	X
Lajos Kürthy	19.92	19.76	20.02
Maksim Sidorov	18.56	19.95	X
Pavel Lyzhyn	19.91	X	X
Hamza Alic	19.70	X	X
Ming-Huang Chang	19.60	X	18.98
Amin Nikfar	18.69	18.95	19.18
Milan Jotanovic	18.39	X	18.21

FINAL   02 September 2011

Position	Athlete	Country	Distance
GOLD	David Storl	Germany	21.78
SILVER	Dylan Armstrong	Canada	21.64
BRONZE	Andrei Mikhnevich	Belarus	21.40
4	Christian Cantwell	United States	21.36
5	Reese Hoffa	United States	20.99
6	Marco Fortes	Portugal	20.83
7	Ryan Whiting	United States	20.75
8	Adam Nelson	United States	20.29
9	Tomasz Majewski	Poland	20.18
10	Ralf Bartels	Germany	20.14
11	Asmir Kolašinac	Serbia	19.84
12	Carlos Véliz	Cuba	19.70

Athlete	Throw 1	Throw 2	Throw 3	Throw 4	Throw 5	Throw 6
David Storl	X	21.60	20.82	X	X	21.78
Dylan Armstrong	20.79	20.58	20.82	21.64	21.40	X
Andrei Mikhnevich	20.45	20.49	21.40	20.72	20.64	21.37
Christian Cantwell	20.50	20.73	20.83	X	21.36	X
Reese Hoffa	20.90	20.99	20.97	20.84	X	X
Marco Fortes	20.59	X	19.36	20.83	20.25	20.04
Ryan Whiting	X	20.48	20.66	20.75	X	X
Adam Nelson	20.29	20.14	19.73	X	20.02	X
Tomasz Majewski	X	20.03	20.18			
Ralf Bartels	20.03	20.14	20.12			
Asmir Kolašinac	19.84	X	19.77			
Carlos Véliz	19.70	X	X			

Women's Shot Put

Qualification for the Final: Minimum achieved distance 18.65m or 12 best qualifiers.

Group A   28 August 2011

Position	Athlete	Country		Distance
1	Valerie Adams	New Zealand	Q	19.79
2	Jillian Camarena-Williams	United States	Q	19.09
3	Cleopatra Borel-Brown	Trinidad & Tobago	Q	18.95
4	Anna Avdeeva	Russia	Q	18.92
5	Natallia Mikhnevich	Belarus	Q	18.88
6	Nadine Kleinert	Germany	Q	18.75
7	Ling Li	China	Q	18.67
8	Misleydis González	Cuba		18.24
9	Julie Labonté	Canada		18.04
10	Josephine Terlecki	Germany		17.85
11	Sarah Stevens-Walker	United States		17.20
12	Radoslava Mavrodieva	Bulgaria		15.76

Athlete	Throw 1	Throw 2	Throw 3
Valerie Adams	19.79	-	-
Jillian Camarena-Williams	19.09	-	-
Cleopatra Borel-Brown	18.20	18.41	18.95
Anna Avdeeva	18.32	18.33	18.92
Natallia Mikhnevich	18.88	-	-
Nadine Kleinert	18.75	-	-
Ling Li	18.67	-	-
Misleydis González	18.24	17.96	17.83
Julie Labonté	17.66	18.04	X
Josephine Terlecki	17.85	17.72	17.20
Sarah Stevens-Walker	16.50	X	17.20
Radoslava Mavrodieva	X	15.76	X

Group B   28 August 2011

Position	Athlete	Country		Distance
1	Lijiao Gong	China	Q	19.21
2	Christina Schwanitz	Germany	Q	19.20
3	Nadzeya Ostapchuk	Belarus	Q	19.11
4	Anna Omarova	Russia	Q	19.03
5	Yevgeniya Kolodko	Russia	Q	18.90
6	Michelle Carter	United States	Q	18.85
7	Chiara Rosa	Italy		18.28
8	Mailín Vargas	Cuba		18.27
9	Xiangrong Liu	China		18.22
10	Natalia Ducó	Chile		17.42
11	Anita Márton	Hungary		17.04
12	Mi-young Lee	South Korea		16.18
13	Simoné du Toit	South Africa		15.83

Women's Shot Put (continued)

Athlete	Throw 1	Throw 2	Throw 3
Lijiao Gong	19.21	-	-
Christina Schwanitz	19.20	-	-
Nadzeya Ostapchuk	19.11	-	-
Anna Omarova	17.86	18.01	19.03
Yevgeniya Kolodko	18.58	18.9	-
Michelle Carter	18.85	-	
Chiara Rosa	17.69	18.27	18.28
Mailín Vargas	X	18.27	X
Xiangrong Liu	17.59	17.96	18.22
Natalia Ducó	17.42	X	17.42
Anita Márton	X	16.33	17.04
Mi-young Lee	16.08	16.18	15.96
Simoné du Toit	15.83	X	X

FINAL   29 August 2011

Position	Athlete	Country		Distance
GOLD	Valerie Adams	New Zealand	(CR	21.24
SILVER	Nadzeya Ostapchuk	Belarus		20.05
BRONZE	Jillian Camarena-Williams	United States		20.02
4	Lijiao Gong	China		19.97
5	Yevgeniya Kolodko	Russia		19.78
6	Ling Li	China		19.71
7	Anna Avdeeva	Russia		19.54
8	Nadine Kleinert	Germany		19.26
9	Michelle Carter	United States		18.76
10	Anna Omarova	Russia		18.67
11	Natallia Mikhnevich	Belarus		18.47
12	Christina Schwanitz	Germany		17.96
13	Cleopatra Borel-Brown	Trinidad & Tobago		17.62

Athlete	Throw 1	Throw 2	Throw 3	Throw 4	Throw 5	Throw 6
Valerie Adams	19.37	X	20.04	20.72	X	21.24
Nadzeya Ostapchuk	19.58	19.34	19.87	19.87	20.05	19.60
Jillian Camarena-Williams	19.63	18.53	19.24	20.02	18.80	19.44
Lijiao Gong	19.64	X	X	19.82	19.97	X
Yevgeniya Kolodko	18.42	18.28	19.78	X	X	19.26
Ling Li	19.12	19.71	19.23	19.60	19.50	19.49
Anna Avdeeva	18.80	18.65	19.16	18.96	19.54	18.51
Nadine Kleinert	19.26	X	18.83	X	X	-
Michelle Carter	18.76	X	18.13			
Anna Omarova	18.67	X	X			
Natallia Mikhnevich	18.44	X	18.47			
Christina Schwanitz	17.96	X	X			
Cleopatra Borel-Brown	X	17.62	17.53			

Men's Discus

Qualification for the Final: Minimum achieved distance 65.50m or 12 best qualifiers.

Group A   29 August 2011

Position	Athlete	Country		Distance
1	Ehsan Hadadi	Iran	q	65.21
2	Robert Harting	Germany	q	64.93
3	Virgilijus Alekna	Lithuania	q	64.21
4	Vikas Gowda	India	q	63.99
5	Gerd Kanter	Estonia	q	63.50
6	Benn Harradine	Australia	q	63.49
7	Jason Young	United States	q	63.14
8	Jarred Rome	United States		62.22
9	Jian Wu	China		62.07
10	Jason Morgan	Jamaica		61.75
11	Erik Cadee	Netherlands		61.62
12	Niklas Arrhenius	Sweden		60.57
13	Abdul Buhari	Great Britain		60.21
14	Roland Varga	Croatia		59.09
	Róbert Fazekas	Hungary		-
	Yennifer Frank Casañas	Spain		DNS

Athlete	Throw 1	Throw 2	Throw 3
Ehsan Hadadi	65.21	64.74	-
Robert Harting	64.93	63.75	-
Virgilijus Alekna	64.21	63.57	X
Vikas Gowda	62.37	63.99	61.85
Gerd Kanter	62.77	63.50	X
Benn Harradine	X	63.49	51.86
Jason Young	61.75	X	63.14
Jarred Rome	58.86	62.22	61.00
Jian Wu	59.51	62.07	X
Jason Morgan	58.51	57.56	61.75
Erik Cadee	61.03	X	61.62
Niklas Arrhenius	60.57	X	X
Abdul Buhari	X	60.21	58.37
Roland Varga	X	59.09	X
Róbert Fazekas	X	X	X

Group B   29 August 2011

Position	Athlete	Country		Distance
1	Piotr Malachowski	Poland	q	65.48
2	Mario Pestano	Spain	q	65.13
3	Jorge Y Fernández	Cuba	q	64.94
4	Märt Israel	Estonia	q	64.19
5	Brett Morse	Great Britain	q	62.38
6	Jan Marcell	Czech Republic		62.29
7	Zoltán Kővágó	Hungary		62.16
8	Rutger Smith	Netherlands		62.12
9	Martin Wierig	Germany		61.68
10	Gerhard Mayer	Austria		61.47
11	Leif Arrhenius	Sweden		61.33
12	Mohammad Samimi	Iran		61.10
13	Lance Brooks	United States		61.07
14	Ercüment Olgundeniz	Turkey		60.86
15	Markus Münch	Germany		60.80
16	Martin Maric	Croatia		60.61
17	Carl Myerscough	Great Britain		60.29

Men's Discus (continued)

Athlete	Throw 1	Throw 2	Throw 3
Piotr Malachowski	64.22	X	65.48
Mario Pestano	65.13	-	-
Jorge Y Fernández	64.94	-	-
Märt Israel	63.49	64.19	X
Brett Morse	60.62	62.38	59.29
Jan Marcell	60.46	62.29	59.26
Zoltán Kővágó	58.14	62.16	X
Rutger Smith	60.17	59.64	62.12
Martin Wierig	X	X	61.68
Gerhard Mayer	61.47	55.33	59.6
Leif Arrhenius	61.33	X	X
Mohammad Samimi	X	X	61.10
Lance Brooks	60.55	61.01	61.07
Ercüment Olgundeniz	53.34	X	60.86
Markus Münch	58.27	60.80	60.59
Martin Maric	59.72	X	60.61
Carl Myerscough	60.29	57.65	59.40

FINAL 30 August 2011

Position	Athlete	Country	Distance
GOLD	Robert Harting	Germany	68.97
SILVER	Gerd Kanter	Estonia	66.95
BRONZE	Ehsan Hadadi	Iran	66.08
4	Märt Israel	Estonia	65.20
5	Benn Harradine	Australia	64.77
6	Virgilijus Alekna	Lithuania	64.09
7	Vikas Gowda	India	64.05
8	Jorge Y. Fernández	Cuba	63.54
9	Piotr Malachowski	Poland	63.37
10	Jason Young	United States	63.20
11	Mario Pestano	Spain	63.00
12	Brett Morse	Great Britain	62.69

Athlete	Throw 1	Throw 2	Throw 3	Throw 4	Throw 5	Throw 6
Robert Harting	68.49	X	68.10	68.97	66.33	X
Gerd Kanter	62.79	66.95	66.13	66.90	X	65.83
Ehsan Hadadi	65.29	64.07	X	X	65.50	66.08
Märt Israel	61.87	63.60	64.31	63.73	65.20	X
Benn Harradine	64.43	64.02	62.08	X	64.18	64.77
Virgilijus Alekna	62.75	X	64.09	62.62	X	61.25
Vikas Gowda	60.79	61.51	64.05	62.81	62.16	62.16
Jorge Y. Fernández	61.05	63.54	63.10	X	60.11	61.77
Piotr Malachowski	58.28	X	63.37			
Jason Young	62.54	X	63.20			
Mario Pestano	62.97	63.00	62.74			
Brett Morse	60.84	62.69	57.87			

Women's Discus

Qualification for the Final: Minimum achieved distance 62.00m or 12 best qualifiers.

Group A   27 August 2011

Position	Athlete	Country		Distance
1	Nadine Müller	Germany	Q	65.54
2	Yarelys Barrios	Cuba	Q	63.80
3	Jian Tan	China	Q	62.26
4	Zinaida Sendriute	Lithuania	q	61.72
5	Dragana Tomaševic	Serbia	q	60.45
6	Dani Samuels	Australia	q	60.05
7	Darya Pishchalnikova	Russia	q	59.94
8	Xuejun Ma	China		59.71
9	Gia Lewis-Smallwood	United States		59.49
10	Natalya Fokina-Semenova	Ukraine		58.27
11	Andressa de Morais	Brazil		57.93
12	Vera Pospíšilová-Cechlová	Czech Republic		53.87

Athlete	Throw 1	Throw 2	Throw 3
Nadine Müller	65.54	-	-
Yarelys Barrios	63.80	-	-
Jian Tan	62.26	-	-
Zinaida Sendriute	X	56.61	61.72
Dragana Tomaševic	60.45	X	X
Dani Samuels	59.77	60.05	59.98
Darya Pishchalnikova	54.11	59.94	59.53
Xuejun Ma	55.80	59.34	59.71
Gia Lewis-Smallwood	X	56.91	59.49
Natalya Fokina-Semenova	56.73	55.16	58.27
Andressa de Morais	X	44.41	57.93
Vera Pospíšilová-Cechlová	53.87	51.52	X

Group B   27 August 2011

Position	Athlete	Country		Distance
1	Yanfeng Li	China	Q	64.44
2	Zaneta Glanc	Poland	Q	63.44
3	Stephanie Brown Trafton	United States	q	61.89
4	Denia Caballero	Cuba	q	60.36
5	Nicoleta Grasu	Romania	q	60.13
6	Aretha Thurmond	United States		59.88
7	Monique Jansen	Netherlands		58.23
8	Kazai Suzanne Kragbé	Ivory Coast		57.55
9	Kateryna Karsak	Ukraine		57.54
10	Harwant Kaur	India		56.49
11	Elisângela Adriano	Brazil		56.45
12	Karen Gallardo	Chile		53.69

Women's Discus (continued)

Athlete	Throw 1	Throw 2	Throw 3
Yanfeng Li	X	64.44	-
Zaneta Glanc	59.48	63.44	-
Stephanie Brown Trafton	61.89	X	59.87
Denia Caballero	X	52.93	60.36
Nicoleta Grasu	60.13	58.25	59.58
Aretha Thurmond	59.88	X	59.48
Monique Jansen	58.23	58.06	57.96
Kazai Suzanne Kragbé	57.55	55.75	X
Kateryna Karsak	57.54	X	57.29
Harwant Kaur	55.50	56.49	52.98
Elisângela Adriano	56.28	53.70	56.45
Karen Gallardo	51.32	52.33	53.69

FINAL   28 August 2011

Position	Athlete	Country	Distance
GOLD	Yanfeng Li	China	66.52
SILVER	Nadine Müller	Germany	65.97
BRONZE	Yarelys Barrios	Cuba	65.73
4	Zaneta Glanc	Poland	63.91
5	Stephanie Brown Trafton	United States	63.85
6	Jian Tan	China	62.96
7	Dragana Tomaševic	Serbia	62.48
8	Nicoleta Grasu	Romania	62.08
9	Denia Caballero	Cuba	60.73
10	Dani Samuels	Australia	59.14
11	Darya Pishchalnikova	Russia	58.10
12	Zinaida Sendriute	Lithuania	57.30

Athlete	Throw 1	Throw 2	Throw 3	Throw 4	Throw 5	Throw 6
Yanfeng Li	65.28	66.52	65.50	64.32	64.34	63.83
Nadine Müller	65.06	65.97	64.08	62.55	X	X
Yarelys Barrios	X	61.87	65.73	63.93	X	63.90
Zaneta Glanc	63.91	62.30	63.11	62.69	62.17	60.32
Stephanie Brown Trafton	60.20	60.97	60.24	63.85	60.26	X
Jian Tan	60.46	61.44	61.79	62.96	X	61.12
Dragana Tomaševic	62.26	58.97	62.48	X	59.03	58.63
Nicoleta Grasu	57.95	60.34	62.08	60.79	60.45	60.72
Denia Caballero	60.73	60.46	X			
Dani Samuels	58.08	59.14	X			
Darya Pishchalnikova	56.89	58.10	57.61			
Zinaida Sendriute	X	57.30	53.53			

Men's Hammer

Qualification for the Final: Minimum achieved distance 77.00m or 12 best qualifiers.

Group A   27 August 2011

Position	Athlete	Country		Distance
1	Koji Murofushi	Japan	Q	78.56
2	Krisztián Pars	Hungary	Q	77.21
3	Szymon Ziólkowski	Poland	Q	77.19
4	Dilshod Nazarov	Tajikistan	q	76.93
5	Olli-Pekka Karjalainen	Finland	q	76.60
6	Kirill Ikonnikov	Russia	q	75.36
7	Ali Mohamed Al-Zinkawi	Kuwait		75.35
8	Kibwe Johnson	United States		75.06
9	Esref Apak	Turkey		73.38
10	Igors Sokolovs	Latvia		72.95
11	Marcel Lomnický	Slovakia		72.68
12	Valeriy Sviatokha	Belarus		71.58
13	Eivind Henriksen	Norway		71.27
14	András Haklits	Croatia		70.93
15	Dzmitry Marshin	Azerbaijan		70.04
16	Yun-chul Lee	South Korea		68.98
17	Mostafa Al-Gamel	Egypt		68.38
18	Kaveh Sadegh Mousavi	Iran		68.01

Athlete	Throw 1	Throw 2	Throw 3
Koji Murofushi	78.56	-	-
Krisztián Pars	77.21	-	-
Szymon Ziólkowski	X	77.19	-
Dilshod Nazarov	75.34	75.17	76.93
Olli-Pekka Karjalainen	X	75.09	76.6
Kirill Ikonnikov	75.36	X	X
Ali Mohamed Al-Zinkawi	75.35	X	X
Kibwe Johnson	75.06	X	X
Esref Apak	73.38	71.99	X
Igors Sokolovs	71.90	71.64	72.95
Marcel Lomnický	72.68	71.44	72.16
Valeriy Sviatokha	X	X	71.58
Eivind Henriksen	68.24	71.27	70.02
András Haklits	X	70.93	X
Dzmitry Marshin	70.04	68.94	68.99
Yun-chul Lee	X	67.14	68.98
Mostafa Al-Gamel	X	64.17	68.38
Kaveh Sadegh Mousavi	X	68.01	X

Men's Hammer (continued)

Group B 27 August 2011

Position	Athlete	Country	Distance
1	Pavel Kryvitski	Belarus	78.16 Q
2	Markus Esser	Germany	77.60 Q
3	Yury Shayunou	Belarus	76.74 q
4	Nicola Vizzoni	Italy	76.74 q
5	Primož Kozmus	Slovenia	76.54 q
6	Pawel Fajdek	Poland	76.10 q
7	Sergej Litvinov	Russia	74.80
8	Kristóf Németh	Hungary	74.09
9	Olexiy Sokyrskiyy	Ukraine	73.81
10	James Steacy	Canada	73.32
11	Libor Charfreitag	Slovakia	72.20
12	Michael Mai	United States	69.96
13	Fatih Eryildirim	Turkey	69.37
14	Mattias Jons	Sweden	67.93
15	Javier Cienfuegos	Spain	67.49
16	Juan Ignacio Cerra	Argentina	64.27
17	Amanmurad Hommadov	Turkmenistan	62.97

Athlete	Throw 1	Throw 2	Throw 3
Pavel Kryvitski	X	76.80	78.16
Markus Esser	77.60	-	-
Yury Shayunou	76.74	76.63	76.07
Nicola Vizzoni	75.41	76.30	76.74
Primož Kozmus	76.21	76.54	76.44
Pawel Fajdek	75.83	76.10	75.66
Sergej Litvinov	74.80	X	73.11
Kristóf Németh	73.36	74.09	73.87
Olexiy Sokyrskiyy	X	X	73.81
James Steacy	73.32	71.74	X
Libor Charfreitag	X	71.87	72.20
Michael Mai	68.35	X	69.96
Fatih Eryildirim	X	69.37	69.04
Mattias Jons	67.93	X	X
Javier Cienfuegos	X	66.78	67.49
Juan Ignacio Cerra	63.04	X	64.27
Amanmurad Hommadov	61.31	59.94	62.97

Men's Hammer (continued)

FINAL   29 August 2011

Position	Athlete	Country	Distance
GOLD	Koji Murofushi	Japan	81.24
SILVER	Krisztián Pars	Hungary	81.18
BRONZE	Primož Kozmus	Slovenia	79.39
4	Markus Esser	Germany	79.12
5	Pavel Kryvitski	Belarus	78.53
6	Kirill Ikonnikov	Russia	78.37
7	Szymon Ziółkowski	Poland	77.64
8	Nicola Vizzoni	Italy	77.04
9	Olli-Pekka Karjalainen	Finland	76.60
10	Dilshod Nazarov	Tajikistan	76.58
11	Pawel Fajdek	Poland	75.20
	Yury Shayunou	Belarus	-

Athlete	Throw 1	Throw 2	Throw 3	Throw 4	Throw 5	Throw 6
Koji Murofushi	79.72	81.03	81.24	79.42	81.24	80.83
Krisztián Pars	77.26	78.84	79.14	79.97	60.34	81.18
Primož Kozmus	77.50	79.39	78.93	X	76.01	78.19
Markus Esser	X	78.56	76.71	75.01	79.12	77.88
Pavel Kryvitski	73.98	78.24	78.53	X	77.35	X
Kirill Ikonnikov	X	X	77.22	X	78.37	78.12
Szymon Ziółkowski	75.04	77.64	76.75	X	74.99	75.10
Nicola Vizzoni	77.04	76.31	76.94	76.01	75.82	X
Olli-Pekka Karjalainen	75.38	76.60	71.34			
Dilshod Nazarov	75.05	74.34	76.58			
Pawel Fajdek	74.86	X	75.20			
Yury Shayunou	X	X	X			

Women's Hammer

Qualification for the Final: Minimum achieved distance 71.00m or 12 best qualifiers.

Group A 02 September 2011

Position	Athlete	Country		Distance
1	Wenxiu Zhang	China	Q	74.17
2	Tatyana Lysenko	Russia	Q	71.94
3	Kathrin Klaas	Germany	Q	71.69
4	Jessica Cosby	United States	Q	71.06
5	Zalina Marghieva	Moldova	q	70.09
6	Bianca Perie	Romania	q	69.66
7	Stéphanie Falzon	France	q	68.92
8	Amber Campbell	United States		68.87
9	Joanna Fiodorow	Poland		66.88
10	Alexándra Papayeoryíou	Greece		66.77
11	Amy Séné	Senegal		66.15
12	Merja Korpela	Finland		65.64
13	Vânia Silva	Portugal		65.40
14	Heather Steacy	Canada		63.39
15	Na-ru Kang	South Korea		61.05

Athlete	Throw 1	Throw 2	Throw 3
Wenxiu Zhang	74.17	-	-
Tatyana Lysenko	71.94	-	-
Kathrin Klaas	69.26	69.57	71.69
Jessica Cosby	71.06	-	-
Zalina Marghieva	X	70.09	69.85
Bianca Perie	68.12	69.66	69.01
Stéphanie Falzon	X	68.92	67.37
Amber Campbell	68.26	68.87	X
Joanna Fiodorow	X	66.88	X
Alexándra Papayeoryíou	64.38	65.58	66.77
Amy Séné	66.15	X	61.31
Merja Korpela	63.93	X	65.64
Vânia Silva	64.46	65.40	64.18
Heather Steacy	63.39	X	X
Na-ru Kang	61.05	X	X

Group B 02 September 2011

Position	Athlete	Country		Distance
1	Yipsi Moreno	Cuba	Q	73.29
2	Jennifer Dahlgren	Argentina	Q	72.70
3	Betty Heidler	Germany	Q	71.48
4	Anita Wlodarczyk	Poland	Q	71.09
5	Silvia Salis	Italy	q	69.82
6	Éva Orbán	Hungary		68.89
7	Jeneva McCall	United States		68.26
8	Alena Matoshka	Belarus		68.23
9	Marina Marghieva	Moldova		67.95
10	Berta Castells	Spain		67.74
11	Nataliya Zolotukhina	Ukraine		67.57
12	Mona Christine Holm	Norway		67.16
13	Sophie Hitchon	Great Britain		64.93
14	Masumi Aya	Japan		64.09
15	Tingting Liu	China		63.12

Women's Hammer (continued)

Athlete	Throw 1	Throw 2	Throw 3
Yipsi Moreno	73.29	-	-
Jennifer Dahlgren	67.81	X	72.70
Betty Heidler	71.48	-	-
Anita Wlodarczyk	71.09	-	-
Silvia Salis	69.82	66.58	X
Éva Orbán	68.89	68.28	X
Jeneva McCall	68.26	65.22	65.45
Alena Matoshka	X	68.23	67.88
Marina Marghieva	X	67.95	X
Berta Castells	67.74	65.22	67.02
Nataliya Zolotukhina	67.44	67.57	65.93
Mona Christine Holm	67.16	66.97	X
Sophie Hitchon	61.91	X	64.93
Masumi Aya	60.14	64.09	X
Tingting Liu	61.45	62.17	63.12

FINAL   04 September 2011

Position	Athlete	Country	Distance
GOLD	Tatyana Lysenko	Russia	77.13
SILVER	Betty Heidler	Germany	76.06
BRONZE	Wenxiu Zhang	China	75.03
4	Yipsi Moreno	Cuba	74.48
5	Anita Wlodarczyk	Poland	73.56
6	Bianca Perie	Romania	72.04
7	Kathrin Klaas	Germany	71.89
8	Zalina Marghieva	Moldova	70.27
9	Silvia Salis	Italy	69.88
10	Jennifer Dahlgren	Argentina	69.72
11	Jessica Cosby	United States	68.91
12	Stéphanie Falzon	France	66.57

Athlete	Throw 1	Throw 2	Throw 3	Throw 4	Throw 5	Throw 6
Tatyana Lysenko	76.80	77.09	77.13	74.51	75.05	X
Betty Heidler	X	73.96	74.70	X	76.06	X
Wenxiu Zhang	75.03	74.31	X	73.17	71.86	74.79
Yipsi Moreno	73.29	X	74.48	X	X	X
Anita Wlodarczyk	73.56	X	72.61	X	X	72.65
Bianca Perie	67.73	70.40	67.75	70.24	70.91	72.04
Kathrin Klaas	67.02	70.18	70.67	71.89	70.44	X
Zalina Marghieva	69.99	X	68.13	70.24	70.27	68.76
Silvia Salis	68.61	69.88	X			
Jennifer Dahlgren	68.27	X	69.72			
Jessica Cosby	X	68.91	68.15			
Stéphanie Falzon	66.57	X	X			

Men's Javelin

Qualification for the Final: Minimum achieved distance 82.50m or 12 best qualifiers.

Group A   01 September 2011

Position	Athlete	Country		Distance
1	Guillermo Martínez	Cuba	Q	83.77
2	Dmitri Tarabin	Russia	Q	82.92
3	Matthias de Zordo	Germany	q	82.05
4	Andreas Thorkildsen	Norway	q	81.83
5	Vítezslav Veselý	Czech Republic	q	81.64
6	Jarrod Bannister	Australia	q	81.35
7	Yukifumi Murakami	Japan		80.19
8	Jakub Vadlejch	Czech Republic		80.08
9	Tero Pitkämäki	Finland		79.46
10	Scott Russell	Canada		77.49
11	Eriks Rags	Latvia		77.34
12	Yervásios Filippídis	Greece		76.66
13	Mihkel Kukk	Estonia		76.42
14	Oleksandr Pyatnytsya	Ukraine		73.56
15	Matija Kranjc	Slovenia		73.17
16	John Robert Oosthuizen	South Africa		73.14
17	Ihab Abdelrahman El Sayed	Egypt		71.99
18	Rinat Tarzumanov	Uzbekistan		70.32
	Mike Hazle	United States		DNS

Athlete	Throw 1	Throw 2	Throw 3
Guillermo Martínez	83.77		
Dmitri Tarabin	X	82.92	
Matthias de Zordo	82.05	81.11	X
Andreas Thorkildsen	79.36	80.85	81.83
Vítezslav Veselý	79.99	74.77	81.64
Jarrod Bannister	81.35	X	75.91
Yukifumi Murakami	80.19	78.04	74.93
Jakub Vadlejch	68.32	80.08	X
Tero Pitkämäki	78.21	79.46	76.05
Scott Russell	76.47	77.49	74.23
Eriks Rags	77.34	X	76.23
Yervásios Filippídis	76.66	70.42	73.41
Mihkel Kukk	73.21	72.1	76.42
Oleksandr Pyatnytsya	71.93	72.05	73.56
Matija Kranjc	73.17	X	-
John Robert Oosthuizen	69.65	73.14	72.79
Ihab Abdelrahman El Sayed	71.99	68	X
Rinat Tarzumanov	X	67.07	70.32
Mike Hazle			

Group B   01 September 2011

Position	Athlete	Country		Distance
1	Stuart Farquhar	New Zealand	q	82.10
2	Fatih Avan	Turkey	q	81.94
3	Mark Frank	Germany	q	81.93
4	Roman Avramenko	Ukraine	q	81.46
5	Sergey Makarov	Russia	q	81.42
6	Antti Ruuskanen	Finland	q	81.03
7	Igor Janik	Poland		80.88
8	Ari Mannio	Finland		80.27
9	Qi Chen	China		78.42
10	Leslie Copeland	Fiji		76.57
11	Petr Frydrych	Czech Republic		76.18
12	Vadims Vasilevskis	Latvia		75.23
13	Gabriel Wallin	Sweden		74.44
14	Arley Ibargüen	Colombia		74.02
15	Aleksandr Ivanov	Russia		73.81
16	Spirídon Lebésis	Greece		73.35
17	Zigismunds Sirmais	Latvia		73.16
18	Sangjin Jung	South Korea		72.03

Athlete	Throw 1	Throw 2	Throw 3
Stuart Farquhar	82.10	X	-
Fatih Avan	80.27	77.68	81.94
Mark Frank	80.96	81.93	-
Roman Avramenko	76.30	X	81.46
Sergey Makarov	81.42	80.18	78.33
Antti Ruuskanen	79.54	81.03	78.14
Igor Janik	80.88	76.63	78.98
Ari Mannio	74.09	80.27	79.31
Qi Chen	X	74.28	78.42
Leslie Copeland	76.57	74.54	73.82
Petr Frydrych	75.38	76.18	X
Vadims Vasilevskis	74.67	75.23	X
Gabriel Wallin	72.96	74.44	74.09
Arley Ibargüen	73.22	74.02	X
Aleksandr Ivanov	73.81	X	X
Spirídon Lebésis	X	73.35	70.44
Zigismunds Sirmais	70.20	X	73.16
Sangjin Jung	72.03	X	X

Men's Javelin (continued)

FINAL   03 September 2011

Position	Athlete	Country	Distance
GOLD	Matthias de Zordo	Germany	86.27
SILVER	Andreas Thorkildsen	Norway	84.78
BRONZE	Guillermo Martínez	Cuba	84.30
4	Vítezslav Veselý	Czech Republic	84.11
5	Fatih Avan	Turkey	83.34
6	Roman Avramenko	Ukraine	82.51
7	Jarrod Bannister	Australia	82.25
8	Mark Frank	Germany	81.81
9	Antti Ruuskanen	Finland	79.46
10	Dmitri Tarabin	Russia	79.06
11	Stuart Farquhar	New Zealand	78.99
12	Sergey Makarov	Russia	78.76

Athlete	Throw 1	Throw 2	Throw 3	Throw 4	Throw 5	Throw 6
Matthias de Zordo	86.27	85.51	-	-	82.88	81.40
Andreas Thorkildsen	80.75	80.46	80.60	84.78	X	80.28
Guillermo Martínez	84.30	80.12	80.09	76.99	-	78.69
Vítezslav Veselý	81.19	X	84.11	79.64	76.28	X
Fatih Avan	78.24	83.34	78.96	79.87	X	77.58
Roman Avramenko	82.51	X	82.20	79.71	78.87	X
Jarrod Bannister	82.25	X	-	X	76.60	X
Mark Frank	78.78	X	81.81	78.48	80.98	77.73
Antti Ruuskanen	X	79.46	79.06			
Dmitri Tarabin	X	79.06	X			
Stuart Farquhar	78.99	75.18	77.13			
Sergey Makarov	77.73	78.76	78.05			

Women's Javelin

Qualification for the Final: Minimum achieved distance 61.00m or 12 best qualifiers.

Group A   01 September 2011

Position	Athlete	Country		Distance
1	Christina Obergföll	Germany	Q	68.76
2	Kathrina Molitor	Germany	Q	63.52
3	Maria Abakumova	Russia	Q	62.49
4	Goldie Sayers	Great Britain	Q	62.19
5	Yuki Ebihara	Japan	q	59.88
6	Madara Palameika	Latvia	q	59.78
7	Jarmila Klimešová	Czech Republic	q	59.65
8	Ásdís Hjálmsdóttir	Iceland		59.15
9	Rachel Yurkovich	United States		58.84
10	Justine Robbeson	South Africa		58.08
11	Indré Jakubaityté	Lithuania		56.92
12	Yanet Cruz	Cuba		56.73
13	Elisabeth Eberl	Austria		56.48
14	Kyung-ae Kim	South Korea		54.96

Athlete	Throw 1	Throw 2	Throw 3
Christina Obergföll	68.76		
Kathrina Molitor	63.52		
Maria Abakumova	X	62.49	
Goldie Sayers	56.61	62.19	
Yuki Ebihara	57.36	59.66	59.88
Madara Palameika	59.78	X	59.33
Jarmila Klimešová	55.90	59.65	56.01
Ásdís Hjálmsdóttir	59.15	57.62	X
Rachel Yurkovich	58.84	58.01	57.92
Justine Robbeson	57.87	55.27	58.08
Indré Jakubaityté	X	56.01	56.92
Yanet Cruz	55.91	56.73	55.48
Elisabeth Eberl	56.48	54.39	X
Kyung-ae Kim	51.64	53.75	54.96

Group B   01 September 2011

Position	Athlete	Country		Distance
1	Sunette Viljoen	South Africa	Q	65.34
2	Barbora Špotáková	Czech Republic	Q	63.40
3	Martina Ratej	Slovenia	Q	61.58
4	Kimberley Mickle	Australia	q	60.50
5	Linda Stahl	Germany	q	60.21
6	Zahra Bani	Italy		58.92
7	Vira Rebryk	Ukraine		58.50
8	Mercedes Chilla	Spain		58.34
9	Sinta Ozolina-Kovala	Latvia		58.15
10	Chunhua Liu	China		57.52
11	Kara Patterson	United States		57.14
12	Tatjana Jelaca	Serbia		56.68
13	Risa Miyashita	Japan		55.62
14	María Murillo	Colombia		52.83

Women's Javelin (continued)

Athlete	Throw 1	Throw 2	Throw 3
Sunette Viljoen	65.34	-	-
Barbora Špotáková	63.40	-	-
Martina Ratej	61.58	-	-
Kimberley Mickle	60.50	57.80	60.12
Linda Stahl	60.21	59.85	58.25
Zahra Bani	X	X	58.92
Vira Rebryk	X	55.69	58.50
Mercedes Chilla	58.34	X	52.01
Sinta Ozolina-Kovala	56.18	58.15	54.02
Chunhua Liu	56.73	56.37	57.52
Kara Patterson	56.41	55.25	57.14
Tatjana Jelaca	56.68	X	54.58
Risa Miyashita	55.62	55.52	55.40
María Murillo	X	X	52.83

FINAL 02 September 2011

Position	Athlete	Country		Distance
GOLD	Maria Abakumova	Russia	(CR	71.99
SILVER	Barbora Špotáková	Czech Republic		71.58
BRONZE	Sunette Viljoen	South Africa		68.38
4	Christina Obergföll	Germany		65.24
5	Kathrina Molitor	Germany		64.32
6	Kimberley Mickle	Australia		61.96
7	Martina Ratej	Slovenia		61.65
8	Jarmila Klimešová	Czech Republic		59.27
9	Yuki Ebihara	Japan		59.08
10	Goldie Sayers	Great Britain		58.18
11	Madara Palameika	Latvia		58.08
	Linda Stahl	Germany		DNS

Athlete	Throw 1	Throw 2	Throw 3	Throw 4	Throw 5	Throw 6
Maria Abakumova	60.38	71.25	-	X	71.99	64.27
Barbora Špotáková	68.80	67.90	68.64	67.12	71.58	66.80
Sunette Viljoen	64.36	65.20	63.12	58.48	68.38	62.68
Christina Obergföll	61.74	64.39	64.80	65.24	63.51	X
Kathrina Molitor	59.88	58.19	57.94	60.31	58.85	64.32
Kimberley Mickle	59.33	57.07	60.87	X	61.96	61.33
Martina Ratej	58.87	X	60.58	X	61.65	X
Jarmila Klimešová	59.27	X	57.37	X	X	55.87
Yuki Ebihara	59.08	58.39	57.96			
Goldie Sayers	57.32	57.52	58.18			
Madara Palameika	55.69	58.08	X			
Linda Stahl						

Heptathlon - 100m Hurdles

Heat 1   29 August 2011

Position	Lane	Athlete	Country	Time	Points
1	1	Hyleas Fountain	United States	12.93	1135
2	7	Jessica Ennis	Great Britain	12.94	1133
3	5	Jessica Zelinka	Canada	13.01	1123
4	2	Louise Hazel	Great Britain	13.24	1089
5	6	Jennifer Oeser	Germany	13.33	1075
6	3	Antoinette Nana Djimou Ida	France	13.48	1053
7	4	Lilli Schwarzkopf	Germany	13.65	1028

Heat 2   29 August 2011

Position	Lane	Athlete	Country	Time	Points
1	3	Karolina Tyminska	Poland	13.12	1106
2	5	Tatyana Chernova	Russia	13.32	1077
3	6	Anna Bogdanova	Russia	13.44	1059
4	4	Grit Šadeiko	Estonia	13.44	1059
5	1	Francesca Doveri	Italy	13.44	1059
6	2	Lyudmyla Yosypenko	Ukraine	13.49	1052
7	7	Aiga Grabuste	Latvia	14.06	970

Heat 3   29 August 2011

Position	Lane	Athlete	Country	Time	Points
1	7	Margaret Simpson	Ghana	13.43	1060
2	2	Remona Fransen	Netherlands	13.57	1040
3	4	Ruky Abdulai	Canada	13.60	1036
4	1	Wassana Winatho	Thailand	13.62	1033
5	3	Sharon Day	United States	13.69	1023
6	5	Jessica Samuelsson	Sweden	13.77	1011
7	6	Katerina Cachová	Czech Republic	13.81	1005

Heat 4   29 August 2011

Position	Lane	Athlete	Country	Time	Points
1	2	Sara Aerts	Belgium	13.38	1068
2	5	Natallia Dobrynska	Ukraine	13.43	1060
3	3	Ida Marcussen	Norway	13.96	984
4	7	Austra Skujyte	Lithuania	13.96	984
5	4	Alina Fyodorova	Ukraine	14.06	970
6	1	Julia Mächtig	Germany	14.15	957
7	6	Györgyi Farkas	Hungary	14.32	934

Heptathlon - High Jump

Group A   29 August 2011

Position	Athlete	Country	Height	Points
1	Hyleas Fountain	United States	1.89	1093
2	Austra Skujyte	Lithuania	1.86	1054
3	Jessica Ennis	Great Britain	1.86	1054
4	Natallia Dobrynska	Ukraine	1.83	1016
5	Anna Bogdanova	Russia	1.83	1016
6	Antoinette Nana Djimou Ida	France	1.83	1016
7	Lyudmyla Yosypenko	Ukraine	1.83	1016
8	Tatyana Chernova	Russia	1.83	1016
9	Jennifer Oeser	Germany	1.83	1016
10	Remona Fransen	Netherlands	1.80	978
11	Ruky Abdulai	Canada	1.80	978
12	Alina Fyodorova	Ukraine	1.80	978
13	Sharon Day	United States	1.80	978
14	Katerina Cachová	Czech Republic	1.77	941

Athlete	1.65	1.68	1.71	1.74	1.77	1.80	1.83	1.86	1.89	1.92
Hyleas Fountain	-	-	O	O	O	O	O	O	XXO	XXX
Austra Skujyte	-	-	O	O	O	XO	XO	XO	XXX	
Jessica Ennis	-	-	-	O	O	XO	XO	XXO	XXX	
Natallia Dobrynska	-	-	O	O	O	O	O	XXX		
Anna Bogdanova	-	-	-	XO	O	O	O	XXX		
Antoinette Nana Djimou Ida	-	-	XO	O	XXO	XO	O	XXX		
Lyudmyla Yosypenko	O	O	O	O	XO	XO	XO	XXX		
Tatyana Chernova	-	-	O	O	O	O	XXO	XXX		
Jennifer Oeser	-	-	O	O	XO	XO	XXO	XXX		
Remona Fransen	-	-	O	O	O	O	XXX			
Ruky Abdulai	O	O	O	XO	O	O	XXX			
Alina Fyodorova	O	O	O	O	O	XO	XXX			
Sharon Day	-	-	-	XO	O	XO	XXX			
Katerina Cachová	O	O	XXO	XO	O	XXX				

Heptathlon - High Jump (continued)

Group B 29 August 2011

Position	Athlete	Country	Height	Points
1	Lilli Schwarzkopf	Germany	1.80	978
2	Margaret Simpson	Ghana	1.80	978
3	Julia Mächtig	Germany	1.80	978
3	Györgyi Farkas	Hungary	1.80	978
5	Grit Šadeiko	Estonia	1.74	903
6	Louise Hazel	Great Britain	1.74	903
7	Karolina Tyminska	Poland	1.74	903
8	Sara Aerts	Belgium	1.74	903
9	Ida Marcussen	Norway	1.71	867
10	Aiga Grabuste	Latvia	1.71	867
11	Francesca Doveri	Italy	1.71	867
12	Jessica Zelinka	Canada	1.68	830
12	Jessica Samuelsson	Sweden	1.68	830
14	Wassana Winatho	Thailand	1.68	830

Athlete	1.59	1.62	1.65	1.68	1.71	1.74	1.77	1.80	1.83
Lilli Schwarzkopf	-	-	O	O	O	O	O	O	XXX
Margaret Simpson	-	-	O	O	O	O	XO	O	XX
Julia Mächtig	-	-	-	O	O	O	XO	XXO	XXX
Györgyi Farkas	-	O	O	O	O	XO	O	XXO	XXX
Grit Šadeiko	-	O	O	O	O	XO	XXX		
Louise Hazel	O	O	O	O	XO	XXO	XXX		
Karolina Tyminska	-	-	XO	O	XXO	XXO	XXX		
Sara Aerts	-	XO	O	XXO	XXO	XXO	X		
Ida Marcussen	-	-	O	XO	O	XXX			
Aiga Grabuste	-	-	XO	XO	O	XXX			
Francesca Doveri	O	XO	O	XO	XXO	XXX			
Jessica Zelinka	-	O	O	O	XXX				
Jessica Samuelsson	-	O	O	O	XXX				
Wassana Winatho	XO	O	O	XXO	XXX				

Heptathlon - Shot Put

Group A   29 August 2011

Position	Athlete	Country	Distance	Points
1	Austra Skujyte	LTU	16.71	976
2	Natallia Dobrynska	UKR	16.14	937
3	Julia Mächtig	GER	15.24	877
4	Jessica Zelinka	CAN	14.91	855
5	Lilli Schwarzkopf	GER	14.89	854
6	Karolina Tyminska	POL	14.70	841
7	Jessica Ennis	GBR	14.67	839
8	Jessica Samuelsson	SWE	14.52	829
9	Anna Bogdanova	RUS	14.52	829
10	Aiga Grabuste	LAT	14.46	825
11	Alina Fyodorova	UKR	14.18	806
12	Antoinette Nana Djimou Ida	FRA	14.07	799
13	Jennifer Oeser	GER	13.70	774
14	Remona Fransen	NED	13.67	772

Athlete	Throw 1	Throw 2	Throw 3
Austra Skujyte	16.71	16.33	16.34
Natallia Dobrynska	15.62	16.14	15.67
Julia Mächtig	12.20	14.67	15.24
Jessica Zelinka	14.91	14.33	14.67
Lilli Schwarzkopf	14.08	14.56	14.89
Karolina Tyminska	14.53	14.40	14.70
Jessica Ennis	14.67	14.51	14.57
Jessica Samuelsson	14.12	14.30	14.52
Anna Bogdanova	13.55	13.42	14.52
Aiga Grabuste	12.13	X	14.46
Alina Fyodorova	14.09	14.18	X
Antoinette Nana Djimou Ida	13.97	14.07	13.42
Jennifer Oeser	13.30	13.70	13.56
Remona Fransen	13.67	13.02	13.06

Heptathlon - Shot Put (continued)

Group B 29 August 2011

Position	Athlete	Country	Distance	Points
1	Sharon Day	USA	14.28	813
2	Tatyana Chernova	RUS	14.17	805
3	Lyudmyla Yosypenko	UKR	13.16	738
4	Ida Marcussen	NOR	12.81	715
5	Györgyi Farkas	HUN	12.75	711
6	Sara Aerts	BEL	12.49	694
7	Margaret Simpson	GHA	12.48	693
8	Louise Hazel	GBR	12.36	685
9	Hyleas Fountain	USA	12.20	674
10	Francesca Doveri	ITA	11.76	645
11	Ruky Abdulai	CAN	11.72	643
12	Katerina Cachová	CZE	11.64	637
13	Grit Šadeiko	EST	11.46	625
	Wassana Winatho	THA	DNS	

Athlete	Throw 1	Throw 2	Throw 3
Sharon Day	14.28	12.74	X
Tatyana Chernova	13.47	13.84	14.17
Lyudmyla Yosypenko	11.99	13.02	13.16
Ida Marcussen	12.15	12.09	12.81
Györgyi Farkas	12.59	12.45	12.75
Sara Aerts	11.84	11.55	12.49
Margaret Simpson	12.47	12.48	12.39
Louise Hazel	12.28	X	12.36
Hyleas Fountain	11.73	12.20	12.19
Francesca Doveri	11.30	11.25	11.76
Ruky Abdulai	11.37	11.72	10.81
Katerina Cachová	11.23	11.64	10.97
Grit Šadeiko	11.46	X	11.41

Heptathlon - 200m

Heat 1   29 August 2011

Position	Lane	Athlete	Country	Time	Points
1	4	Jessica Ennis	Great Britain	23.27	1052
2	1	Tatyana Chernova	Russia	23.50	1029
3	2	Karolina Tyminska	Poland	23.87	993
4	6	Hyleas Fountain	United States	23.96	985
5	5	Jessica Zelinka	Canada	24.06	975
6	7	Lyudmyla Yosypenko	Ukraine	24.09	972
7	3	Jennifer Oeser	Germany	24.58	926

Heat 2   29 August 2011

Position	Lane	Athlete	Country	Time	Points
1	1	Louise Hazel	Great Britain	24.25	957
2	7	Grit Šadeiko	Estonia	24.39	944
3	5	Ruky Abdulai	Canada	24.50	933
4	4	Jessica Samuelsson	Sweden	24.55	929
5	3	Aiga Grabuste	Latvia	24.83	902
6	6	Antoinette Nana Djimou Ida	France	25.19	869
7	2	Francesca Doveri	Italy	25.45	846

Heat 3   29 August 2011

Position	Lane	Athlete	Country	Time	Points
1	3	Sharon Day	United States	25.01	886
2	6	Remona Fransen	Netherlands	25.17	871
3	1	Margaret Simpson	Ghana	25.23	866
4	2	Natallia Dobrynska	Ukraine	25.35	855
5	5	Katerina Cachová	Czech Republic	25.36	854
6	4	Lilli Schwarzkopf	Germany	25.82	813
	7	Wassana Winatho	Thailand	DNS	

Heat 4   29 August 2011

Position	Lane	Athlete	Country	Time	Points
1	1	Alina Fyodorova	Ukraine	25.35	855
2	2	Julia Mächtig	Germany	25.54	838
3	3	Anna Bogdanova	Russia	25.64	829
4	4	Ida Marcussen	Norway	25.74	820
5	5	Austra Skujyte	Lithuania	26.04	794
6	6	Györgyi Farkas	Hungary	26.35	767
7		Sara Aerts	Belgium	DNS	

Heptathlon - Long Jump

Group A   30 August 2011

Position	Athlete	Country	Wind	Distance	Points
1	Tatyana Chernova	Russia	-0.7	6.61	1043
2	Jessica Ennis	Great Britain	0.0	6.51	1010
3	Aiga Grabuste	Latvia	-0.4	6.45	991
4	Hyleas Fountain	United States	-0.6	6.45	991
5	Karolina Tyminska	Poland	-0.5	6.39	972
6	Anna Bogdanova	Russia	-0.4	6.38	969
7	Ruky Abdulai	Canada	-0.7	6.30	943
8	Jennifer Oeser	Germany	-0.2	6.28	937
9	Grit Šadeiko	Estonia	-0.1	6.28	937
10	Louise Hazel	Great Britain	-0.3	6.25	927
11	Antoinette Nana Djimou Ida	France	-0.3	6.13	890
12	Remona Fransen	Netherlands	-0.7	6.06	868
13	Austra Skujyte	Lithuania	-1.6	6.05	865
14	Julia Mächtig	Germany	0.0	5.98	843

Athlete	Jump 1	Jump 2	Jump 3
Tatyana Chernova	6.38	6.61	X
Jessica Ennis	6.27	6.51	6.30
Aiga Grabuste	6.31	5.96	6.45
Hyleas Fountain	6.45	X	6.28
Karolina Tyminska	6.39	6.32	6.28
Anna Bogdanova	6.38	5.60	6.09
Ruky Abdulai	6.11	6.30	5.99
Jennifer Oeser	X	6.28	6.14
Grit Šadeiko	X	X	6.28
Louise Hazel	6.15	6.25	6.12
Antoinette Nana Djimou Ida	6.13	6.02	5.86
Remona Fransen	6.06	X	X
Austra Skujyte	X	6.05	5.85
Julia Mächtig	5.98	5.92	X

Heptathlon - Long Jump (continued)

Group B   30 August 2011

Position	Athlete	Country	Wind	Distance	Points
1	Natallia Dobrynska	Ukraine	-1.0	6.18	905
2	Lilli Schwarzkopf	Germany	-0.5	6.18	905
3	Jessica Zelinka	Canada	-0.6	6.16	899
4	Francesca Doveri	Italy	-0.1	6.09	877
5	Jessica Samuelsson	Sweden	-0.7	6.05	865
6	Lyudmyla Yosypenko	Ukraine	-0.7	6.03	859
7	Alina Fyodorova	Ukraine	-0.1	5.98	843
8	Katerina Cachová	Czech Republic	-0.5	5.97	840
9	Ida Marcussen	Norway	-1.3	5.88	813
10	Margaret Simpson	Ghana	-0.9	5.88	813
11	Sharon Day	United States	-0.4	5.87	810
12	Györgyi Farkas	Hungary	0.0	5.78	783
	Sara Aerts	Belgium		DNS	
	Wassana Winatho	Thailand		DNS	

Athlete	Jump 1	Jump 2	Jump 3
Natallia Dobrynska	6.18	6.10	6.10
Lilli Schwarzkopf	6.18	6.04	5.95
Jessica Zelinka	6.16	5.78	X
Francesca Doveri	6.09	X	5.82
Jessica Samuelsson	6.01	6.05	X
Lyudmyla Yosypenko	6.03	5.97	5.87
Alina Fyodorova	5.98	5.44	5.63
Katerina Cachová	5.65	5.49	5.97
Ida Marcussen	5.70	X	5.88
Margaret Simpson	4.70	X	5.88
Sharon Day	5.64	X	5.87
Györgyi Farkas	5.58	5.78	5.58

Heptathlon - Javelin

Group A   30 August 2011

Position	Athlete	Country	Distance	Points
1	Antoinette Nana Djimou Ida	France	55.79	973
2	Margaret Simpson	Ghana	53.13	921
3	Tatyana Chernova	Russia	52.95	917
4	Jennifer Oeser	Germany	51.30	885
5	Lilli Schwarzkopf	Germany	49.69	854
6	Austra Skujyte	Lithuania	49.19	844
7	Natallia Dobrynska	Ukraine	48.00	821
8	Ruky Abdulai	Canada	46.35	790
9	Aiga Grabuste	Latvia	45.82	779
10	Ida Marcussen	Norway	44.90	762
11	Julia Mächtig	Germany	43.74	739
12	Lyudmyla Yosypenko	Ukraine	42.94	724
13	Grit Šadeiko	Estonia	42.84	722
14	Györgyi Farkas	Hungary	42.15	709

Athlete	Throw 1	Throw 2	Throw 3
Antoinette Nana Djimou Ida	55.79	50.77	54.17
Margaret Simpson	53.13	52.53	51.37
Tatyana Chernova	46.63	52.95	X
Jennifer Oeser	51.30	-	-
Lilli Schwarzkopf	49.69	47.81	43.97
Austra Skujyte	49.19	47.57	48.90
Natallia Dobrynska	48.00	X	46.74
Ruky Abdulai	44.48	45.67	46.35
Aiga Grabuste	43.46	44.71	45.82
Ida Marcussen	44.90	X	40.38
Julia Mächtig	43.74	42.26	42.31
Lyudmyla Yosypenko	42.94	X	42.49
Grit Šadeiko	41.23	42.84	X
Györgyi Farkas	41.66	42.15	X

Heptathlon - Javelin (continued)

Group B   30 August 2011

Position	Athlete	Country	Distance	Points
1	Katerina Cachová	Czech Republic	43.98	744
2	Hyleas Fountain	United States	43.42	733
3	Louise Hazel	Great Britain	41.75	701
4	Anna Bogdanova	Russia	41.38	694
5	Karolina Tyminska	Poland	41.32	693
6	Jessica Samuelsson	Sweden	41.32	693
7	Jessica Ennis	Great Britain	39.95	666
8	Jessica Zelinka	Canada	39.59	659
9	Sharon Day	United States	39.14	651
10	Remona Fransen	Netherlands	38.03	630
11	Alina Fyodorova	Ukraine	37.13	612
12	Francesca Doveri	Italy	35.09	573
	Sara Aerts	Belgium	DNS	
	Wassana Winatho	Thailand	DNS	

Athlete	Throw 1	Throw 2	Throw 3
Katerina Cachová	43.89	36.66	43.98
Hyleas Fountain	42.09	42.85	43.42
Louise Hazel	40.53	41.75	39.37
Anna Bogdanova	41.38	37.87	39.93
Karolina Tyminska	39.87	X	41.32
Jessica Samuelsson	41.32	38.12	X
Jessica Ennis	38.17	39.95	39.14
Jessica Zelinka	35.31	39.59	37.85
Sharon Day	39.14	38.41	35.88
Remona Fransen	38.03	37.66	33.38
Alina Fyodorova	34.22	33.84	37.13
Francesca Doveri	35.09	33.55	X

Heptathlon - 800m

Heat 1   30 August 2011

Position	Lane	Athlete	Country	Time	Points
1	7	Jessica Samuelsson	Sweden	2:10.20	962
2	7	Ida Marcussen	Norway	2:11.01	950
3	4	Francesca Doveri	Italy	2:13.14	919
4	5	Györgyi Farkas	Hungary	2:14.33	902
5	1	Katerina Cachová	Czech Republic	2:15.43	887
6	6	Sharon Day	United States	2:15.74	882
7	2	Remona Fransen	Netherlands	2:16.80	868
8	3	Alina Fyodorova	Ukraine	2:18.51	844
	8	Grit Šadeiko	Estonia	DNF	

Heat 2   30 August 2011

Position	Lane	Athlete	Country	Time	Points
1	6	Jessica Zelinka	Canada	2:12.62	927
2	5	Lyudmyla Yosypenko	Ukraine	2:14.37	902
3	4	Aiga Grabuste	Latvia	2:14.82	895
4	7	Lilli Schwarzkopf	Germany	2:15.26	889
5	3	Ruky Abdulai	Canada	2:15.29	889
6	2	Louise Hazel	Great Britain	2:15.44	887
7	8	Julia Mächtig	Germany	2:17.14	863
8	1	Margaret Simpson	Ghana	2:17.91	852
9	7	Anna Bogdanova	Russia	2:18.34	846

Heat 3   30 August 2011

Position	Lane	Athlete	Country	Time	Points
1	3	Karolina Tyminska	Poland	2:05.21	1036
2	1	Jessica Ennis	Great Britain	2:07.81	997
3	6	Tatyana Chernova	Russia	2:08.04	993
4	7	Jennifer Oeser	Germany	2:10.39	959
5	4	Natallia Dobrynska	Ukraine	2:11.34	945
6	2	Austra Skujyte	Lithuania	2:23.21	780
7	8	Antoinette Nana Djimou Ida	France	2:28.74	709
	5	Hyleas Fountain	United States	DNF	

Heptathlon - Final Standings

Position	Athlete	Country	Points
GOLD	Tatyana Chernova	Russia	6880
SILVER	Jessica Ennis	Great Britain	6751
BRONZE	Jennifer Oeser	Germany	6571
4	Karolina Tyminska	Poland	6544
5	Natallia Dobrynska	Ukraine	6539
6	Lilli Schwarzkopf	Germany	6321
7	Antoinette Nana Djimou Ida	France	6309
8	Austra Skujyte	Lithuania	6297
9	Jessica Zelinka	Canada	6268
10	Lyudmyla Yosypenko	Ukraine	6263
11	Anna Bogdanova	Russia	6242
12	Aiga Grabuste	Latvia	6229
13	Ruky Abdulai	Canada	6212
14	Margaret Simpson	Ghana	6183
15	Louise Hazel	Great Britain	6149
16	Jessica Samuelsson	Sweden	6119
17	Julia Mächtig	Germany	6095
18	Sharon Day	United States	6043
19	Remona Fransen	Netherlands	6027
20	Ida Marcussen	Norway	5911
21	Alina Fyodorova	Ukraine	5908
22	Katerina Cachová	Czech Republic	5908
23	Francesca Doveri	Italy	5786
24	Györgyi Farkas	Hungary	5784
25	Hyleas Fountain	United States	5611
26	Grit Šadeiko	Estonia	5190
	Wassana Winatho	Thailand	DNF
	Sara Aerts	Belgium	DNF

Decathlon - 100m

Heat 1   27 August 2011

Position	Lane	Athlete	Country	Time	Points
1	3	Ashton Eaton	United States	10.46	985
2	1	Trey Hardee	United States	10.55	963
3	5	Damian Warner	Canada	10.56	961
4	4	Luiz Alberto de Araújo	Brazil	10.71	926
5	6	Oleksiy Kasyanov	Ukraine	10.75	917
6	7	Mihail Dudaš	Serbia	10.81	903
7	2	Rico Freimuth	Germany	10.83	899

Heat 2   27 August 2011

Position	Lane	Athlete	Country	Time	Points
1	5	Eelco Sintnicolaas	Netherlands	10.76	915
2	3	Ingmar Vos	Netherlands	10.82	901
3	1	Yordani García	Cuba	10.85	894
4	6	Andres Raja	Estonia	10.85	894
5	7	Darius Draudvila	Lithuania	10.90	883
6	4	Jamie Adjetey-Nelson	Canada	10.97	867
7	2	Maurice Smith	Jamaica	10.98	865

Heat 3   27 August 2011

Position	Lane	Athlete	Country	Time	Points
1	3	Brent Newdick	New Zealand	11.00	861
2	2	Leonel Suárez	Cuba	11.07	845
3	8	Pascal Behrenbruch	Germany	11.08	843
4	7	Kun-Woo Kim	South Korea	11.11	836
5	1	Willem Coertzen	South Africa	11.16	825
6	5	Romain Barras	France	11.20	817
7	4	Dmitriy Karpov	Kazakhstan	11.24	808
8	6	Mikk Pahapill	Estonia	11.28	799

Heat 4   27 August 2011

Position	Lane	Athlete	Country	Time	Points
1	1	Larbi Bouraada	Algeria	10.88	888
2	2	Jan Felix Knobel	Germany	11.18	821
3	3	Hadi Sepehrzad	Iran	11.19	819
4	6	Thomas van der Plaetsen	Belgium	11.20	817
5	4	Roman Šebrle	Czech Republic	11.25	806
6	8	Ryan Harlan	United States	11.29	797
7	7	Aleksey Drozdov	Russia	11.34	786
8	5	Keisuke Ushiro	Japan	11.42	769

Decathlon - Long Jump

Group A   27 August 2011

Position	Athlete	Country	Wind	Distance	Points
1	Thomas van der Plaetsen	Belgium	-0.9	7.79	1007
2	Oleksiy Kasyanov	Ukraine	-0.6	7.59	957
3	Ashton Eaton	United States	0.0	7.46	925
4	Aleksey Drozdov	Russia	-0.3	7.45	922
5	Trey Hardee	United States	-0.1	7.45	922
6	Mihail Dudaš	Serbia	-0.5	7.41	913
7	Ingmar Vos	Netherlands	-0.4	7.41	913
8	Willem Coertzen	South Africa	-0.2	7.37	903
9	Damian Warner	Canada	-1.1	7.35	898
10	Brent Newdick	New Zealand	-0.7	7.31	888
11	Roman Šebrle	Czech Republic	-0.4	7.30	886
12	Eelco Sintnicolaas	Netherlands	-0.3	7.29	883
13	Andres Raja	Estonia	-0.2	7.21	864
14	Darius Draudvila	Lithuania	-0.7	7.19	859
15	Mikk Pahapill	Estonia	-0.3	7.12	842

Athlete	Jump 1	Jump 2	Jump 3
Thomas van der Plaetsen	7.79	-	-
Oleksiy Kasyanov	7.46	7.59	X
Ashton Eaton	X	7.46	7.21
Aleksey Drozdov	7.05	7.30	7.45
Trey Hardee	X	7.45	X
Mihail Dudaš	7.41	7.15	7.33
Ingmar Vos	7.41	-	-
Willem Coertzen	X	7.37	7.33
Damian Warner	7.35	X	X
Brent Newdick	7.31	7.14	X
Roman Šebrle	7.30	7.18	7.22
Eelco Sintnicolaas	X	X	7.29
Andres Raja	7.21	7.21	7.16
Darius Draudvila	7.14	7.19	X
Mikk Pahapill	X	X	7.12

Decathlon - Long Jump (continued)

Group B   27 August 2011

Position	Athlete	Country	Wind	Distance	Points
1	Larbi Bouraada	Algeria	-0.2	7.42	915
2	Leonel Suárez	Cuba	0.0	7.33	893
3	Jan Felix Knobel	Germany	-0.4	7.30	886
4	Kun-Woo Kim	South Korea	-0.2	7.24	871
5	Jamie Adjetey-Nelson	Canada	-0.2	7.21	864
6	Romain Barras	France	0.0	7.06	828
7	Maurice Smith	Jamaica	-0.5	7.06	828
8	Keisuke Ushiro	Japan	-0.2	6.96	804
9	Dmitriy Karpov	Kazakhstan	-0.1	6.86	781
10	Pascal Behrenbruch	Germany	-0.5	6.80	767
11	Luiz Alberto de Araújo	Brazil	-0.3	6.74	753
12	Ryan Harlan	United States	-0.3	6.68	739
13	Hadi Sepehrzad	Iran	-0.3	6.65	732
14	Yordani García	Cuba	-0.3	6.56	711
	Rico Freimuth	Germany			-

Athlete	Jump 1	Jump 2	Jump 3
Larbi Bouraada	X	7.41	7.42
Leonel Suárez	6.95	6.66	7.33
Jan Felix Knobel	7.15	7.30	7.27
Kun-Woo Kim	7.22	7.24	X
Jamie Adjetey-Nelson	X	7.21	X
Romain Barras	7.05	X	7.06
Maurice Smith	X	X	7.06
Keisuke Ushiro	6.87	6.76	6.96
Dmitriy Karpov	6.69	6.86	6.64
Pascal Behrenbruch	6.67	6.80	6.76
Luiz Alberto de Araújo	X	6.74	X
Ryan Harlan	6.55	6.68	X
Hadi Sepehrzad	6.43	6.27	6.65
Yordani García	X	6.56	6.24
Rico Freimuth	X	X	X

Decathlon - Shot Put

Group A   27 August 2011

Position	Athlete	Country	Distance	Points
1	Ryan Harlan	United States	16.49	882
2	Aleksey Drozdov	Russia	16.17	862
3	Jan Felix Knobel	Germany	16.06	855
4	Pascal Behrenbruch	Germany	16.01	852
5	Dmitriy Karpov	Kazakhstan	15.69	832
6	Hadi Sepehrzad	Iran	15.65	830
7	Roman Šebrle	Czech Republic	15.20	802
8	Maurice Smith	Jamaica	15.15	799
9	Trey Hardee	United States	15.09	795
10	Yordani García	Cuba	14.93	785
11	Romain Barras	France	14.92	785
12	Darius Draudvila	Lithuania	14.81	778
13	Luiz Alberto de Araújo	Brazil	14.77	776
14	Mikk Pahapill	Estonia	14.76	775
15	Andres Raja	Estonia	14.61	766

Athlete	Throw 1	Throw 2	Throw 3
Ryan Harlan	16.49	16.23	X
Aleksey Drozdov	X	16.17	X
Jan Felix Knobel	14.72	15.86	16.06
Pascal Behrenbruch	15.91	15.73	16.01
Dmitriy Karpov	15.69	X	14.91
Hadi Sepehrzad	15.31	15.2	15.65
Roman Šebrle	15.05	X	15.20
Maurice Smith	15.15	15.14	X
Trey Hardee	15.09	X	15.09
Yordani García	14.52	14.12	14.93
Romain Barras	14.61	14.66	14.92
Darius Draudvila	X	14.38	14.81
Luiz Alberto de Araújo	14.45	14.77	14.76
Mikk Pahapill	14.76	14.08	X
Andres Raja	14.39	X	14.61

Decathlon - Shot Put (continued)

Group B 27 August 2011

Position	Athlete	Country	Distance	Points
1	Leonel Suárez	Cuba	14.54	761
2	Ashton Eaton	United States	14.44	755
3	Oleksiy Kasyanov	Ukraine	14.43	755
4	Eelco Sintnicolaas	Netherlands	14.13	736
5	Ingmar Vos	Netherlands	13.86	720
6	Mihail Dudaš	Serbia	13.76	714
7	Brent Newdick	New Zealand	13.75	713
8	Willem Coertzen	South Africa	13.48	697
9	Damian Warner	Canada	13.26	683
10	Larbi Bouraada	Algeria	13.11	674
11	Kun-Woo Kim	South Korea	12.96	665
12	Keisuke Ushiro	Japan	12.88	660
13	Thomas van der Plaetsen	Belgium	12.76	653
	Rico Freimuth	Germany	-	
	Jamie Adjetey-Nelson	Canada	DNS	

Athlete	Throw 1	Throw 2	Throw 3
Leonel Suárez	14.54	13.57	14.25
Ashton Eaton	14.44	X	X
Oleksiy Kasyanov	14.29	14.43	X
Eelco Sintnicolaas	13.50	12.98	14.13
Ingmar Vos	13.72	13.73	13.86
Mihail Dudaš	13.67	13.76	X
Brent Newdick	13.75	X	13.25
Willem Coertzen	X	13.48	13.01
Damian Warner	12.92	X	13.26
Larbi Bouraada	13.11	13.10	X
Kun-Woo Kim	12.61	12.59	12.96
Keisuke Ushiro	X	12.88	12.71
Thomas van der Plaetsen	11.99	12.76	12.63
Rico Freimuth	X	-	-

Decathlon - High Jump

Group A   27 August 2011

Position	Athlete	Country	Height	Points
1	Thomas van der Plaetsen	Belgium	2.17	963
2	Aleksey Drozdov	Russia	2.14	934
3	Leonel Suárez	Cuba	2.05	850
4	Roman Šebrle	Czech Republic	2.05	850
5	Ryan Harlan	United States	2.02	822
6	Yordani García	Cuba	2.02	822
7	Mikk Pahapill	Estonia	2.02	822
7	Willem Coertzen	South Africa	2.02	822
7	Mihail Dudaš	Serbia	2.02	822
7	Ashton Eaton	United States	2.02	822
11	Keisuke Ushiro	Japan	2.02	822
12	Andres Raja	Estonia	1.99	794
13	Oleksiy Kasyanov	Ukraine	1.99	794
14	Larbi Bouraada	Algeria	1.96	767
	Ingmar Vos	Netherlands	DNS	

Athlete	1.75	1.78	1.81	1.84	1.87	1.90	1.93	1.96
Thomas van der Plaetsen	-	-	-	-	-	-	-	O
Aleksey Drozdov	-	-	-	-	-	-	O	-
Leonel Suárez	-	-	-	-	-	-	O	-
Roman Šebrle	-	-	-	-	-	-	-	O
Ryan Harlan	-	-	-	-	-	-	O	O
Yordani García	-	-	-	-	-	O	-	XO
Mikk Pahapill	-	-	-	-	-	O	-	O
Willem Coertzen	-	-	-	-	-	O	O	O
Mihail Dudaš	-	-	-	-	-	O	-	O
Ashton Eaton	-	-	-	-	-	-	-	O
Keisuke Ushiro	-	-	-	-	-	O	-	XO
Andres Raja	-	-	-	-	-	O	-	O
Oleksiy Kasyanov	-	-	-	-	-	XO	-	O
Larbi Bouraada	-	-	-	-	-	-	XO	O

Athlete	1.99	2.02	2.05	2.08	2.11	2.14	2.17
Thomas van der Plaetsen	-	O	O	XO	O	O	XXO
Aleksey Drozdov	O	O	O	XXO	XO	XO	XXX
Leonel Suárez	XO	O	XO	XXX			
Roman Šebrle	O	O	XXO	XXX			
Ryan Harlan	O	O	XXX				
Yordani García	XXO	O	XXX				
Mikk Pahapill	-	XO	XXX				
Willem Coertzen	O	XO	XXX				
Mihail Dudaš	O	XO	XXX				
Ashton Eaton	O	XO	XXX				
Keisuke Ushiro	O	XXO	XXX				
Andres Raja	O	XXX					
Oleksiy Kasyanov	O	XXX					
Larbi Bouraada	XXX						

Group B   27 August 2011

Position	Athlete	Country	Height	Points
1	Trey Hardee	United States	2.02	822
2	Damian Warner	Canada	2.02	822
3	Romain Barras	France	1.99	794
4	Darius Draudvila	Lithuania	1.96	767
5	Jan Felix Knobel	Germany	1.96	767
6	Kun-Woo Kim	South Korea	1.96	767
7	Brent Newdick	New Zealand	1.96	767
8	Maurice Smith	Jamaica	1.93	740
9	Eelco Sintnicolaas	Netherlands	1.93	740
10	Dmitriy Karpov	Kazakhstan	1.93	740
11	Pascal Behrenbruch	Germany	1.93	740
12	Luiz Alberto de Araújo	Brazil	1.90	714
13	Hadi Sepehrzad	Iran	1.90	714
	Jamie Adjetey-Nelson	Canada	DNS	
	Rico Freimuth	Germany	DNS	

Athlete	1.78	1.81	1.84	1.87	1.90	1.93	1.96	1.99	2.02	2.05
Trey Hardee	-	-	-	-	-	O	-	XXO	XO	XXX
Damian Warner	-	-	O	O	O	O	XXO	XXO	XXO	XXX
Romain Barras	-	-	-	O	-	O	XXO	XXO	XXX	
Darius Draudvila	-	-	-	-	O	O	O	XXX		
Jan Felix Knobel	-	-	O	XO	O	XO	XO	XXX		
Kun-Woo Kim	-	-	-	O	O	O	XXO	XXX		
Brent Newdick	-	-	O	-	O	XO	XXO	XXX		
Maurice Smith	-	-	-	O	XO	O	XXX			
Eelco Sintnicolaas	-	-	XO	XO	XO	O	XXX			
Dmitriy Karpov	-	-	-	O	XO	XXO	XXX			
Pascal Behrenbruch	-	-	O	XXO	O	XXO	XXX			
Luiz Alberto de Araújo	-	O	-	O	O	XXX				
Hadi Sepehrzad	-	O	O	XO	XO	XXX				

Decathlon - 400m

Heat 1   27 August 2011

Position	Lane	Athlete	Country	Time	Points
1	6	Ashton Eaton	United States	46.99	959
2	4	Larbi Bouraada	Algeria	47.34	941
3	5	Mihail Dudaš	Serbia	47.73	922
4	3	Trey Hardee	United States	48.37	891
5	2	Oleksiy Kasyanov	Ukraine	48.46	887
6	1	Kun-Woo Kim	South Korea	49.24	850
	7	Rico Freimuth	Germany	DNS	

Heat 2   27 August 2011

Position	Lane	Athlete	Country	Time	Points
1	6	Eelco Sintnicolaas	Netherlands	48.35	892
2	3	Luiz Alberto de Araújo	Brazil	48.48	886
3	5	Leonel Suárez	Cuba	49.17	853
4	2	Willem Coertzen	South Africa	49.20	852
5	1	Thomas van der Plaetsen	Belgium	49.46	840
6	7	Andres Raja	Estonia	49.47	839
7	4	Yordani García	Cuba	49.64	831

Heat 3   27 August 2011

Position	Lane	Athlete	Country	Time	Points
1	8	Jan Felix Knobel	Germany	49.46	840
2	1	Romain Barras	France	49.50	838
3	2	Brent Newdick	New Zealand	49.95	817
4	3	Damian Warner	Canada	50.12	809
5	6	Maurice Smith	Jamaica	50.27	802
6	5	Darius Draudvila	Lithuania	50.55	789
7	7	Dmitriy Karpov	Kazakhstan	52.01	724
	4	Jamie Adjetey-Nelson	Canada	DNS	

Heat 4   27 August 2011

Position	Lane	Athlete	Country	Time	Points
1	4	Pascal Behrenbruch	Germany	49.90	819
2	5	Mikk Pahapill	Estonia	50.65	785
3	7	Keisuke Ushiro	Japan	50.89	774
4	8	Hadi Sepehrzad	Iran	50.92	773
5	2	Roman Šebrle	Czech Republic	51.18	761
6	1	Aleksey Drozdov	Russia	51.35	753
7	3	Ryan Harlan	United States	51.57	744
	6	Ingmar Vos	Netherlands	DNS	

Decathlon - 110m Hurdles

Heat 1   28 August 2011

Position	Lane	Athlete	Country	Time	Points
1	3	Ashton Eaton	United States	13.85	994
2	2	Trey Hardee	United States	13.97	978
3	1	Andres Raja	Estonia	14.04	969
4	6	Damian Warner	Canada	14.19	950
5	5	Maurice Smith	Jamaica	14.68	889
6	4	Yordani García	Cuba	14.70	886

Heat 2   28 August 2011

Position	Lane	Athlete	Country	Time	Points
1	7	Luiz Alberto de Araújo	Brazil	14.25	942
2	6	Leonel Suárez	Cuba	14.29	937
3	3	Romain Barras	France	14.37	927
4	1	Eelco Sintnicolaas	Netherlands	14.42	921
5	5	Willem Coertzen	South Africa	14.48	913
6	4	Oleksiy Kasyanov	Ukraine	14.65	892
7	2	Darius Draudvila	Lithuania	14.93	858

Heat 3   28 August 2011

Position	Lane	Athlete	Country	Time	Points
1	2	Pascal Behrenbruch	Germany	14.33	932
2	1	Mikk Pahapill	Estonia	14.54	906
3	6	Larbi Bouraada	Algeria	14.56	903
4	3	Dmitriy Karpov	Kazakhstan	14.64	894
5	5	Ryan Harlan	United States	14.71	885
6	4	Thomas van der Plaetsen	Belgium	14.79	875
7	7	Brent Newdick	New Zealand	14.86	867

Heat 4   28 August 2011

Position	Lane	Athlete	Country	Time	Points
1	1	Roman Šebrle	Czech Republic	14.75	880
2	6	Mihail Dudaš	Serbia	14.89	863
3	5	Jan Felix Knobel	Germany	14.92	859
4	2	Kun-Woo Kim	South Korea	14.95	856
5	4	Hadi Sepehrzad	Iran	14.95	856
6	7	Keisuke Ushiro	Japan	15.20	825
7	3	Aleksey Drozdov	Russia	15.49	791

Decathlon - Discus

Group A   28 August 2011

Position	Athlete	Country	Distance	Points
1	Aleksey Drozdov	Russia	50.29	876
2	Hadi Sepehrzad	Iran	50.06	872
3	Trey Hardee	United States	49.89	868
4	Pascal Behrenbruch	Germany	48.56	840
5	Jan Felix Knobel	Germany	47.93	827
6	Mikk Pahapill	Estonia	47.16	811
7	Dmitriy Karpov	Kazakhstan	47.10	810
8	Roman Šebrle	Czech Republic	46.93	807
9	Luiz Alberto de Araújo	Brazil	46.46	797
10	Leonel Suárez	Cuba	46.25	793
11	Ashton Eaton	United States	46.17	791
12	Maurice Smith	Jamaica	45.63	780
13	Oleksiy Kasyanov	Ukraine	43.74	741

Athlete	Throw 1	Throw 2	Throw 3
Aleksey Drozdov	X	X	50.29
Hadi Sepehrzad	45.36	50.06	X
Trey Hardee	49.89	49.73	X
Pascal Behrenbruch	48.56	48.28	46.84
Jan Felix Knobel	47.93	46.16	X
Mikk Pahapill	47.16	46.77	46.07
Dmitriy Karpov	45.40	47.10	X
Roman Šebrle	44.98	46.93	X
Luiz Alberto de Araújo	45.05	45.12	46.46
Leonel Suárez	41.13	46.25	X
Ashton Eaton	46.17	X	45.70
Maurice Smith	45.20	45.63	44.57
Oleksiy Kasyanov	X	43.74	X

Decathlon - Discus (continued)

Group B   28 August 2011

Position	Athlete	Country	Distance	Points
1	Brent Newdick	New Zealand	45.65	780
2	Mihail Dudaš	Serbia	43.97	746
3	Keisuke Ushiro	Japan	43.84	743
4	Ryan Harlan	United States	43.52	736
5	Andres Raja	Estonia	43.39	734
6	Willem Coertzen	South Africa	43.13	728
7	Eelco Sintnicolaas	Netherlands	42.23	710
8	Damian Warner	Canada	41.71	699
9	Romain Barras	France	41.65	698
10	Kun-Woo Kim	South Korea	39.53	655
11	Larbi Bouraada	Algeria	37.84	621
12	Thomas van der Plaetsen	Belgium	37.2	608
	Darius Draudvila	Lithuania	-	
	Yordani García	Cuba	DNS	

Athlete	Throw 1	Throw 2	Throw 3
Brent Newdick	40.26	45.65	44.22
Mihail Dudaš	42.86	43.97	X
Keisuke Ushiro	42.59	39.43	43.84
Ryan Harlan	43.52	42.61	X
Andres Raja	43.38	42.58	43.39
Willem Coertzen	42.02	43.13	X
Eelco Sintnicolaas	X	38.28	42.23
Damian Warner	X	40.75	41.71
Romain Barras	35.19	X	41.65
Kun-Woo Kim	35.00	37.14	39.53
Larbi Bouraada	X	26.65	37.84
Thomas van der Plaetsen	34.76	37.20	36.83
Darius Draudvila	X	X	X

Decathlon - Pole Vault

Group A   28 August 2011

Position	Athlete	Country	Height	Points
1	Eelco Sintnicolaas	Netherlands	5.20	972
2	Thomas van der Plaetsen	Belgium	5.10	941
3	Aleksey Drozdov	Russia	5.00	910
4	Leonel Suárez	Cuba	5.00	910
5	Mikk Pahapill	Estonia	4.90	880
6	Dmitriy Karpov	Kazakhstan	4.80	849
6	Trey Hardee	United States	4.80	849
8	Roman Šebrle	Czech Republic	4.80	849
9	Jan Felix Knobel	Germany	4.70	819
10	Ashton Eaton	United States	4.60	790
11	Keisuke Ushiro	Japan	4.40	731
	Ryan Harlan	United States	-	
	Yordani García	Cuba	DNS	

Athlete	4.30	4.40	4.50	4.60	4.70	4.80	4.90	5.00	5.10	5.20	5.30
Eelco Sintnicolaas	-	-	-	-	-	-	-	-	-	XO	-
Thomas van der Plaetsen	-	-	-	-	-	-	O	-	O	XXX	
Aleksey Drozdov	-	-	-	O	-	XO	O	O	XXX		
Leonel Suárez	-	-	XO	-	XO	-	XO	O	XXX		
Mikk Pahapill	-	-	O	XXO	-	O	XXO	XXX			
Dmitriy Karpov	-	-	-	O	-	XO	-	XXX			
Trey Hardee	-	-	-	-	-	XO	-	XXX			
Roman Šebrle	O	-	XO	-	XXO	XXO	XX-	-	X		
Jan Felix Knobel	-	-	-	XXO	O	XXX					
Ashton Eaton	-	-	-	O	-	XXX					
Keisuke Ushiro	-	XO	-	XXX							
Ryan Harlan	-	-	-	XXX							

Decathlon - Pole Vault (continued)

Group B   28 August 2011

Position	Athlete	Country	Height	Points
1	Romain Barras	France	5.00	910
2	Kun-Woo Kim	South Korea	4.90	880
3	Mihail Dudaš	Serbia	4.90	880
4	Pascal Behrenbruch	Germany	4.90	880
5	Larbi Bouraada	Algeria	4.90	880
6	Andres Raja	Estonia	4.70	819
7	Oleksiy Kasyanov	Ukraine	4.70	819
8	Luiz Alberto de Araújo	Brazil	4.70	819
9	Brent Newdick	New Zealand	4.50	760
10	Damian Warner	Canada	4.50	760
	Hadi Sepehrzad	Iran	-	
	Willem Coertzen	South Africa	-	
	Maurice Smith	Jamaica	DNS	
	Darius Draudvila	Lithuania	DNS	

Athlete	4.00	4.10	4.20	4.30	4.40	4.50	4.60	4.70	4.80	4.90	5.00	5.10
Romain Barras	-	-	-	-	-	-	-	-	O	O	XXO	XXX
Kun-Woo Kim	-	-	-	-	-	XO	XO	-	XO	O	XXX	
Mihail Dudaš	-	-	-	-	O	O	XO	XO	XXO	XO	XXX	
Pascal Behrenbruch	-	-	O	-	O	O	O	O	XO	XXO	XXX	
Larbi Bouraada	-	-	-	-	-	XXO	-	O	XO	XXO	XXX	
Andres Raja	-	-	-	-	O	-	O	O	XXX			
Oleksiy Kasyanov	-	-	-	-	XO	O	XXO	O	XXX			
Luiz Alberto de Araújo	-	-	-	-	-	O	XO	XXO	XXX			
Brent Newdick	-	-	-	O	-	O	-	XXX				
Damian Warner	-	-	XXO	XO	O	O	XXX					
Hadi Sepehrzad	XXX											
Willem Coertzen	-	XXX										

Decathlon - Javelin

Group A 28 August 2011

Position	Athlete	Country	Distance	Points
1	Leonel Suárez	Cuba	69.12	876
2	Trey Hardee	United States	68.99	874
3	Jan Felix Knobel	Germany	68.42	865
4	Keisuke Ushiro	Japan	67.73	855
5	Mikk Pahapill	Estonia	66.40	835
6	Aleksey Drozdov	Russia	64.80	810
7	Ryan Harlan	United States	58.43	714
8	Andres Raja	Estonia	57.35	698
9	Brent Newdick	New Zealand	55.69	673
10	Ashton Eaton	United States	55.17	665
11	Damian Warner	Canada	54.61	657
12	Dmitriy Karpov	Kazakhstan	46.91	543
	Hadi Sepehrzad	Iran	DNS	

Athlete	Throw 1	Throw 2	Throw 3
Leonel Suárez	69.12	67.01	69.08
Trey Hardee	68.99	66.40	64.03
Jan Felix Knobel	68.42	X	64.78
Keisuke Ushiro	X	67.73	X
Mikk Pahapill	65.11	64.32	66.40
Aleksey Drozdov	64.80	63.40	63.80
Ryan Harlan	58.43	-	-
Andres Raja	56.59	56.51	57.35
Brent Newdick	54.02	54.92	55.69
Ashton Eaton	46.94	55.07	55.17
Damian Warner	52.11	X	54.61
Dmitriy Karpov	46.91	45.92	-

Group B 28 August 2011

Position	Athlete	Country	Distance	Points
1	Roman Šebrle	Czech Republic	67.28	848
2	Pascal Behrenbruch	Germany	66.50	836
3	Romain Barras	France	63.25	787
4	Eelco Sintnicolaas	Netherlands	61.07	754
5	Larbi Bouraada	Algeria	59.00	723
6	Mihail Dudaš	Serbia	58.93	722
7	Thomas van der Plaetsen	Belgium	58.91	721
8	Luiz Alberto de Araújo	Brazil	54.38	654
9	Kun-Woo Kim	South Korea	53.33	638
10	Oleksiy Kasyanov	Ukraine	52.16	621
	Yordani García	Cuba	DNS	
	Maurice Smith	Jamaica	DNS	
	Darius Draudvila	Lithuania	DNS	
	Willem Coertzen	South Africa	DNS	

Athlete	Throw 1	Throw 2	Throw 3
Roman Šebrle	61.11	67.28	63.13
Pascal Behrenbruch	62.14	61.85	66.50
Romain Barras	61.81	63.25	61.55
Eelco Sintnicolaas	57.99	61.07	60.4
Larbi Bouraada	59.00	-	-
Mihail Dudaš	56.40	55.86	58.93
Thomas van der Plaetsen	58.91	53.58	53.27
Luiz Alberto de Araújo	51.13	54.38	53.48
Kun-Woo Kim	49.42	48.63	53.33
Oleksiy Kasyanov	51.54	49.71	52.16

Decathlon - 1500m

Heat 1   28 August 2011

Position	Athlete	Country	Time	Points
1	Larbi Bouraada	Algeria	4:14.97	846
2	Kun-Woo Kim	South Korea	4:15.65	842
3	Romain Barras	France	4:29.19	750
4	Oleksiy Kasyanov	Ukraine	4:29.35	749
5	Keisuke Ushiro	Japan	4:43.87	656
6	Luiz Alberto de Araújo	Brazil	4:47.29	635
7	Brent Newdick	New Zealand	4:47.30	635
8	Andres Raja	Estonia	4:52.28	605
9	Damian Warner	Canada	4:54.37	593
10	Dmitriy Karpov	Kazakhstan	4:58.41	569
11	Ryan Harlan	United States	5:21.63	442

Heat 2   28 August 2011

Position	Athlete	Country	Time	Points
1	Ashton Eaton	United States	4:18.94	819
2	Leonel Suárez	Cuba	4:24.16	783
3	Eelco Sintnicolaas	Netherlands	4:25.40	775
4	Mihail Dudaš	Serbia	4:26.06	771
5	Mikk Pahapill	Estonia	4:35.41	709
6	Pascal Behrenbruch	Germany	4:36.64	702
7	Aleksey Drozdov	Russia	4:41.73	669
8	Jan Felix Knobel	Germany	4:43.12	661
9	Trey Hardee	United States	4:45.68	645
10	Thomas van der Plaetsen	Belgium	4:45.86	644
11	Roman Šebrle	Czech Republic	4:56.50	580

Decathlon - Final Standings

Position	Athlete	Country	Points
GOLD	Trey Hardee	United States	8607
SILVER	Ashton Eaton	United States	8505
BRONZE	Leonel Suárez	Cuba	8501
4	Aleksey Drozdov	Russia	8313
5	Eelco Sintnicolaas	Netherlands	8298
6	Mihail Dudaš	Serbia	8256
7	Pascal Behrenbruch	Germany	8211
8	Jan Felix Knobel	Germany	8200
9	Mikk Pahapill	Estonia	8164
10	Larbi Bouraada	Algeria	8158
11	Romain Barras	France	8134
12	Oleksiy Kasyanov	Ukraine	8132
13	Thomas van der Plaetsen	Belgium	8069
14	Roman Šebrle	Czech Republic	8069
15	Andres Raja	Estonia	7982
16	Luiz Alberto de Araújo	Brazil	7902
17	Kun-Woo Kim	South Korea	7860
18	Damian Warner	Canada	7832
19	Brent Newdick	New Zealand	7761
20	Keisuke Ushiro	Japan	7639
21	Dmitriy Karpov	Kazakhstan	7550
22	Ryan Harlan	United States	6761
23	Maurice Smith	Jamaica	DNF
24	Jamie Adjetey-Nelson	Canada	DNF
25	Darius Draudvila	Lithuania	DNF
26	Ingmar Vos	Netherlands	DNF
27	Yordani García	Cuba	DNF
28	Hadi Sepehrzad	Iran	DNF
29	Rico Freimuth	Germany	DNF
30	Willem Coertzen	South Africa	DNF

Men's 20 Kilometres Walk

FINAL   28 August 2011

Position	Athlete	Country	Time
GOLD	Valeriy Borchin	Russia	1:19:56
SILVER	Vladimir Kanaykin	Russia	1:20:27
BRONZE	Luis Fernando López	Colombia	1:20:38
4	Zhen Wang	China	1:20:54
5	Stanislav Emelyanov	Russia	1:21:11
6	Hyunsub Kim	South Korea	1:21:17
7	Ruslan Dmytrenko	Ukraine	1:21:31
8	Yusuke Suzuki	Japan	1:21:39
9	Alex Schwazer	Italy	1:21:50
10	Erick Barrondo	Guam	1:22:08
11	Yafei Chu	China	1:22:10
12	Sergey Morozov	Russia	1:22:37
13	Hao Wang	China	1:22:49
14	Matej Tóth	Slovakia	1:22:55
15	Eder Sánchez	Mexico	1:23:05
16	João Vieira	Portugal	1:23:26
17	Miguel Ángel López	Spain	1:23:41
18	Anton Kucmin	Slovakia	1:23:57
19	James Rendón	Colombia	1:24:08
20	Horacio Nava	Mexico	1:24:15
21	Christopher Linke	Germany	1:24:17
22	Caio Bonfim	Brazil	1:24:29
23	Trevor Barron	United States	1:24:33
24	Rafal Augustyn	Poland	1:24:47
25	Youngjun Byun	South Korea	1:24:48
26	Hassanine Sebei	Tunisia	1:25:17
27	Jared Tallent	Australia	1:25:25
28	Recep Çelik	Turkey	1:25:39
29	Nazar Kovalenko	Ukraine	1:25:50
30	Gurmeet Singh	India	1:26:34
31	Babubhai Kesharabhai Panucha	India	1:26:53
32	David Kimutai Rotich	Kenya	1:27:20
33	Yerko Araya	Chile	1:27:47
34	Hédi Teraoui	Tunisia	1:29:48
35	Diego Flores	Mexico	1:30:00
36	Juan Manuel Cano	Argentina	1:30:00
37	Emerson Hernandez	El Salvador	1:30:48
38	Ronal Quispe	Bolivia	1:32:09
	Moacir Zimmermann	Brazil	DQ
	Gustavo Restrepo	Colombia	DQ
	Giorgio Rubino	Italy	DQ
	Anatole Ibañez	Sweden	DQ
	Adam Rutter	Australia	DNF
	Mauricio Arteaga	Ecuador	DNF
	Francisco Javier Fernández	Spain	DNF
	Chil-sung Park	South Korea	DNF

Women's 20 Kilometres Walk

FINAL   31 August 2011

Position	Athlete	Country	Time
GOLD	Olga Kaniskina	Russia	1:29:42
SILVER	Hong Liu	China	1:30:00
BRONZE	Anisya Kirdyapkina	Russia	1:30:13
4	Elisa Rigaudo	Italy	1:30:44
5	Shenjie Qieyang	China	1:31:14
6	Susana Feitor	Portugal	1:31:26
7	Ana Cabecinha	Portugal	1:31:36
8	Kristina Saltanovic	Lithuania	1:31:40
9	Beatriz Pascual	Spain	1:31:46
10	Inês Henriques	Portugal	1:32:06
11	Vera Sokolova	Russia	1:32:13
12	Olena Shumkina	Ukraine	1:32:17
13	María Vasco	Spain	1:32:42
14	Ni Gao	China	1:32:49
15	Regan Lamble	Australia	1:33:38
16	Olive Loughnane	Ireland	1:34:02
17	Tatiana Mineeva	Russia	1:34:08
18	Nastassia Yatsevich	Belarus	1:34:09
19	Jamy Franco	Guam	1:34:36
20	Kumi Otoshi	Japan	1:34:37
21	Claire Tallent	Australia	1:34:46
22	Mayumi Kawasaki	Japan	1:35:03
23	Johanna Jackson	Great Britain	1:35:32
24	Nadiia Borovska-Prokopuk	Ukraine	1:35:38
25	Lucie Pelantová	Czech Republic	1:35:45
26	Yong-eun Jeon	South Korea	1:35:52
27	Claudia Stef	Romania	1:36:55
28	Agnese Pastare	Latvia	1:37:48
29	Brigita Virbalyté	Lithuania	1:38:39
30	Maria Michta	United States	1:38:54
31	Maria Czaková	Slovakia	1:39:07
32	Arabelly Orjuela	Colombia	1:39:28
33	Ingrid Hernández	Colombia	1:39:53
34	Zuzana Schindlerová	Czech Republic	1:39:57
35	Marie Polli	Switzerland	1:40:28
36	Milángela Rosales	Venezuela	1:40:49
37	Rachel Lavallée Seaman	Canada	1:43:31
38	Grace Wanjiru Njue	Kenya	1:43:59
39	Yadira Guamán	Ecuador	1:45:15
40	Chaima Trabelsi	Tunisia	1:46:29
	Claudia Balderrama	Bolivia	DQ
	María José Poves	Spain	DQ
	Viktória Madarász	Hungary	DQ
	Neringa Aidietyte	Lithuania	DQ
	Maria Guadalupe Sánchez	Mexico	DQ
	Olga Iakovenko	Ukraine	DQ
	Sabine Krantz	Germany	DNF
	Melanie Seeger	Germany	DNF
	Masumi Fuchise	Japan	DNF
	Semiha Mutlu	Turkey	DNF

Men's 50 Kilometres Walk

FINAL   03 September 2011

Position	Athlete	Country	Time
GOLD	Sergey Bakulin	Russia	3:41:24
SILVER	Denis Nizhegorodov	Russia	3:42:45
BRONZE	Jared Tallent	Australia	3:43:36
4	Tianfeng Si	China	3:44:40
5	Luke Adams	Australia	3:45:31
6	Koichiro Morioka	Japan	3:46:21
7	Chil-sung Park	South Korea	3:47:13
8	Faguang Xu	China	3:47:19
9	Takayuki Tanii	Japan	3:48:03
10	Hirooki Arai	Japan	3:48:40
11	Andrés Chocho	Ecuador	3:49:32
12	Marco De Luca	Italy	3:49:40
13	Rafal Sikora	Poland	3:50:24
14	Dong-young Kim	South Korea	3:51:12
15	Jarkko Kinnunen	Finland	3:52:32
16	Jean-Jacques Nkouloukidi	Italy	3:52:35
17	Trond Nymark	Norway	3:54:26
18	Edgar Hernández	Mexico	3:54:46
19	José Leyver	Mexico	3:55:37
20	Oleksiy Kazanin	Ukraine	3:56:18
21	Omar Zepeda	Mexico	3:56:41
22	Andreas Gustafsson	Sweden	4:00:05
23	Bertrand Moulinet	France	4:07:58
24	Quentin Rew	New Zealand	4:08:46
25	Jianbo Li	China	4:10:26
	Jesús Angel García	Spain	DQ
	Mikel Odriozola	Spain	DQ
	Antti Kempas	Finland	DQ
	Yohan Diniz	France	DQ
	Cedric Houssaye	France	DQ
	Colin Griffin	Ireland	DQ
	Junghyun Yim	South Korea	DQ
	Tadas Šuškevicius	Lithuania	DQ
	Rafal Fedaczynski	Poland	DQ
	Igor Erokhin	Russia	DQ
	Nenad Filipovic	Serbia	DQ
	Miloš Bátovský	Slovakia	DQ
	Nathan Deakes	Australia	DNF
	José Ignacio Díaz	Spain	DNF
	Igors Kazakevics	Latvia	DNF
	Grzegorz Sudol	Poland	DNF
	Sergey Kirdyapkin	Russia	DNF
	Matej Tóth	Slovakia	DNF
	Christopher Linke	Germany	DNS
	Robert Heffernan	Ireland	DNS

Men's 4x100m Relay

Qualification for the Final: first two in each heat plus the next two fastest finishers.

Heat 1   04 September 2011

Position	Lane	Athletes	Country		Time
1	5	Trell Kimmons; Justin Gatlin; Maurice Mitchell; Travis Padgett	United States	Q	37.79
2	1	Teddy Tinmar; Christophe Lemaitre; Yannick Lesourd; Jimmy Vicaut	France	Q	38.38
3	2	Ricardo Monteiro; João Ferreira; Arnaldo Abrantes; Yazalde Nascimento	Portugal		39.09
4	4	Emmanuel Kubi; Tim Abeyie; Ashhad Agyapong; Aziz Zakari	Ghana		39.17
5	7	Wen-Tang Wang; Yuan-Kai Liu; Meng-Lin Tsai; Wei-Chen Yi	Chinese Taipei		39.30
	3	Diego Cavalcanti; Sandro Viana; Nilson Andrè; Bruno de Barros	Brazil		DQ
	6	Pascal Mancini; Reto Schenkel; Alex Wilson; Marc Schneeberger	Switzerland		DNF

Heat 2   04 September 2011

Position	Lane	Athletes	Country		Time
1	4	Keston Bledman; Marc Burns; Aaron Armstrong; Richard Thompson	Trinidad & Tobago	Q	37.91
2	8	Nesta Carter; Michael Frater; Yohan Blake; Dexter Lee	Jamaica	Q	38.07
3	2	Jason Rogers; Kim Collins; Antoine Adams; Brijesh Lawrence	St Kitts & Nevis	q	38.47
4	5	Yuichi Kobayashi; Masashi Eriguchi; Shinji Takahira; Hitoshi Saito	Japan		38.66
5	6	Hannes Dreyer; Ofentse Mogawane; Roscoe Engel; Thuso Mpuang	South Africa		38.72
6	1	Qiang Chen; Jiahong Liang; Bingtian Su; Yi Lao	China		38.87
7	7	Marcos Amalbert; Carlos Rodríguez; Marquis Holston; Miguel López	Puerto Rico		39.04
	3	Tobias Unger; Marius Broening; Sebastian Ernst; Alex Schaf	Germany		DNF

Heat 3   04 September 2011

Position	Lane	Athletes	Country		Time
1	5	Christian Malcolm; Craig Pickering; Marlon Devonish; Harry Aikines-Aryeetey	Great Britain	Q	38.29
2	4	Pawel Stempel; Dariusz Kuc; Robert Kubaczyk; Kamil Krynski	Poland	Q	38.37
3	8	Michael Tumi; Simone Collio; Emanuele Di Gregorio; Fabio Cerutti	Italy	q	38.41
4	3	Anthony Alozie; Matt Davies; Aaron Rouge-Serret; Isaac Ntiamoah	Australia		38.69
5	1	Ho-suah Yeo; Kyu-won Cho; Kukyoung Kim; Hee-nam Lim	South Korea		38.94
6	6	Sam Effah; Gavin Smellie; Jared Connaughton; Justyn Warner	Canada		39.28
7	7	Weerawat Pharueang; Suppachai Chimdee; Sompote Suwannarangsri; Jirapong Meenapra	Thailand		39.54
	2	Giovanni Codrington; Brian Mariano; Jerrel Feller; Patrick van Luijk	Netherlands		DQ

Men's 4x100m Relay (continued)

FINAL   04 September 2011

Position	Lane	Athletes	Country		Time
GOLD	6	Nesta Carter; Michael Frater; Yohan Blake; Usain Bolt	Jamaica	WR	37.04
SILVER	8	Teddy Tinmar; Christophe Lemaitre; Yannick Lesourd; Jimmy Vicaut	France		38.20
BRONZE	1	Jason Rogers; Kim Collins; Antoine Adams; Brijesh Lawrence	St Kitts & Nevis		38.49
4	7	Pawel Stempel; Dariusz Kuc; Robert Kubaczyk; Kamil Krynski	Poland		38.50
5	2	Michael Tumi; Simone Collio; Emanuele Di Gregorio; Fabio Cerutti	Italy		38.96
6	5	Keston Bledman; Marc Burns; Aaron Armstrong; Richard Thompson	Trinidad & Tobago		39.01
	3	Christian Malcolm; Craig Pickering; Marlon Devonish; Harry Aikines-Aryeetey	Great Britain		DNF
	4	Trell Kimmons; Justin Gatlin; Darvis Patton; Walter Dix	United States		DNF

Women's 4x100m Relay

Qualification for the Final: first two in each heat plus the next two fastest finishers.

Heat 1   04 September 2011

Position	Lane	Athletes	Country		Time
1	2	Shelly-Ann Fraser-Pryce; Kerron Stewart; Sherone Simpson; Jura Levy	Jamaica	Q	42.23
2	4	Myriam Soumaré; Céline Distel; Lina Jacques-Sébastien; Véronique Mang	France	Q	42.60
3	3	Ana Claudia Silva; Vanda Gomes; Franciela Krasucki; Rosângela Santos	Brazil	q	42.92
4	1	Yomara Hinestroza; Maria Alejandra Idrobo; Darlenis Obregón; Norma González	Colombia		43.53
5	6	Nao Okabe; Momoko Takahashi; Chisato Fukushima; Saori Imai	Japan		43.83
6	5	Plácida Martínez; Amparo Cotán; Concepción Montaner; Ruth Beitia	Spain		46.24
	7	Yongli Wei; Qiuping Liang; Lan Jiang; Yujia Tao	China		DQ

Heat 2   04 September 2011

Position	Lane	Athletes	Country		Time
1	2	Kai Selvon; Kelly-Ann Baptiste; Semoy Hackett; Michelle-Lee Ahye	Trinidad & Tobago	Q	42.50
2	7	Olesya Povh; Nataliya Pohrebnyak; Mariya Ryemyen; Hrystyna Stuy	Ukraine	Q	42.63
3	5	Yulia Gushchina; Natalia Rusakova; Elizabeta Savlinis; Aleksandra Fedoriva	Russia	q	42.78
4	6	Hayley Butler; Melissa Breen; Charlotte Van Veenendaal; Sally Pearson	Australia		43.79
5	4	Tiffany Porter; Anyika Onuora; Laura Turner; Jeanette Kwakye	Great Britain		43.95
6	1	Jeesu Eum; So-Yeon Kim; Sunae Lee; So-Yeun Park	South Korea		46.14
	3	Anna Kielbasinska; Marika Popowicz; Marta Jeschke; Agnieszka Ligieza	Poland		DNF

Women's 4x100m Relay (continued)

Heat 3   04 September 2011

Position	Lane	Athletes	Country		Time
1	1	Bianca Knight; Shalonda Solomon; Marshevet Myers; Alexandria Anderson	United States	Q	41.94
2	4	Gloria Asumnu; Oludamola Osayomi; Agnes Osazuwa; Blessing Okagbare	Nigeria	Q	42.74
3	7	Kadene Vassell; Dafne Schippers; Anouk Hagen; Jamile Samuel	Netherlands		43.44
4	5	Clélia Reuse; Jacqueline Gasser; Ellen Sprunger; Léa Sprunger	Switzerland		44.04
5	3	Hanna Bahdanovich; Yuliya Balykina; Alena Neumiarzhitskaya; Hanna Liapeshka	Belarus		44.38
6	2	Sheniqua Ferguson; Nivea Smith; Anthonique Strachan; Debbie Ferguson-McKenzie	Bahamas		50.62
	6	Yasmin Kwadwo; Anne Möllinger; Cathleen Tschirch; Marion Wagner	Germany		DNF

FINAL   04 September 2011

Position	Lane	Athletes	Country	Time
GOLD	4	Bianca Knight; Allyson Felix; Marshevet Myers; Carmelita Jeter	United States	41.56
SILVER	6	Shelly-Ann Fraser-Pryce; Kerron Stewart; Sherone Simpson; Veronica Campbell-Brown	Jamaica	41.70
BRONZE	8	Olesya Povh; Nataliya Pohrebnyak; Mariya Ryemyen; Hrystyna Stuy	Ukraine	42.51
4	3	Kai Selvon; Kelly-Ann Baptiste; Semoy Hackett; Michelle-Lee Ahye	Trinidad & Tobago	42.58
5	5	Myriam Soumaré; Céline Distel; Lina Jacques-Sébastien; Véronique Mang	France	42.70
6	1	Yulia Gushchina; Natalia Rusakova; Elizabeta Savlinis; Aleksandra Fedoriva	Russia	42.93
7	7	Gloria Asumnu; Oludamola Osayomi; Agnes Osazuwa; Blessing Okagbare	Nigeria	42.93
8	2	Ana Claudia Silva; Vanda Gomes; Franciela Krasucki; Rosângela Santos	Brazil	43.10

Men's 4x400m Relay

Qualification for the Final: first three in each heat plus the next two fastest finishers.

Heat 1   01 September 2011

Position	Lane	Athletes	Country		Time
1	6	Greg Nixon; Jamaal Torrance; Michael Berry; LaShawn Merritt	United States	Q	2:58.82
2	7	Allodin Fothergill; Riker Hylton; Lansford Spence; Leford Green	Jamaica	Q	2:59.13
3	1	Oscar Pistorius; Ofentse Mogawane; Willem de Beer; Shane Victor	South Africa	Q	2:59.21
4	5	Richard Strachan; Nigel Levine; Christopher Clarke; Martyn Rooney	Great Britain	q	3:00.38
5	2	Jonas Plass; Kamghe Gaba; Eric Krüger; Thomas Schneider	Germany	q	3:00.68
6	8	Zwede Hewitt; Jarrin Solomon; Deon Lendore; Renny Quow	Trinidad & Tobago		3:02.47
7	3	Kei Takase; Yuzo Kanemaru; Yusuke Ishitsuka; Hideyuki Hirose	Japan		3:02.64
8	4	Bonggo Park; Chanho Lim; Jun Lee; Hyeokje Seong	South Korea		3:04.05

Heat 2   01 September 2011

Position	Lane	Athletes	Country		Time
1	1	Antoine Gillet; Jonathan Borlée; Nils Duerinck; Kévin Borlée	Belgium	Q	3:00.71
2	2	Maksim Dyldin; Konstantin Svechkar; Pavel Trenikhin; Denis Alekseyev	Russia	Q	3:00.81
3	4	Vincent Kiplangat Kosgei; Anderson Mureta Mutegi; Vincent Mumo Kiilu; Mark Kiprotich Mutai	Kenya	Q	3:00.97
4	8	Ramon Miller; Avard Moncur; Andrae Williams; LaToy Williams	Bahamas		3:01.54
5	6	Ben Offereins; Tristan Thomas; Steven Solomon; Sean Wroe	Australia		3:01.56
6	7	Kacper Kozlowski; Piotr Wiaderek; Jakub Krzewina; Marcin Marciniszyn	Poland		3:01.84
7	5	Nicolas Fillon; Teddy Venel; Mamoudou Hanne; Yoann Décimus	France		3:03.68
8	3	Ismail Alsabani; Yousef Ahmed Masrahi; Hamed Hamdan Al Bishi; Mohammed Al-Salhi	Saudi Arabia		3:05.65

Men's 4x400m Relay (continued)

FINAL 02 September 2011

Position	Lane	Athletes	Country		Time
GOLD	5	Greg Nixon; Bershawn Jackson; Angelo Taylor; LaShawn Merritt	United States		2:59.31
SILVER	8	Shane Victor; Ofentse Mogawane; Willem de Beer; Louis van Zyl	South Africa		2:59.87
BRONZE	4	Allodin Fothergill; Jermaine Gonzales; Riker Hylton; Leford Green	Jamaica		3:00.10
4	3	Maksim Dyldin; Konstantin Svechkar; Pavel Trenikhin; Denis Alekseyev	Russia		3:00.22
5	6	Jonathan Borlée; Antoine Gillet; Nils Duerinck; Kévin Borlée	Belgium		3:00.41
6	7	Vincent Kiplangat Kosgei; Vincent Mumo Kiilu; Anderson Mureta Mutegi; Mark Kiprotich Mutai	Kenya		3:01.15
7	1	Richard Strachan; Nigel Levine; Christopher Clarke; Martyn Rooney	Great Britain		3:01.16
8	2	Jonas Plass; Kamghe Gaba; Miguel Rigau; Thomas Schneider	Germany		3:01.37

Women's 4x400m Relay

Qualification for the Final: first two in each heat plus the next two fastest finishers.

Heat 1 02 September 2011

Position	Lane	Athletes	Country		Time
1	7	Natasha Hastings; Jessica Beard; Francena McCorory; Keshia Baker	United States	Q	3:23.57
2	5	Nataliya Pyhyda; Olha Zavhorodnya; Hanna Yaroshchuk; Antonina Yefremova	Ukraine	Q	3:24.13
3	3	Hanna Tashpulatava; Yulyana Yushchanka; Ilona Usovich; Sviatlana Usovich	Belarus	q	3:24.28
4	6	Janin Lindenberg; Esther Cremer; Lena Schmidt; Claudia Hoffmann	Germany		3:27.31
5	1	Phara Anacharsis; Muriel Hurtis; Marie Gayot; Floria Guei	France		3:28.02
6	2	Caitlin Sargent; Caitlin Willis-Pincott; Lauren Boden; Anneliese Rubie	Australia		3:32.27
	4	Alexandra Kuzina; Viktoriya Yalovtseva; Marina Maslenko; Tatyana Khadjimuradova	Kazakhstan		DNF

Heat 2 02 September 2011

Position	Lane	Athletes	Country		Time
1	2	Kseniya Vdovina; Ksenia Zadorina; Lyudmila Litvinova; Antonina Krivoshapka	Russia	Q	3:20.94
2	3	Omolara Omotosho; Muizat Ajoke Odumosu; Margaret Etim; Bukola Abogunloko	Nigeria	Q	3:25.59
3	6	Denisa Rosolová; Zuzana Bergrová; Jitka Bartonicková; Zuzana Hejnová	Czech Republic	q	3:26.01
4	1	Aymeé Martínez; Diosmely Peña; Susana Clement; Daisurami Bonne	Cuba		3:26.74
5	4	Adrienne Power; Esther Akinsulie; Jenna Martin; Lemlem Bereket	Canada		3:27.92
6	5	Geisa Aparecida Coutinho; Bárbara de Oliveira; Joelma Sousa; Jailma de Lima	Brazil		3:32.43

Women's 4x400m Relay

Heat 3   02 September 2011

Position	Lane	Athletes	Country		Time
1	6	Rosemarie Whyte; Shereefa Lloyd; Patricia Hall; Davita Prendergast	Jamaica	Q	3:22.01
2	1	Christine Ohuruogu; Nicola Sanders; Lee McConnell; Perri Shakes-Drayton	Great Britain	Q	3:23.05
3	4	Chiara Bazzoni; Maria Enrica Spacca; Libania Grenot; Marta Milani	Italy		3:26.48
4	2	Marian Andrews-Heffernan; Joanne Cuddihy; Claire Bergin; Michelle Carey	Ireland		3:27.48
5	3	Nagihan Karadere; Birsen Engin; Meliz Redif; Pinar Saka	Turkey		3:32.15
6	7	Yanmei Chen; Xiaoyin Tang; Zhihui Zheng; Jingwen Chen	China		3:32.39
7	5	Yu-jin Woo; Ha-Nee Lee; Seongmyun Park; Se-Ra Oh	South Korea		3:43.22

FINAL   03 September 2011

Position	Lane	Athletes	Country	Time
GOLD	6	Sanya Richards-Ross; Allyson Felix; Jessica Beard; Francena McCorory	United States	3:18.09
SILVER	4	Rosemarie Whyte; Davita Prendergast; Novlene Williams-Mills; Shericka Williams	Jamaica	3:18.71
BRONZE	5	Antonina Krivoshapka; Natalya Antyukh; Lyudmila Litvinova; Anastasiya Kapachinskaya	Russia	3:19.36
4	3	Perri Shakes-Drayton; Nicola Sanders; Christine Ohuruogu; Lee McConnell	Great Britain	3:23.63
5	7	Nataliya Pyhyda; Anastasiya Rabchenyuk; Hanna Yaroshchuk; Antonina Yefremova	Ukraine	3:23.86
6	1	Hanna Tashpulatava; Yulyana Yushchanka; Ilona Usovich; Sviatlana Usovich	Belarus	3:25.64
7	2	Denisa Rosolová; Zuzana Bergrová; Jitka Bartoničková; Zuzana Hejnová	Czech Republic	3:26.57
8	8	Omolara Omotosho; Muizat Ajoke Odumosu; Margaret Etim; Bukola Abogunloko	Nigeria	3:29.82

Athlete Index

Forenames	Surname	Born	Country	Events	Prev Apps
Maria	Abakumova	15/01/1986	Russia	Javelin (w)	07 09
Emanuele	Abate	08/07/1985	Italy	110m Hurdles (m)	0
Youcef	Abdi	07/12/1977	Australia	3000m SC (m)	03 07 09
Ruky	Abdulai	08/08/1985	Canada	Heptathlon	09
Abdishakur Nageye	Abdulle	23/06/1993	Somalia	5000m (m)	0
Takatoshi	Abe	12/11/1991	Japan	400m Hurdles (m)	0
Tim	Abeyie	07/11/1982	Ghana	4x100m (m)	0
Endurance	Abinuwa	31/07/1987	Nigeria	200m (w)	09
Bukola	Abogunloko	18/08/1994	Nigeria	4x400m (w)	0
Rabah	Aboud	01/01/1981	Algeria	5000m (m)	0
Arnaldo	Abrantes	27/11/1986	Portugal	200m (m), 4x100m (m)	07 09
Antoine	Adams	31/08/1988	St Kitts & Nevis	4x100m (m)	0
Luke	Adams	22/10/1976	Australia	50km Walk (m)	03 05 07 09
Valerie	Adams	06/10/1984	New Zealand	Shot Put (w)	03 05 07 09
Birtukan	Adamu	29/04/1992	Ethiopia	3000m SC (w)	0
Seun	Adigun	03/01/1987	Nigeria	100m Hurdles (w)	09
Jamie	Adjetey-Nelson	20/05/1984	Canada	Decathlon	0
Elisângela	Adriano	27/07/1972	Brazil	Discus (w)	99 01 03 05 07 09
Sara	Aerts	25/01/1984	Belgium	Heptathlon	09
Alessandra	Aguilar	01/07/1978	Spain	Marathon (w)	09
Jessica	Aguilera	27/10/1987	Nicaragua	400m Hurdles (w)	07 09
Ashhad	Agyapong	23/09/1985	Ghana	4x100m (m)	0
Feta	Ahamada	24/06/1987	Comoros	100m (w)	0
Farhan	Ahmad	11/01/1990	Pakistan	800m (m)	0
Michelle-Lee	Ahye	10/04/1992	Trinidad & Tobago	4x100m (w)	0
Neringa	Aidietyte	05/06/1983	Lithuania	20km Walk (w)	0
Harry	Aikines-Aryeetey	29/08/1988	Great Britain	100m (m), 4x100m (m)	09
Marina	Aitova	13/09/1982	Kazakhstan	High Jump (w)	03 07 09
Yukiko	Akaba	18/10/1979	Japan	Marathon (w)	09
Esther	Akinsulie	22/04/1984	Canada	4x400m (w)	09
Malika	Akkaoui	25/12/1987	Morocco	1500m (w)	0
Hamed Hamdan	Al Bishi	03/03/1982	Saudi Arabia	4x400m (m)	03 05 09
Bahaa	Al Farra	10/03/1991	Palestine	400m (m)	0
Salima El Ouali	Alami	29/12/1983	Morocco	3000m SC (w)	0
Ali Ahmed	Al-Amri	17/07/1978	Saudi Arabia	3000m SC (m)	05 07 09
Mohammad	Al-Azemi	16/06/1982	Kuwait	800m (m)	05 07 09
Dailenys	Alcántara	10/08/1991	Cuba	Triple Jump (w)	0
Yamilé	Aldama	14/08/1972	Great Britain	Triple Jump (w)	99 05 07 09
Virgilijus	Alekna	13/02/1972	Lithuania	Discus (m)	99 01 03 05 07 09
Denis	Alekseyev	26/12/1987	Russia	4x400m (m)	0
Zebene	Alemayehu	04/09/1992	Ethiopia	1500m (m)	0
Mostafa	Al-Gamel	01/10/1988	Egypt	Hammer (m)	0
Nabil Mohammed	Al-Garbi	03/11/1992	Yemen	1500m (m)	0
Hussain Jamaan	Alhamdah	04/08/1983	Saudi Arabia	5000m (m)	09
Zourah	Ali	06/08/1983	Djibouti	800m (w)	09
Hamza	Alic	20/01/1979	Bosnia & Herzegovina	Shot Put (m)	05 07 09
Abdullah Abdulaziz	Aljoud	10/07/1975	Saudi Arabia	5000m (m)	0
Ahmed Mohamed	Al-Merjabi	09/09/1990	Oman	400m (m)	0
Anthony	Alozie	18/08/1986	Australia	4x100m (m)	09
Alaa Hikmat	Al-Qaysi	14/09/1985	Iraq	400m (w)	0
Ismail	Alsabani	25/04/1989	Saudi Arabia	4x400m (m)	0
Omar Jouma Bilal	Al-Salfa	15/10/1989	United Arab Emirates	200m (m)	09
Mohammed	Al-Salhi	11/05/1986	Saudi Arabia	4x400m (m)	03 05 07 09
Francisco Javier	Alves	02/09/1980	Spain	5000m (m)	07
Ali Mohamed	Al-Zinkawi	27/02/1984	Kuwait	Hammer (m)	05 07 09
Marcos	Amalbert	09/04/1988	Puerto Rico	4x100m (m)	0
Mohammed	Aman	10/01/1994	Ethiopia	800m (m)	0
Doreen	Amata	06/05/1988	Nigeria	High Jump (w)	09
Phara	Anacharsis	17/12/1983	France	4x400m (w)	0
Alexandria	Anderson	28/01/1987	United States	4x100m (w)	0
Jeshua	Anderson	22/06/1989	United States	400m Hurdles (m)	0
Marvin	Anderson	12/05/1982	Jamaica	200m (m)	07
Isabellah	Andersson	12/11/1980	Sweden	Marathon (w)	0

Forenames	Surname	Born	Country	Events	Prev Apps
Nilson	Andrè	30/01/1986	Brazil	100m (m), 200m (m), 4x100m (m)	0
Marian	Andrews-Heffernan	16/04/1982	Ireland	4x400m (w)	0
Tonje	Angelsen	17/01/1990	Norway	High Jump (w)	0
Natalya	Antyukh	26/06/1981	Russia	400m Hurdles (w), 4x400m (w)	01 05 07 09
Esref	Apak	03/01/1982	Turkey	Hammer (m)	05 07 09
Demetra	Arachovití	18/07/1987	Cyprus	100m Hurdles (w)	0
Hirooki	Arai	18/05/1988	Japan	50km Walk (m)	0
Ronalds	Arajs	29/11/1987	Latvia	100m (m)	09
Jacob	Araptany	11/02/1992	Uganda	3000m SC (m)	0
Yerko	Araya	14/02/1986	Chile	20km Walk (m)	09
Nicholas	Arciniaga	30/06/1983	United States	Marathon (m)	0
Aaron	Armstrong	14/10/1977	Trinidad & Tobago	100m (m)	05 09
Aaron	Armstrong	14/10/1977	Trinidad & Tobago	4x100m (m)	05 09
Dylan	Armstrong	15/01/1981	Canada	Shot Put (m)	01 07 09
Leif	Arrhenius	15/07/1986	Sweden	Discus (m)	0
Niklas	Arrhenius	10/09/1982	Sweden	Discus (m)	05 07
Mauricio	Arteaga	08/08/1988	Ecuador	20km Walk (m)	09
Maryna	Arzamasava	17/12/1982	Belarus	800m (w)	0
Nickel	Ashmeade	07/04/1990	Jamaica	200m (m)	0
Yared	Asmerom	04/02/1980	Eritrea	Marathon (m)	05 07 09
Meskerem	Assefa	28/09/1986	Ethiopia	1500m (w)	03 09
Sofia	Assefa	14/11/1987	Ethiopia	3000m SC (w)	09
Jonathan	Åstrand	09/09/1985	Finland	200m (m)	0
Gloria	Asumnu	22/05/1985	Nigeria	4x100m (w)	0
Delphine	Atangana	16/08/1984	Cameroon	100m (w)	05 07
Jessica	Augusto	08/11/1981	Portugal	10000m (w)	05 07 09
Rafal	Augustyn	14/05/1984	Poland	20km Walk (m)	07 09
Fatih	Avan	01/01/1989	Turkey	Javelin (m)	09
Anna	Avdeeva	06/04/1985	Russia	Shot Put (w)	07 09
Roman	Avramenko	23/03/1988	Ukraine	Javelin (m)	09
Masumi	Aya	01/01/1980	Japan	Hammer (w)	01 03 07
Merve	Aydin	17/03/1990	Turkey	800m (w)	0
Bimbo Miel	Ayedou	17/08/1991	Benin	400m Hurdles (w)	0
Simon	Ayeko	10/05/1987	Uganda	3000m SC (m)	09
Massoud	Azizi	02/02/1985	Afghanistan	100m (m)	09
Mehdi	Baala	17/08/1978	France	1500m (m)	99 01 03 05 07 09
Jaroslav	Bába	02/09/1984	Czech Republic	High Jump (m)	03 05 07 09
Ahmed	Baday	12/01/1979	Morocco	Marathon (m)	07 09
Seung-Ho	Baek	16/12/1990	South Korea	5000m (m)	0
Hanna	Bahdanovich	14/10/1983	Belarus	4x100m (w)	09
Daniel	Bailey	09/09/1986	Antigua & Barbuda	100m (m)	05 09
Balázs	Baji	09/06/1989	Hungary	110m Hurdles (m)	0
Keshia	Baker	30/01/1988	United States	4x400m (w)	0
Sergey	Bakulin	13/11/1986	Russia	50km Walk (m)	0
Egle	Balciünaité	03/04/1979	Lithuania	800m (w)	07 09
Claudia	Balderrama	13/11/1983	Bolivia	20km Walk (w)	0
Erik	Balnuweit	21/09/1988	Germany	110m Hurdles (m)	0
Yuliya	Balykina	12/04/1984	Belarus	4x100m (w)	0
Zahra	Bani	31/12/1979	Italy	Javelin (w)	05 07
Konstadínos	Baniótis	06/11/1986	Greece	High Jump (m)	09
Jarrod	Bannister	03/10/1984	Australia	Javelin (m)	07
Andriyana	Bânova	01/05/1987	Bulgaria	Triple Jump (w)	0
Kelly-Ann	Baptiste	14/01/2008	Trinidad & Tobago	4x100m (w)	05 09
Vera	Barbosa	13/01/1989	Portugal	400m Hurdles (w)	07
Bryan	Barnett	10/02/1987	Canada	200m (m)	07 09
Romain	Barras	01/08/1980	France	Decathlon	05 07 09
Brigetta	Barrett	24/12/1990	United States	High Jump (w)	0
Yarelys	Barrios	24/06/1983	Cuba	Discus (w)	07 09
Trevor	Barron	30/09/1992	United States	20km Walk (m)	0
Erick	Barrondo	14/06/1991	Guam	20km Walk (m)	0
Marisa	Barros	25/02/1980	Portugal	Marathon (w)	09
Trevor	Barry	14/06/1983	Bahamas	High Jump (m)	09
Mutaz Essa	Barshim	24/06/1991	Qatar	High Jump (m)	0
Ralf	Bartels	21/02/1978	Germany	Shot Put (m)	01 03 05 07 09
Rondell	Bartholomew	07/04/1990	Grenada	400m (m)	09
Jitka	Bartonicková	22/12/1985	Czech Republic	4x400m (w)	0

Forenames	Surname	Born	Country	Events	Prev Apps
Dimitri	Bascou	20/07/1987	France	110m Hurdles (m)	09
Ser-Od	Bat-Ochir	07/10/1981	Mongolia	Marathon (m)	03 05 07 09
Miloš	Bátovský	26/05/1979	Slovakia	50km Walk (m)	05 07 09
Scott	Bauhs	11/05/1986	United States	10000m (m)	0
Sebastian	Bayer	11/06/1986	Germany	Long Jump (m)	09
Atsede	Baysa	16/04/1987	Ethiopia	Marathon (w)	09
Mario	Bazán	01/08/1997	Peru	3000m SC (m)	09
Chiara	Bazzoni	05/07/1984	Italy	4x400m (w)	0
Jessica	Beard	08/01/1989	United States	400m (w), 4x400m (w)	09
Kierre	Beckles	21/05/1990	Barbados	100m Hurdles (w)	0
Pascal	Behrenbruch	19/01/1985	Germany	Decathlon	09
Ruth	Beitia	01/04/1979	Spain	High Jump (w), 4x100m (w)	03 05 07 09
Alemitu	Bekele	17/09/1977	Turkey	5000m (w)	09
Bezunesh	Bekele	29/01/1983	Ethiopia	Marathon (w)	05 09
Kenenisa	Bekele	13/06/1982	Ethiopia	5000m (m), 10000m (m)	03 05 07 09
Emir	Bekric	14/03/1991	Serbia	400m Hurdles (m)	0
Mimi	Belete	09/06/1988	Brunei	1500m (w)	09
Amor	Ben Yahia	01/07/1985	Tunisia	3000m SC (m)	0
Yvonne	Bennett	29/07/1990	Northern Mariana Islands	100m (w)	07 09
Lemlem	Bereket	10/12/1987	Canada	800m (w), 4x400m (w)	0
Claire	Bergin	01/02/1985	Ireland	4x400m (w)	0
Jere	Bergius	04/04/1987	Finland	Pole Vault (m)	0
Zuzana	Bergrová	24/11/1984	Czech Republic	4x400m (w)	0
Martyn	Bernard	15/12/1984	Great Britain	High Jump (m)	07
Jeimy	Bernárdez	03/09/1986	Honduras	100m Hurdles (w)	05 07 09
Yahya	Berrabah	13/10/1981	Morocco	Long Jump (m)	03 05 07 09
Michael	Berry	10/12/1991	United States	4x400m (m)	0
Yoandris	Betanzos	15/02/1982	Cuba	Triple Jump (m)	03 05 07 09
Beraki	Beyene	06/02/1980	Eritrea	Marathon (m)	0
Cindy	Billaud	11/03/1986	France	100m Hurdles (w)	09
Collis	Birmingham	27/12/1984	Australia	5000m (m)	09
Richard	Blagg	03/11/1988	Gibraltar	800m (m)	0
Yohan	Blake	26/12/1989	Jamaica	100m (m), 4x100m (m)	0
Holly	Bleasdale	02/11/1991	Great Britain	Pole Vault (w)	0
Keston	Bledman	08/03/1988	Trinidad & Tobago	100m (m), 4x100m (m)	07 09
Adrian	Blincoe	04/11/1979	New Zealand	5000m (m)	03 05 09
Dominik	Bochenek	14/05/1987	Poland	110m Hurdles (m)	0
Lauren	Boden	03/08/1988	Australia	400m Hurdles (w), 4x400m (w)	0
Anna	Bogdanova	21/10/1984	Russia	Heptathlon	07
Usain	Bolt	21/08/1986	Jamaica	100m (m) 200m (m), 4x100m (m)	03 05 07 09
Bohdan	Bondarenko	30/08/1989	Ukraine	High Jump (m)	0
Caio	Bonfim	19/03/1991	Brazil	20km Walk (m)	0
Daisurami	Bonne	09/03/1988	Cuba	400m (w), 4x400m (w)	09
Wanida	Boonwan	30/08/1986	Thailand	High Jump (w)	0
Valeriy	Borchin	11/09/1986	Russia	20km Walk (m)	07 09
Cleopatra	Borel-Brown	03/10/1979	Trinidad & Tobago	Shot Put (w)	05 07 09
Diane	Borg	12/09/1990	Malta	100m (w)	05
Lázaro	Borges	19/06/1986	Cuba	Pole Vault (m)	0
Jonathan	Borlée	22/02/1988	Belgium	400m (m), 4x400m (w)	0
Kévin	Borlée	22/02/1988	Belgium	400m (m), 4x400m (m)	09
Nadiia	Borovska-Prokopuk	25/02/1981	Ukraine	20km Walk (w)	0
Yuriy	Borzakovskiy	12/04/1981	Russia	800m (m)	03 05 07 09
Tarek	Boukensa	19/11/1981	Algeria	1500m (m)	03 05 07 09
Larbi	Bouraada	10/05/1988	Algeria	Decathlon	09
Abderrahime	Bouramdane	01/01/1978	Morocco	Marathon (m)	05 07
Zahra	Bouras	13/01/1987	Algeria	800m (w)	0
Ingvill Måkestad	Bovim	07/08/1981	Norway	1500m (w)	0
Alana	Boyd	10/05/1984	Australia	Pole Vault (w)	07
Mahfoud	Brahimi	24/02/1985	Algeria	800m (m)	0
Ryan	Brathwaite	06/06/1988	Barbados	110m Hurdles (m)	07 09
Melissa	Breen	17/09/1990	Australia	4x100m (w)	0
Nery	Brenes	25/09/1985	Costa Rica	400m (m)	05 07 09
Fionnuala	Britton	24/09/1984	Ireland	3000m SC (w)	07
Marius	Broening	24/10/1983	Germany	4x100m (m)	09
Lance	Brooks	01/01/1984	United States	Discus (m)	0
Chris	Brown	15/10/1978	Bahamas	400m (m)	01 03 05 07 09

Forenames	Surname	Born	Country	Events	Prev Apps
Ben	Bruce	10/09/1982	United States	3000m SC (m)	0
Anna Giordano	Bruno	13/12/1980	Italy	Pole Vault (w)	09
Elyzaveta	Bryzgina	28/11/1989	Ukraine	200m (w)	09
Andreas	Bube	13/07/1987	Denmark	800m (m)	0
Nicole	Büchler	17/12/1983	Switzerland	Pole Vault (w)	07 09
Abdul	Buhari	26/06/1982	Great Britain	Discus (m)	0
Andrew	Bumbalough	14/03/1987	United States	5000m (m)	0
Gelete	Burka	23/01/1986	Ethiopia	1500m (w)	05 07 09
Olena	Burkovska	09/08/1981	Ukraine	Marathon (w)	0
Marc	Burns	07/01/1983	Trinidad & Tobago	4x100m (m)	03 05 07 09
Betty	Burua	24/11/1986	Papua New Guinea	400m (w)	0
Janeth Jepkosgei	Busienei	13/12/1983	Kenya	800m (w)	07 09
Urige	Buta	28/11/1982	Norway	Marathon (m)	0
Hayley	Butler	21/04/1984	Australia	4x100m (w)	0
Igor	Bychkov	07/03/1987	Spain	Pole Vault (m)	0
Youngjun	Byun	20/03/1984	South Korea	20km Walk (m)	09
Dailis	Caballero	06/03/1988	Cuba	Pole Vault (w)	0
Denia	Caballero	13/01/1990	Cuba	Discus (w)	0
Ana	Cabecinha	29/04/1984	Portugal	20km Walk (w)	0
Eusebio	Cáceres	10/09/1991	Spain	Long Jump (m)	0
Katerina	Cachová	26/02/1990	Czech Republic	Heptathlon	0
Erik	Cadee	15/02/1984	Netherlands	Discus (m)	07 09
Asli	Cakir	20/08/1985	Turkey	1500m (w)	09
Emmanuel	Callender	10/05/1984	Trinidad & Tobago	200m (w)	09
Bonko	Camara	06/02/1988	Mauritania	100m (w)	07
Kerfalla	Camara	07/05/1988	Guinea	400m (m)	0
Moussa	Camara	12/02/1988	Mali	800m (m)	0
Youlia	Camara	27/12/1991	Guinea	100m (w)	0
Jillian	Camarena-Williams	02/08/1982	United States	Shot Put (w)	07 09
Amber	Campbell	05/06/1981	United States	Hammer (w)	05 09
Veronica	Campbell-Brown	15/05/1982	Jamaica	200m (w), 4x100m (w)	05 07 09
Juan Manuel	Cano	12/12/1987	Argentina	20km Walk (m)	09
Christian	Cantwell	30/09/1980	United States	Shot Put (m)	03 05 07 09
Marzia	Caravelli	23/10/1981	Italy	100m Hurdles (w)	0
Michelle	Carey	20/03/1981	Ireland	4x400m (w)	07 09
Javier	Carriqueo	29/05/1979	Argentina	5000m (m)	07
Danielle	Carruthers	22/12/1979	United States	100m Hurdles (w)	0
Michelle	Carter	12/10/1985	United States	Shot Put (w)	09
Nesta	Carter	10/11/1985	Jamaica	100m (m)	07
Nesta	Carter	10/11/1985	Jamaica	4x100m (m)	07
Florian	Carvalho	09/03/1989	France	1500m (m)	0
Nelkis	Casabona	12/05/1984	Cuba	100m (w), 200m (w)	0
Jhon Lennon	Casallo	17/05/1984	Peru	Marathon (m)	0
Yennifer Frank	Casañas	18/10/1978	Spain	Discus (m)	03 05 09
Cristina	Casandra	01/02/1977	Romania	3000m SC (w)	05 07 09
Berta	Castells	24/01/1984	Spain	Hammer (w)	03 05 07 09
Diego	Cavalcanti	18/03/1991	Brazil	4x100m (m)	0
Recep	Çelik	10/06/1983	Turkey	20km Walk (m)	0
Matthew	Centrowitz	18/10/1989	United States	1500m (m)	0
Juan Ignacio	Cerra	16/10/1976	Argentina	Hammer (m)	99 01 03 05 09
Fabio	Cerutti	26/09/1985	Italy	4x100m (m)	09
Dwain	Chambers	05/04/1978	Great Britain	100m (m)	99 01 03 09
Seyha	Chan	09/08/1994	Cambodia	200m (w)	0
Jasmine	Chaney	25/08/1988	United States	400m Hurdles (w)	0
Ming-Huang	Chang	22/04/1983	Chinese Taipei	Shot Put (m)	07 09
Libor	Charfreitag	11/09/1977	Slovakia	Hammer (m)	99 01 03 05 07 09
Jingwen	Chen	08/02/1990	China	4x400m (w)	0
Qi	Chen	10/03/1982	China	Javelin (m)	0
Qiang	Chen	12/06/1990	China	4x100m (m)	0
Rong	Chen	18/05/1988	China	Marathon (w)	09
Yanmei	Chen	01/01/1987	China	4x400m (w)	0
Wen	Cheng	18/03/1992	China	400m Hurdles (m)	0
Daniel Kipkorir	Chepyegon	01/06/1986	Uganda	Marathon (m)	09
Tatyana	Chernova	29/01/1988	Russia	Heptathlon	07 09
Mercy	Cherono	07/05/1991	Kenya	5000m (w)	0
Priscah Jepleting	Cherono	27/06/1980	Kenya	10000m (w)	05 07

Forenames	Surname	Born	Country	Events	Prev Apps
Sharon Jemutai	Cherop	16/03/1984	Kenya	Marathon (w)	0
Vivian Jepkemoi	Cheruiyot	11/09/1983	Kenya	5000m (w), 10000m (w)	07 09
Silvano	Chesani	17/07/1988	Italy	High Jump (m)	0
Milcah Chemos	Cheywa	24/02/1986	Kenya	3000m SC (w)	09
Anna	Chicherova	22/07/1982	Russia	High Jump (w)	03 05 07 09
Eilidh	Child	20/02/1987	Great Britain	400m Hurdles (w)	09
Mercedes	Chilla	19/01/1980	Spain	Javelin (w)	05 07 09
Suppachai	Chimdee	05/01/1991	Thailand	4x100m (m)	09
Abraham Kipkirong	Chirchir	01/08/1980	Kenya	3000m SC (m)	0
Kyu-won	Cho	01/09/1991	South Korea	4x100m (m)	0
Andrés	Chocho	04/11/1983	Ecuador	50km Walk (m)	07 09
Bo-ra	Choi	15/07/1991	South Korea	Marathon (w)	0
Yun-hee	Choi	28/05/1986	South Korea	Pole Vault (w)	0
Dimítrios	Chondrokoúkis	26/01/1988	Greece	High Jump (m)	0
Ah Chong Sam	Chong	06/07/1978	Samoa	100m (m)	0
Kim	Christensen	04/01/1984	Denmark	Shot Put (m)	0
Brendan	Christian	11/12/1983	Antigua & Barbuda	200m (m)	07 09
Yafei	Chu	05/09/1988	China	20km Walk (w)	09
Yun-hee	Chung	03/01/1983	South Korea	Marathon (w)	0
Elena	Churakova	16/12/1986	Russia	400m Hurdles (w)	09
Marcos	Chuva	08/08/1989	Portugal	Long Jump (m)	0
Javier	Cienfuegos	15/07/1990	Spain	Hammer (m)	09
Omar	Cisneros	19/11/1989	Cuba	400m Hurdles (m)	09
Christopher	Clarke	25/01/1990	Great Britain	4x400m (m)	0
Lawrence	Clarke	12/03/1990	Great Britain	110m Hurdles (m)	0
Jérôme	Clavier	03/05/1983	France	Pole Vault (m)	07 09
Will	Claye	13/06/1991	United States	Long Jump (m), Triple Jump (m)	0
Kerron	Clement	31/10/1985	United States	400m Hurdles (m)	05 07 09
Susana	Clement	18/08/1989	Cuba	4x400m (w)	0
Helen	Clitheroe	02/01/1974	Great Britain	5000m (w)	99 01 05 07 09
Pollara	Cobb	29/01/1992	Guam	100m (w)	0
Emma	Coburn	19/10/1990	United States	3000m SC (w)	0
Giovanni	Codrington	17/07/1988	Netherlands	4x100m (m)	0
Willem	Coertzen	30/12/1982	South Africa	Decathlon	09
William	Collazo	31/08/1986	Cuba	400m (m)	07 09
Kim	Collins	05/04/1976	St Kitts & Nevis	100m (m), 200m (m), 4x100m (m)	99 01 03 05 07 09
Simone	Collio	27/12/1979	Italy	4x100m (m)	05 07 09
Benjamin	Compaoré	05/08/1987	France	Triple Jump (m)	0
Jared	Connaughton	20/07/1985	Canada	200m (m), 4x100m (m)	09
Leslie	Copeland	23/04/1988	Fiji	Javelin (m)	0
Alexis	Copello	12/08/1985	Cuba	Triple Jump (m)	09
Edgar	Cortez	08/10/1989	Nicaragua	800m (m)	0
Jessica	Cosby	31/05/1982	United States	Hammer (w)	07 09
Keila	Costa	06/02/1983	Brazil	Long Jump (w), Triple Jump (w)	07 09
Amparo	Cotán	13/05/1988	Spain	4x100m (w)	0
Héctor	Cotto	08/08/1984	Puerto Rico	110m Hurdles (m)	09
Geisa Aparecida	Coutinho	01/06/1980	Brazil	400m (w), 4x400m (w)	03 09
Kurt	Couto	14/05/1985	Mozambique	400m Hurdles (m)	05 07 09
Alistair Ian	Cragg	13/06/1980	Ireland	5000m (m)	07 09
Esther	Cremer	29/03/1988	Germany	4x400m (w)	09
Robert	Crowther	02/08/1987	Australia	Long Jump (m)	0
Yanet	Cruz	08/02/1988	Cuba	Javelin (w)	09
Joanne	Cuddihy	11/05/1984	Ireland	400m (w), 4x400m (w)	07
Javier	Culson	25/07/1984	Puerto Rico	400m Hurdles (m)	07 09
Maria	Czaková	02/10/1988	Slovakia	20km Walk (w)	0
Christopher Lima	da Costa	19/01/1988	São Tomé and Príncipe	100m (m)	0
Fábio Gomes	da Silva	04/08/1983	Brazil	Pole Vault (m)	07 09
Fernando	da Silva	10/10/1986	Brazil	800m (m)	0
Holder	da Silva	22/01/1988	Guinea-Bissau	200m (m)	07
Tejitu	Daba	29/07/1988	Brunei	5000m (w)	07 09
Henry	Dagmil	07/12/1981	Philippines	Long Jump (m)	09
Jennifer	Dahlgren	21/04/1984	Argentina	Hammer (w)	05 07 09
Malin	Dahlström	26/08/1989	Sweden	Pole Vault (w)	0
Fatima Sulaiman	Dahman	10/11/1991	Yemen	400m Hurdles (w)	0
Djénébou	Danté	07/08/1989	Mali	100m (w)	0
Calvin	Dascent	05/04/1989	US Virgin Islands	200m (m)	0

Forenames	Surname	Born	Country	Events	Prev Apps
Christelle	Daunay	05/12/1974	France	10000m (w)	0
Kleberson	Davide	20/07/1985	Brazil	800m (m)	07 09
Matt	Davies	18/04/1985	Australia	4x100m (m)	09
Walter	Davis	23/05/1976	United States	Triple Jump (m)	09
Sharon	Day	23/08/1986	United States	Heptathlon	09
Luiz Alberto	de Araújo	27/06/1987	Brazil	Decathlon	0
Bruno	de Barros	07/01/1987	Brazil	200m (m), 4x100m (m)	0
Willem	de Beer	14/03/1988	South Africa	4x400m (m)	0
Ribeiro Pinto	de Carvalho	02/02/1993	East Timor	1500m (m)	0
Jailma	de Lima	04/06/1977	Brazil	400m Hurdles (w), 4x400m (w)	99 07 09
Marco	De Luca	12/05/1981	Italy	50km Walk (m)	05 07 09
Andressa	de Morais	21/12/1990	Brazil	Discus (w)	0
Bárbara	de Oliveira	04/02/1986	Brazil	4x400m (w)	09
Colleen	De Reuck	13/04/1964	United States	Marathon (w)	0
Matthias	de Zordo	21/02/1988	Germany	Javelin (m)	0
Nathan	Deakes	17/08/1977	Australia	50km Walk (m)	01 05 07
Chala	Dechase	13/06/1984	Ethiopia	Marathon (m)	0
Yoann	Décimus	30/11/1987	France	4x400m (m)	09
Meseret	Defar	19/11/1983	Ethiopia	5000m (w), 10000m (w)	03 05 07 09
Tatyana	Dektyareva	08/05/1981	Russia	100m Hurdles (w)	09
Janay	DeLoach	12/10/1985	United States	Long Jump (w)	0
Charles	Delys	09/04/1982	French Polynesia	1500m (m)	0
Lashinda	Demus	10/03/1983	United States	400m Hurdles (w)	05 09
Dmytro	Dem'yanyuk	30/06/1983	Ukraine	High Jump (m)	07
Kate	Dennison	07/05/1984	Great Britain	Pole Vault (w)	07 09
Aleksandr	Derevyagin	24/03/1979	Russia	400m Hurdles (m)	07 09
Lovelite	Detenamo	22/12/1993	Nauru	100m (w)	0
Marlon	Devonish	01/06/1976	Great Britain	100m (m), 4x100m (m)	99 01 05 07 09
Jeroen	D'Hoedt	10/01/1990	Belgium	1500m (m)	0
Emanuele	Di Gregorio	13/12/1980	Italy	4x100m (m)	09
Antonietta	Di Martino	01/06/1978	Italy	High Jump (w)	01 07 09
José Ignacio	Díaz	22/11/1979	Spain	50km Walk (m)	05 07 09
Maximiliano	Díaz	15/11/1988	Argentina	Triple Jump (m)	0
Genzebe	Dibaba	08/02/1991	Ethiopia	5000m (w)	09
Mateusz	Didenkow	22/04/1987	Poland	Pole Vault (m)	0
Mohamed Fathalla	Difallah	26/08/1987	Egypt	Long Jump (m)	0
Karsten	Dilla	17/07/1989	Germany	Pole Vault (m)	0
Yohan	Diniz	01/01/1978	France	50km Walk (m)	05 07 09
Gloria	Diogo	13/01/1983	São Tomé and Príncipe	100m (w)	05 07 09
Céline	Distel	25/05/1987	France	4x100m (w)	0
Walter	Dix	31/01/1986	United States	100m (m), 200m (m), 4x100m (m)	0
Alyson	Dixon	24/09/1978	Great Britain	Marathon (w)	0
Vonette	Dixon	26/11/1975	Jamaica	100m Hurdles (w)	01 03 05 07
Aleksey	Dmitrik	12/04/1984	Russia	High Jump (m)	0
Ruslan	Dmytrenko	22/03/1986	Ukraine	20km Walk (m)	09
Teresa	Dobija	09/10/1982	Poland	Long Jump (w)	09
Lisa	Dobriskey	23/12/1983	Great Britain	1500m (w)	07 09
Natallia	Dobrynska	29/05/1982	Ukraine	Heptathlon	05 07 09
Jeremy	Dodson	30/08/1987	United States	200m (m)	0
Bahar	Dogan	02/09/1974	Turkey	Marathon (w)	07
Fabrizio	Donato	14/08/1976	Italy	Triple Jump (m)	03 07 09
Guojian	Dong	16/03/1987	China	Marathon (m)	0
Konstadínos	Douvalídis	10/03/1987	Greece	110m Hurdles (m)	07
Francesca	Doveri	21/12/1982	Italy	Heptathlon	0
Darius	Draudvila	29/03/1983	Lithuania	Decathlon	0
Hannes	Dreyer	13/01/1985	South Africa	4x100m (m)	09
Hamza	Driouch	16/11/1994	Qatar	1500m (m)	0
Aleksey	Drozdov	03/12/1983	Russia	Decathlon	05 07
Simoné	du Toit	27/09/1988	South Africa	Shot Put (w)	0
Natalia	Ducó	31/01/1989	Chile	Shot Put (w)	09
Mihail	Dudaš	01/11/1989	Serbia	Decathlon	0
Nils	Duerinck	20/03/1984	Belgium	4x400m (m)	09
Lishan	Dula	17/02/1987	Brunei	Marathon (w)	0
Maksim	Dyldin	19/05/1987	Russia	4x400m (m)	09
Ashton	Eaton	21/01/1988	United States	Decathlon	09
Elisabeth	Eberl	25/03/1988	Austria	Javelin (w)	0

Forenames	Surname	Born	Country	Events	Prev Apps
Yuki	Ebihara	28/10/1985	Japan	Javelin (w)	09
Alonso	Edward	08/12/1989	Panama	200m (m)	09
Darvin	Edwards	07/05/1981	St Lucia	High Jump (m)	09
Sam	Effah	29/12/1988	Canada	4x100m (m)	09
Jeff	Eggleston	01/10/1984	United States	Marathon (m)	0
Ogho-Oghene	Egwero	26/11/1988	Nigeria	100m (m)	09
Sentayehu	Ejigu	28/06/1985	Ethiopia	5000m (w)	03 05 09
Yevgeniy	Ektov	01/09/1986	Kazakhstan	Triple Jump (m)	09
Irina Litvinenko	Ektova	08/01/1987	Kazakhstan	Triple Jump (w)	09
Mouhcine	El Amine	08/01/1982	Morocco	800m (m)	0
Ihab Abdelrahman	El Sayed	01/05/1989	Egypt	Javelin (m)	0
Ali Mabrouk	El Zaidi	13/01/1978	Lebanon	Marathon (m)	99 01 07 09
Andrew	Ellerton	18/11/1983	Canada	800m (m)	0
James	Ellington	06/09/1985	Great Britain	200m (m)	0
Sheryf	El-Sheryf	02/01/1989	Ukraine	Triple Jump (m)	0
Peter	Emelieze	19/04/1988	Nigeria	100m (m)	09
Stanislav	Emelyanov	23/10/1990	Russia	20km Walk (m)	0
Roscoe	Engel	06/03/1989	South Africa	4x100m (m)	0
Birsen	Engin	18/10/1980	Turkey	400m Hurdles (w), 4x400m (w)	0
Hannah	England	06/03/1987	Great Britain	1500m (w)	09
Adil	Ennani	30/06/1980	Morocco	Marathon (m)	09
Jessica	Ennis	28/01/1986	Great Britain	Heptathlon	07 09
Dedeh	Erawati	25/05/1980	Indonesia	100m Hurdles (w)	0
Masashi	Eriguchi	17/12/1988	Japan	4x100m (m)	09
Sandra	Eriksson	04/06/1989	Finland	3000m SC (w)	09
Sebastian	Ernst	11/10/1984	Germany	200m (m), 4x100m (m)	05
Igor	Erokhin	04/09/1986	Russia	50km Walk (m)	07
Fatih	Eryildirim	01/03/1979	Turkey	Hammer (m)	07
Shitaye	Eshete	21/05/1990	Brunei	10000m (w)	0
Jesús	España	21/08/1978	Spain	5000m (m)	05 07 09
Markus	Esser	03/02/1980	Germany	Hammer (m)	05 07 09
Brice	Etes	11/04/1984	Monaco	800m (m)	0
Margaret	Etim	28/11/1992	Nigeria	4x400m (w)	0
Jeesu	Eum	13/05/1989	South Korea	4x100m (w)	0
Natalya	Evdokimova	17/03/1978	Russia	1500m (w)	03 09
Nelson	Évora	20/04/1984	Portugal	Triple Jump (m)	05 07 09
Hamid	Ezzine	05/10/1983	Morocco	3000m SC (m)	05 07
Fadlin	Fadlin	28/10/1989	Indonesia	100m (m)	0
Pawel	Fajdek	04/06/1989	Poland	Hammer (m)	0
Stéphanie	Falzon	07/01/1983	France	Hammer (w)	07 09
Mohamed	Farah	23/03/1983	Great Britain	5000m (m), 10000m (m)	07 09
Györgyi	Farkas	13/02/1985	Hungary	Heptathlon	0
Andrey	Farnosov	09/07/1980	Russia	3000m SC (m)	0
Stuart	Farquhar	15/03/1982	New Zealand	Javelin (m)	07 09
Karl	Farrugia	11/01/1981	Malta	100m (m)	0
Jesper	Faurschou	01/07/1983	Denmark	Marathon (m)	0
Róbert	Fazekas	18/08/1975	Hungary	Discus (m)	01 03
Rafal	Fedaczynski	03/12/1980	Poland	50km Walk (m)	05 07 09
Aleksandra	Fedoriva	13/09/1988	Russia	4x100m (w)	09
Aleksey	Fedorov	25/05/1991	Russia	Triple Jump (m)	0
Susana	Feitor	28/01/1975	Portugal	20km Walk (w)	99 01 03 05 07 09
Perdita	Felicien	29/08/1980	Canada	100m Hurdles (w)	01 03 05 09
Allyson	Felix	18/11/1985	United States	200m (w), 400m (w), 4x100m (w), 4x	03 05 07 09
Ana Dulce	Félix	23/10/1982	Portugal	10000m (w)	09
Jerrel	Feller	09/06/1987	Netherlands	4x100m (m)	0
Birtukan	Fente	18/06/1989	Ethiopia	3000m SC (w)	0
Svetlana	Feofanova	16/07/1980	Russia	Pole Vault (w)	01 03 07
Sheniqua	Ferguson	24/11/1989	Bahamas	100m (w), 4x100m (w)	09
Debbie	Ferguson-McKenzie	16/01/1976	Bahamas	200m (w), 4x100m (w)	03 05 07 09
Francisco Javier	Fernández	06/03/1977	Spain	20km Walk (m)	01 03 05 07 09
Jorge Y	Fernández	02/10/1987	Cuba	Discus (m)	0
Nuria	Fernández	16/08/1976	Spain	1500m (w)	01 03 05 09
João	Ferreira	11/12/1980	Portugal	4x100m (m)	09
Diego	Ferrín	21/03/1988	Ecuador	High Jump (m)	0
Ángela	Figueroa	28/06/1984	Colombia	3000m SC (w)	0
Nenad	Filipovic	05/10/1978	Serbia	50km Walk (m)	03 07 09

Forenames	Surname	Born	Country	Events	Prev Apps
Konstadínos	Filippídis	26/11/1986	Greece	Pole Vault (m)	05 09
Yervásios	Filippídis	24/07/1987	Greece	Javelin (m)	0
Nicolas	Fillon	14/01/1986	France	4x400m (m)	0
Joanna	Fiodorow	04/03/1989	Poland	Hammer (w)	0
Sabina	Fischer	29/06/1973	Switzerland	5000m (w)	01
Shalane	Flanagan	08/07/1981	United States	10000m (w)	05 07 09
Georg	Fleischhauer	21/10/1988	Germany	400m Hurdles (m)	0
Lauren	Fleshman	26/09/1981	United States	5000m (w)	03 05
Diego	Flores	23/03/1987	Mexico	20km Walk (m)	0
Lina	Flórez	02/10/1984	Colombia	100m Hurdles (w)	0
Natalya	Fokina-Semenova	07/07/1982	Ukraine	Discus (w)	05 07 09
Damar	Forbes	11/09/1990	Jamaica	Long Jump (m)	0
Ronald	Forbes	05/04/1985	Cayman Islands	110m Hurdles (m)	0
Mario	Forsythe	30/10/1985	Jamaica	200m (m)	0
Marco	Fortes	26/09/1982	Portugal	Shot Put (m)	09
Brigitte	Foster-Hylton	07/11/1974	Jamaica	100m Hurdles (w)	01 03 05 09
Allodin	Fothergill	07/02/1987	Jamaica	4x400m (m)	0
Hyleas	Fountain	14/01/1981	United States	Heptathlon	05 07
Lehann	Fourie	16/02/1987	South Africa	110m Hurdles (m)	09
Jamy	Franco	01/07/1991	Guam	20km Walk (w)	0
Bridget	Franek	08/11/1987	United States	3000m SC (w)	09
Mark	Frank	21/06/1977	Germany	Javelin (m)	05 09
Remona	Fransen	25/11/1985	Netherlands	Heptathlon	0
Shelly-Ann	Fraser-Pryce	27/12/1986	Jamaica	4x100m (w)	09
Michael	Frater	06/10/1982	Jamaica	100m (m), 4x100m (m)	03 05 09
Henry	Frayne	14/04/1990	Australia	Triple Jump (m)	0
Cornel	Fredericks	03/03/1990	South Africa	400m Hurdles (m)	0
Rico	Freimuth	14/03/1988	Germany	Decathlon	0
Danielle	Frenkel	08/09/1987	Israel	High Jump (w)	0
Petr	Frydrych	13/01/1988	Czech Republic	Javelin (m)	09
Masumi	Fuchise	02/09/1986	Japan	20km Walk (w)	07 09
Chisato	Fukushima	27/06/1988	Japan	200m (w), 4x100m (w)	09
Alina	Fyodorova	31/07/1989	Ukraine	Heptathlon	0
Kamghe	Gaba	13/01/1984	Germany	4x400m (m)	09
Rubie Joy	Gabriel	22/11/1994	Palau	100m (w)	0
Kristina	Gadschiew	03/07/1984	Germany	Pole Vault (w)	09
Gérard	Gahungu	05/05/1989	Burundi	5000m (m)	0
Ignisious	Gaisah	20/07/1983	Ghana	Long Jump (m)	03 05
Mumin	Gala	06/09/1986	Djibouti	5000m (m)	0
Karen	Gallardo	06/03/1984	Chile	Discus (w)	0
Tetyana	Gamera-Shmyrko	01/06/1983	Ukraine	Marathon (w)	0
Ni	Gao	28/10/1979	China	20km Walk (w)	01 03 05 07 09
Stephanie	Garcia	03/05/1988	United States	3000m SC (w)	0
Jesús Angel	García	17/10/1969	Spain	50km Walk (m)	01 03 05 07 09
Rosibel	García	13/02/1981	Colombia	800m (w)	07 09
Víctor	García	13/03/1985	Spain	3000m SC (m)	0
Yordani	García	21/11/1988	Cuba	Decathlon	07 09
Roba	Gari	12/04/1982	Ethiopia	3000m SC (m)	07 09
Jacqueline	Gasser	23/02/1990	Switzerland	4x100m (w)	0
Justin	Gatlin	10/02/1982	United States	100m (m), 4x100m (m)	05
Mabel	Gay	09/08/1982	Cuba	Triple Jump (w)	05 07 09
Marie	Gayot	18/12/1989	France	4x400m (w)	0
Stanley	Gbagbeke	24/07/1989	Nigeria	Long Jump (m)	09
Gebregziabher	Gebremariam	10/09/1984	Ethiopia	Marathon (m)	03 05 07 09
Mekonnen	Gebremedhin	11/10/1988	Ethiopia	1500m (m)	07 09
Dejen	Gebremeskel	24/11/1989	Ethiopia	5000m (m)	0
Luiza	Gega	05/11/1988	Albania	800m (w)	0
Elroy	Gelant	25/08/1986	South Africa	5000m (m)	0
Alex	Genest	30/06/1986	Canada	3000m SC (m)	0
Manuela	Gentili	07/02/1978	Italy	400m Hurdles (w)	0
Phylicia	George	16/11/1987	Canada	100m Hurdles (w)	0
Kalkidan	Gezahegne	08/05/1991	Ethiopia	1500m (w)	09
Enas	Gharib	22/05/1972	Egypt	Long Jump (w)	01 03 05 07 09
Majed Aldim	Ghazal	21/04/1987	Syria	High Jump (m)	09
Habiba	Ghribi	09/04/1984	Tunisia	3000m SC (w)	05 09
Antoine	Gillet	22/03/1988	Belgium	4x400m (m)	09

Forenames	Surname	Born	Country	Events	Prev Apps
Arnie David	Girat	26/08/1984	Cuba	Triple Jump (m)	03 05 07 09
Ramon	Gittens	20/07/1987	Barbados	100m (m)	09
Zaneta	Glanc	11/03/1983	Poland	Discus (w)	09
Mathieu	Gnanligo	13/12/1986	Benin	400m (m)	07 09
Geronimo	Goeloe	18/11/1981	Aruba	100m (m)	0
Samuel	Goitom	01/01/1983	Eritrea	Marathon (m)	0
Naide	Gomes	20/11/1979	Portugal	Long Jump (w)	05 07 09
Vanda	Gomes	07/11/1988	Brazil	200m (w), 4x100m (w)	0
Álvaro	Gómez	31/12/1990	Colombia	100m (m)	09
Zoila	Gómez	31/12/1990	United States	Marathon (w)	09
Sandra	Gomis	21/11/1983	France	100m Hurdles (w)	09
Lijiao	Gong	24/01/1989	China	Shot Put (w)	07 09
Jermaine	Gonzales	26/11/1984	Jamaica	400m (m), 4x400m (m)	09
Misleydis	González	19/06/1978	Cuba	Shot Put (w)	05 07 09
Norma	González	11/08/1982	Colombia	400m (w), 4x100m (w)	09
Marquise	Goodwin	19/11/1990	United States	Long Jump (m)	0
Jehue	Gordon	17/09/1988	Trinidad & Tobago	400m Hurdles (m)	09
Federico	Gorrieri	04/10/1985	San Marino	100m (m)	0
Kara	Goucher	09/07/1978	United States	10000m (w)	07 09
Abderrahim	Goumri	21/05/1976	Morocco	Marathon (m)	01 03 05 07 09
Vikas	Gowda	05/07/1983	India	Discus (m)	05 07
Aiga	Grabuste	24/03/1988	Latvia	Heptathlon	07 09
Nicoleta	Grasu	11/09/1971	Romania	Discus (w)	99 01 05 07 09
Elizaveta	Grechishnikova	12/12/1983	Russia	5000m (w)	09
Jack	Green	06/10/1991	Great Britain	400m Hurdles (m)	0
Leford	Green	14/11/1986	Jamaica	400m Hurdles (m), 4x400m (m)	07 09
David	Greene	11/04/1986	Great Britain	400m Hurdles (m)	07 09
Ryan	Gregson	26/04/1990	Australia	1500m (m)	09
Libania	Grenot	12/07/1983	Italy	4x400m (w)	05 09
Colin	Griffin	03/08/1982	Ireland	50km Walk (m)	07 09
Adrian	Griffith	11/11/1984	Bahamas	100m (m)	09
Lauma	Griva	27/10/1984	Latvia	Long Jump (w)	0
Daniel	Grueso	30/07/1985	Colombia	200m (m)	07 09
Yadira	Guamán	08/06/1986	Ecuador	20km Walk (w)	07
Floria	Guei	02/05/1990	France	4x400m (w)	0
Yulia	Gushchina	04/03/1983	Russia	200m (w), 4x100m (w)	05 07 09
Andreas	Gustafsson	10/08/1981	Sweden	50km Walk (m)	07 09
Abdelkader	Hachlaf	03/08/1978	Morocco	3000m SC (m)	01 03 07
Halima	Hachlaf	06/09/1988	Morocco	800m (w)	09
Semoy	Hackett	27/11/1988	Trinidad & Tobago	4x100m (w)	09
Ehsan	Hadadi	20/01/1985	Iran	Discus (m)	07 09
Mohammad Noor	Hadi	31/05/1985	Malaysia	100m (m)	0
Anouk	Hagen	30/04/1990	Netherlands	4x100m (w)	0
Yvonne	Hak	30/06/1986	Netherlands	800m (w)	0
András	Haklits	23/09/1977	Croatia	Hammer (m)	99 05 07 09
Patricia	Hall	16/10/1982	Jamaica	4x400m (w)	0
Nikki	Hamblin	20/05/1988	New Zealand	800m (w), 1500m (w)	09
Da-Rye	Han	20/11/1988	South Korea	High Jump (w)	0
Truong Thanh	Hang	01/05/1986	Vietnam	800m (w)	0
Mamoudou	Hanne	06/03/1988	France	4x400m (m)	0
Trey	Hardee	07/12/1984	United States	Decathlon	09
Ryan	Harlan	25/04/1981	United States	Decathlon	05
Abdouraim	Haroun	12/04/1992	Chad	100m (m)	0
Dawn	Harper	13/05/1984	United States	100m Hurdles (w)	09
Benn	Harradine	14/10/1982	Australia	Discus (m)	09
Queen	Harrison	20/01/1974	United States	400m Hurdles (w)	09
Robert	Harting	18/10/1984	Germany	Discus (m)	05 07 09
Amy	Hastings	21/01/1984	United States	5000m (w)	0
Natasha	Hastings	23/07/1986	United States	4x400m (w)	07
Minori	Hayakari	29/11/1972	Japan	3000m SC (w)	05 07 09
Ashot	Hayrapetyan	14/09/1988	Armenia	800m (m)	0
Louise	Hazel	06/10/1985	Great Britain	Heptathlon	09
Ahmad	Hazer	04/09/1989	Lebanon	110m Hurdles (m)	09
Mike	Hazle	22/03/1979	United States	Javelin (m)	09
Robert	Heffernan	28/02/1978	Ireland	50km Walk (m)	01 05 07 09
Betty	Heidler	14/10/1983	Germany	Hammer (w)	03 05 07 09

Forenames	Surname	Born	Country	Events	Prev Apps
Zuzana	Hejnová	19/12/1986	Czech Republic	400m Hurdles (w), 4x400m (w)	05 07 09
Kelsie	Hendry	29/06/1982	Canada	Pole Vault (w)	05 09
Leeroy	Henriette	07/01/1991	Seychelles	200m (m)	0
Eivind	Henriksen	14/09/1990	Norway	Hammer (m)	0
Inês	Henriques	01/05/1980	Portugal	20km Walk (w)	01 05 07 09
Tabarie	Henry	01/12/1987	US Virgin Islands	400m (m)	09
Emerson	Hernandez	20/01/1989	El Salvador	20km Walk (m)	0
Edgar	Hernández	08/06/1977	Mexico	50km Walk (m)	01
Ingrid	Hernández	29/11/1988	Colombia	20km Walk (w)	0
Michael	Herrera	05/06/1985	Cuba	200m (m)	0
Tjipekapora	Herunga	01/01/1988	Namibia	400m (w)	0
Paul	Hession	27/01/1983	Ireland	200m (m)	05 07 09
Zwede	Hewitt	18/06/1989	Trinidad & Tobago	4x400m (m)	0
Raymond	Higgs	24/01/1991	Bahamas	Long Jump (m)	0
Juan Carlos	Higuero	03/08/1978	Spain	1500m (m)	01 03 05 07 09
Siham	Hilali	02/05/1986	Morocco	1500m (w)	07 09
Andrew	Hinds	25/04/1984	Barbados	100m (m)	09
Korene	Hinds	18/01/1976	Jamaica	3000m SC (w)	05 07
Yomara	Hinestroza	20/05/1988	Colombia	4x100m (w)	09
Hideyuki	Hirose	20/07/1989	Japan	4x400m (m)	09
Sophie	Hitchon	11/07/1991	Great Britain	Hammer (w)	0
Ásdís	Hjálmsdóttir	28/10/1985	Iceland	Javelin (w)	09
Moa	Hjelmer	19/06/1990	Sweden	200m (w), 400m (w)	0
Reese	Hoffa	08/10/1977	United States	Shot Put (m)	03 07 09
Claudia	Hoffmann	10/12/1982	Germany	4x400m (w)	09
Nikkita	Holder	07/05/1987	Canada	100m Hurdles (w)	0
Mark	Hollis	01/12/1984	United States	Pole Vault (m)	09
Caroline Bonde	Holm	19/07/1990	Denmark	Pole Vault (w)	0
Mona Christine	Holm	05/08/1983	Norway	Hammer (w)	07
Tetyana	Holovchenko	13/02/1980	Ukraine	Marathon (w)	07
Marquis	Holston	10/07/1989	Puerto Rico	4x100m (m)	0
Raphael	Holzdeppe	28/09/1989	Germany	Pole Vault (m)	0
Amanmurad	Hommadov	28/01/1989	Turkmenistan	Hammer (m)	09
Steven	Hooker	25/09/1984	Australia	Pole Vault (m)	09
Hiroyuki	Horibata	28/10/1986	Japan	Marathon (m)	0
Nikolina	Horvat	18/09/1986	Croatia	400m Hurdles (w)	0
Cedric	Houssaye	13/12/1979	France	50km Walk (m)	09
John	Howard	21/07/1981	Federated States of Micror	100m (m)	01 03 05
Molly	Huddle	31/08/1984	United States	5000m (w)	09
Matthew	Hughes	03/08/1989	Canada	3000m SC (m)	0
Yeon-jung	Huh	09/10/1980	South Korea	800m (w)	0
Daniel	Huling	16/07/1983	United States	3000m SC (m)	09
Jeff	Hunt	24/07/1982	Australia	Marathon (m)	0
Erison	Hurtault	29/12/1984	Dominica	400m (m)	09
Muriel	Hurtis	25/03/1979	France	4x400m (w)	99 03 07
Kylie	Hutson	27/11/1987	United States	Pole Vault (w)	0
In-sung	Hwang	15/08/1984	South Korea	Shot Put (m)	0
Junhyeon	Hwang	25/05/1987	South Korea	Marathon (m)	09
Jun-Suk	Hwang	23/08/1983	South Korea	Marathon (m)	0
Kimberly	Hyacinthe	28/03/1989	Canada	200m (w)	0
Riker	Hylton	13/12/1988	Jamaica	400m (m), 4x400m (m)	0
Mardrea	Hyman	11/10/1989	Jamaica	3000m SC (w)	09
Olga	Iakovenko	01/06/1987	Ukraine	20km Walk (w)	09
Natalia	Iastrebova	12/10/1984	Ukraine	Triple Jump (w)	09
Anatole	Ibañez	14/11/1985	Sweden	20km Walk (m)	0
Arley	Ibargüen	17/10/1982	Colombia	Javelin (m)	09
Caterine	Ibargüen	12/02/1984	Colombia	Triple Jump (w)	05 09
Antoinette Nana Djimou	Ida	02/08/1985	France	Heptathlon	07 09
Lavonne	Idlette	31/10/1985	Dominica	100m Hurdles (w)	0
Phillips	Idowu	30/12/1978	Great Britain	Triple Jump (m)	01 05 07 09
Maria Alejandra	Idrobo	08/04/1988	Colombia	4x100m (w)	0
Rafael	Iglesias	05/07/1979	Spain	Marathon (m)	09
Abdalaati	Iguider	25/03/1987	Morocco	1500m (m)	07 09
Kirill	Ikonnikov	05/03/1984	Russia	Hammer (m)	0
Dmitrii	Ilin	24/05/1989	Kyrgyzstan	100m (m)	0
Anna	Iljuštšenko	12/10/1985	Estonia	High Jump (w)	09

Forenames	Surname	Born	Country	Events	Prev Apps
Saori	Imai	22/08/1990	Japan	4x100m (w)	0
Yuta	Imazeki	06/11/1987	Japan	400m Hurdles (m)	0
Kyriakos	Ioannou	26/07/1984	Cyprus	High Jump (m)	05 07 09
Marius	Ionescu	18/12/1984	Romania	Marathon (m)	0
Kim Fai	Iong	12/01/1989	Macau	110m Hurdles (m)	0
Yusuke	Ishitsuka	19/06/1987	Japan	4x400m (m)	0
Elena	Isinbaeva	03/06/1982	Russia	Pole Vault (w)	03 05 07 09
Afa	Ismail	01/11/1993	Maldives	200m (w)	0
Ismail Ahmed	Ismail	01/11/1984	Sudan	800m (m)	03 05 07 09
Märt	Israel	23/09/1983	Estonia	Discus (m)	07 09
Mai	Ito	23/05/1984	Japan	Marathon (w)	0
Aleksandr	Ivanov	25/05/1982	Russia	Javelin (m)	01 03 05 07 09
Natalya	Ivoninskaya	22/02/1985	Kazakhstan	100m Hurdles (w)	07 09
Bershawn	Jackson	08/05/1983	United States	400m Hurdles (m), 4x400m (m)	03 05 07 09
Emma	Jackson	07/06/1988	Great Britain	800m (w)	0
Johanna	Jackson	17/01/1985	Great Britain	20km Walk (w)	07 09
Lina	Jacques-Sébastien	10/05/1985	France	4x100m (w)	0
Anna	Jagaciak	10/02/1990	Poland	Triple Jump (w)	0
Indré	Jakubaityté	24/01/1976	Lithuania	Javelin (w)	07 09
Maryam Yusuf	Jamal	16/09/1984	Brunei	1500m (w)	05 07 09
Norjannah Hafiszah	Jamaludin	23/05/1986	Malaysia	100m (w)	0
Kirani	James	01/09/1992	Grenada	400m (m)	0
Igor	Janik	18/01/1983	Poland	Javelin (m)	07 09
Monique	Jansen	03/10/1978	Netherlands	Discus (w)	0
Lacy	Janson	20/02/1983	United States	Pole Vault (w)	07
Jovanee	Jarrett	15/01/1983	Jamaica	Long Jump (w)	09
Bledee	Jarry	17/11/1990	Liberia	100m (m)	0
Ibrahim	Jeilan	12/06/1989	Ethiopia	10000m (m)	0
Tatjana	Jelaca	10/08/1990	Serbia	Javelin (w)	0
Alhaji	Jeng	13/12/1981	SWE	Pole Vault (m)	07 09
Yong-eun	Jeon	24/05/1988	South Korea	20km Walk (w)	0
Jin-hyeok	Jeong	01/06/1990	South Korea	Marathon (m)	0
Priscah	Jeptoo	24/06/1984	Kenya	Marathon (w)	0
Joshua	Jeremiah	05/09/1986	Nauru	100m (m)	0
Marta	Jeschke	02/06/1986	Poland	100m (w), 4x100m (w)	09
Carmelita	Jeter	24/11/1979	United States	100m (w), 200m (w), 4x100m (w)	07 09
Chaofeng	Jia	16/11/1988	China	Marathon (w)	0
Fan	Jiang	16/09/1989	China	110m Hurdles (m)	0
Lan	Jiang	27/06/1989	China	4x100m (w)	0
Funmi	Jimoh	29/05/1984	United States	Long Jump (w)	09
Charles	Jock	23/11/1989	United States	800m (m)	0
Alexander	John	03/05/1986	Germany	110m Hurdles (m)	09
Kibwe	Johnson	05/03/1980	United States	Hammer (m)	05 07 09
Mayookha	Johny	09/04/1988	India	Long Jump (w), Triple Jump (w)	0
Dusty	Jonas	19/04/1986	United States	High Jump (m)	0
Mattias	Jons	19/11/1982	Sweden	Hammer (m)	0
Carlos	Jorge	24/09/1986	Dominican Republic	100m (m)	09
Moise	Joseph	12/08/1989	Haiti	800m (m)	09
Milan	Jotanovic	11/01/1984	Serbia	Shot Put (m)	07
Hye-kyung	Jung	13/04/1981	South Korea	Triple Jump (w)	0
Hye-lim	Jung	01/06/1987	South Korea	100m (w), 100m Hurdles (w)	0
Sangjin	Jung	16/04/1984	South Korea	Javelin (m)	09
Soonok	Jung	23/04/1983	South Korea	Long Jump (w)	07 09
Ebba	Jungmark	10/03/1987	Sweden	High Jump (w)	07
Anastasiya	Juravleva	09/10/1981	Uzbekistan	Triple Jump (w)	03 05 07
Dmitrijs	Jurkevics	07/01/1987	Latvia	1500m (m)	09
Abubaker	Kaki	21/06/1989	Sudan	800m (m)	07 09
René	Kalmer	03/11/1980	South Africa	Marathon (w)	01
Abubaker Ali	Kamal	08/11/1983	Qatar	3000m SC (m)	03 07 09
Béatrice	Kamboulé	25/02/1980	Burkina Faso	100m Hurdles (w)	0
Yusuf Saad	Kamel	29/03/1983	Brunei	1500m (m)	05 07 09
Valeriya	Kanatova	29/08/1992	Uzbekistan	Triple Jump (w)	0
Vladimir	Kanaykin	21/03/1985	Russia	20km Walk (m)	05 07
Yuzo	Kanemaru	18/09/1987	Japan	400m (m), 4x400m (m)	07 09
Na-ru	Kang	25/04/1983	South Korea	Hammer (w)	0
Olga	Kaniskina	19/01/1985	Russia	20km Walk (w)	07 09

Forenames	Surname	Born	Country	Events	Prev Apps
Gerd	Kanter	06/05/1979	Estonia	Discus (m)	03 05 07 09
Anastasiya	Kapachinskaya	21/11/1979	Russia	400m (w), 4x400m (w)	01 03 09
Bianca	Kappler	08/08/1977	Germany	Long Jump (w)	03 05 07 09
Nagihan	Karadere	01/01/1984	Turkey	400m Hurdles (w), 4x400m (w)	0
Tugba	Karakaya	16/02/1991	Turkey	1500m (w)	0
Kseniya	Karandyuk	21/06/1986	Ukraine	400m (w)	0
Bekir	Karayel	10/05/1982	Turkey	Marathon (m)	0
Natallia	Kareiva	14/11/1985	Belarus	1500m (w)	0
Olli-Pekka	Karjalainen	07/03/1980	Finland	Hammer (m)	99 01 03 05 07 09
Dmitriy	Karpov	23/07/1981	Kazakhstan	Decathlon	03 05 07 09
Kateryna	Karsak	26/12/1985	Ukraine	Discus (w)	07 09
Oleksiy	Kasyanov	26/08/1985	Ukraine	Decathlon	09
Harwant	Kaur	05/07/1980	India	Discus (w)	0
Mayumi	Kawasaki	10/05/1980	Japan	20km Walk (w)	05 07 09
Yuki	Kawauchi	05/03/1987	Japan	Marathon (m)	0
Igors	Kazakevics	17/04/1980	Latvia	50km Walk (m)	0
Oleksiy	Kazanin	22/05/1982	Ukraine	50km Walk (m)	05
Tamás	Kazi	16/05/1985	Hungary	800m (m)	09
Aberu	Kebede	15/01/1987	Ethiopia	Marathon (w)	09
Ezekiel	Kemboi	25/11/1983	Kenya	3000m SC (m)	05 09
Antti	Kempas	03/10/1980	Finland	50km Walk (m)	05 07
Jukka	Keskisalo	27/03/1981	Finland	3000m SC (m)	03 05 09
Kabelo	Kgosiemang	07/01/1986	Botswana	High Jump (m)	07 09
Tatyana	Khadjimuradova	28/09/1980	Kazakhstan	4x400m (w)	0
Lyubov	Kharlamova	02/03/1981	Russia	3000m SC (w)	0
Moses	Kibet	23/03/1991	Uganda	5000m (m)	09
Sylvia Jebiwott	Kibet	28/03/1984	Kenya	5000m (w)	07 09
Viola Jelagat	Kibiwot	22/12/1983	Kenya	1500m (w)	07 09
Anna	Kielbasinska	26/06/1990	Poland	200m (w), 4x100m (w)	0
Goitom	Kifle	03/12/1993	Eritrea	5000m (m)	0
Yonas	Kifle	05/11/1977	Eritrea	Marathon (m)	01 05 09
Vincent Mumo	Kiilu	03/08/1982	Kenya	4x400m (m)	03
Gary	Kikaya	04/02/1980	Democratic Republic of Co	400m (m)	03 05 07 09
Deokhyeon	Kim	08/12/1985	South Korea	Long Jump (m)	07 09
Deokhyeon	Kim	08/12/1985	South Korea	Triple Jump (m)	07 09
Dong-young	Kim	06/03/1980	South Korea	50km Walk (m)	05
Hyunsub	Kim	31/05/1985	South Korea	20km Walk (m)	07 09
Kukyoung	Kim	19/04/1991	South Korea	100m (m)	0
Kukyoung	Kim	19/04/1991	South Korea	4x100m (m)	0
Kun-Woo	Kim	29/02/1980	South Korea	Decathlon	07
Kyung-ae	Kim	05/03/1988	South Korea	Javelin (w)	0
Min	Kim	09/05/1989	South Korea	Marathon (m)	0
So-Yeon	Kim	10/11/1990	South Korea	4x100m (w)	0
Sung-eun	Kim	24/02/1989	South Korea	Marathon (w)	0
Yoo Suk	Kim	19/01/1982	South Korea	Pole Vault (m)	05 09
Lucia	Kimani	21/06/1980	Bosnia & Herzegovina	Marathon (w)	07
Delivert Arsene	Kimbembe	14/09/1994	Congo	100m (m)	07 09
Trell	Kimmons	13/07/1985	United States	100m (m), 4x100m (m)	0
Jarkko	Kinnunen	19/01/1984	Finland	50km Walk (m)	07 09
Megumi	Kinukawa	07/08/1989	Japan	5000m (w), 10000m (w)	07
Eliud	Kipchoge	05/11/1984	Kenya	5000m (m)	03 05 07 09
Benjamin	Kiplagat	04/03/1989	Uganda	3000m SC (m)	07 09
Edna Ngeringwony	Kiplagat	15/09/1979	Kenya	Marathon (w)	0
Silas	Kiplagat	20/08/1989	Kenya	1500m (m)	0
Abraham	Kiplimo	14/04/1989	Uganda	5000m (m)	0
Nicholas	Kiprono	07/11/1987	Uganda	Marathon (m)	09
Asbel	Kiprop	30/06/1989	Kenya	1500m (m)	07 09
Stephen	Kiprotich	28/12/1985	Uganda	Marathon (m)	0
Brimin Kiprop	Kipruto	31/07/1985	Kenya	3000m SC (m)	05 07 09
Vincent	Kipruto	13/09/1987	Kenya	Marathon (m)	0
Eliud	Kiptanui	06/06/1989	Kenya	Marathon (m)	0
Benjamin Kolum	Kiptoo	01/01/1979	Kenya	Marathon (m)	09
Sally	Kipyego	16/07/1986	Kenya	10000m (w)	09
Sergey	Kirdyapkin	18/06/1980	Russia	50km Walk (m)	05 07 09
Anisya	Kirdyapkina	23/10/1989	Russia	20km Walk (w)	09
Nikoléta	Kiriakopoúlou	21/03/1986	Greece	Pole Vault (w)	09

Forenames	Surname	Born	Country	Events	Prev Apps
Tigist	Kiros	08/06/1992	Ethiopia	10000m (w)	0
Abel	Kirui	04/06/1982	Kenya	Marathon (m)	09
Peter Cheruiyot	Kirui	02/01/1988	Kenya	10000m (m)	0
Takayuki	Kishimoto	06/05/1990	Japan	400m Hurdles (m)	0
Rachid	Kisri	02/08/1975	Morocco	Marathon (m)	07 09
Yukihiro	Kitaoka	02/11/1982	Japan	Marathon (m)	0
Jackson Mumbwa	Kivuva	11/08/1989	Kenya	800m (m)	09
Kathrin	Klaas	08/02/1984	Germany	Hammer (w)	05 07 09
Nadine	Kleinert	20/10/1975	Germany	Shot Put (w)	99 01 03 05 07 09
Jarmila	Klimešová	09/02/1981	Czech Republic	Javelin (w)	03
Darya	Klishina	15/01/1991	Russia	Long Jump (w)	0
Lucia	Klocová	20/11/1983	Slovakia	800m (w)	03 05 07 09
Carolina	Klüft	02/02/1983	Sweden	Long Jump (w)	03 05 07
Bianca	Knight	02/01/1989	United States	4x100m (w)	0
Jan Felix	Knobel	16/01/1989	Germany	Decathlon	0
Yuichi	Kobayashi	12/12/1988	Japan	200m (m), 4x100m (m)	09
Gérard	Kobéané	24/04/1988	Burundi	100m (m)	0
Cherono	Koech	08/12/1992	Kenya	800m (w)	0
Isiah Kiplangat	Koech	19/12/1993	Kenya	5000m (m)	0
Iríni	Kokkinaríou	14/02/1981	Greece	3000m SC (w)	07 09
Nina	Kolaric	12/12/1986	Slovenia	Long Jump (w)	09
Asmir	Kolašinac	15/10/1984	Serbia	Shot Put (m)	09
Yevgeniya	Kolodko	02/07/1990	Russia	Shot Put (w)	0
Daniel Kipchirchir	Komen	27/11/1984	Kenya	1500m (m)	05 07
Merja	Korpela	15/05/1981	Finland	Hammer (w)	05 07 09
Irene Jerotich	Kosgei	26/10/1986	Kenya	Marathon (w)	0
Vincent Kiplangat	Kosgei	11/11/1985	Kenya	400m Hurdles (m), 4x400m (m)	0
Anton	Kosmac	14/12/1976	Slovenia	Marathon (m)	0
Ekaterina	Kostetskaya	31/12/1986	Russia	800m (w)	0
Aleksandra	Kotlyarova	10/10/1988	Uzbekistan	Triple Jump (w)	0
Kitavanah	Kountavong	01/12/1987	Laos	100m (m)	0
Zoltán	Kővágó	10/04/1979	Hungary	Discus (m)	01 03 05 07 09
Nazar	Kovalenko	09/02/1987	Ukraine	20km Walk (m)	0
Yoann	Kowal	07/10/1980	France	1500m (m)	09
Kacper	Kozlowski	07/12/1986	Poland	4x400m (m)	09
Primož	Kozmus	30/09/1979	Slovenia	Hammer (m)	03 07 09
Kazai Suzanne	Kragbé	22/12/1981	Ivory Coast	Discus (w)	09
Matija	Kranjc	12/06/1984	Slovenia	Javelin (m)	0
Sabine	Krantz	06/02/1981	Germany	20km Walk (w)	03 05 07 09
Franciela	Krasucki	26/04/1988	Brazil	4x100m (w)	0
Gesa Felicitas	Krause	03/08/1992	Germany	3000m SC (w)	0
Yuliya	Krevsun	04/11/1987	Ukraine	800m (w)	09
Bjørnar Ustad	Kristensen	26/01/1982	Norway	3000m SC (m)	07 09
Antonina	Krivoshapka	21/07/1987	Russia	400m (w), 4x400m (w)	09
Dmitry	Kroyter	18/02/1993	Israel	High Jump (m)	0
Eric	Krüger	21/03/1988	Germany	4x400m (m)	09
Kamil	Krynski	12/05/1987	Poland	4x100m (m)	0
Pavel	Kryvitski	17/04/1984	Belarus	Hammer (m)	09
Jakub	Krzewina	10/10/1989	Poland	4x400m (m)	0
Adam	Kszczot	02/09/1989	Poland	800m (m)	09
Robert	Kubaczyk	04/08/1986	Poland	4x100m (m)	09
Emmanuel	Kubi	16/10/1989	Ghana	4x100m (m)	0
Satomi	Kubokura	27/04/1982	Japan	400m Hurdles (w)	07 09
Dariusz	Kuc	24/04/1986	Poland	100m (m), 4x100m (m)	07 09
Olga	Kucherenko	05/11/1985	Russia	Long Jump (w)	09
Anton	Kucmin	07/06/1984	Slovakia	20km Walk (m)	07
Jan	Kudlicka	29/04/1988	Czech Republic	Pole Vault (m)	09
Mihkel	Kukk	08/10/1983	Estonia	Javelin (m)	09
Abera	Kuma	31/08/1990	Ethiopia	5000m (m)	0
Andreas	Kundert	01/10/1984	Switzerland	110m Hurdles (m)	07
Anna	Kuropatkina	03/10/1985	Russia	Triple Jump (w)	0
Lajos	Kürthy	22/10/1986	Hungary	Shot Put (m)	07 09
Geofrey	Kusuro	12/02/1989	Uganda	5000m (m)	09
Phobay	Kutu-Akoi	03/12/1987	Liberia	100m (w)	0
Alexandra	Kuzina	26/12/1990	Kazakhstan	4x400m (w)	0
Yasmin	Kwadwo	09/11/1990	Germany	4x100m (w)	0

Forenames	Surname	Born	Country	Events	Prev Apps
Jeanette	Kwakye	20/03/1983	Great Britain	100m (w), 4x100m (w)	07
Erik	Kynard	03/02/1991	United States	High Jump (m)	0
Simona	La Mantia	14/04/1983	Italy	Triple Jump (w)	03 05
Amine	Laalou	13/05/1982	Morocco	1500m (m)	03 05 07 09
Julie	Labonté	12/01/1990	Canada	Shot Put (w)	0
Bernard	Lagat	12/12/1974	United States	5000m (m)	01 03 07 09
Samyr	Laine	17/07/1984	Haiti	Triple Jump (m)	09
Btissam	Lakhouad	07/12/1980	Morocco	1500m (w)	09
Ivet	Lalova	18/05/1984	Bulgaria	200m (w)	07 09
Regan	Lamble	14/10/1991	Australia	20km Walk (w)	0
Raffaella	Lamera	13/04/1983	Italy	High Jump (w)	0
Giovanni	Lanaro	27/09/1981	Mexico	Pole Vault (m)	05 07 09
Gladys	Landaverde	23/02/1990	El Salvador	1500m (w)	0
Nancy Jebet	Langat	22/08/1981	Kenya	1500m (w)	05 09
Yi	Lao	10/10/1985	China	4x100m (m)	0
Fabrice	Lapierre	17/10/1983	Australia	Long Jump (m)	09
Cathrine	Larsåsen	05/12/1986	Norway	Pole Vault (w)	0
Germán	Lauro	02/04/1984	Argentina	Shot Put (m)	07 09
Renaud	Lavillenie	18/09/1986	France	Pole Vault (m)	09
Brijesh	Lawrence	27/12/1989	St Kitts & Nevis	200m (m), 4x100m (m)	0
Othman Hadj	Lazib	10/05/1983	Algeria	110m Hurdles (m)	0
Spirídon	Lebésis	30/05/1987	Greece	Javelin (m)	0
Dexter	Lee	18/01/1991	Jamaica	4x100m (m)	0
Ha-Nee	Lee	24/04/1989	South Korea	4x400m (w)	0
Jun	Lee	25/01/1991	South Korea	4x400m (m)	0
Mi-young	Lee	19/08/1979	South Korea	Shot Put (w)	05
Myongseung	Lee	14/08/1979	South Korea	Marathon (m)	03 07 09
Seung-yun	Lee	28/02/1989	South Korea	400m Hurdles (m)	0
Sook-Jung	Lee	29/09/1991	South Korea	Marathon (w)	0
Sunae	Lee	28/03/1994	South Korea	4x100m (w)	0
Yun-chul	Lee	28/03/1982	South Korea	Hammer (m)	0
Mosito	Lehata	08/04/1989	Lesotho	200m (m)	0
Christophe	Lemaître	11/06/1990	France	100m (m), 200m (m), 4x100m (m)	09
Deon	Lendore	28/10/1992	Trinidad & Tobago	4x400m (m)	0
Yannick	Lesourd	03/04/1988	France	4x100m (m)	0
Éloyse	Lesueur	15/07/1988	France	Long Jump (w)	09
Nigel	Levine	30/04/1989	Great Britain	4x400m (m)	0
Jura	Levy	04/11/1990	Jamaica	4x100m (w)	0
Marcin	Lewandowski	13/06/1987	Poland	800m (m)	09
Steven	Lewis	20/07/1978	Great Britain	Pole Vault (m)	99 03 07 09
Gia	Lewis-Smallwood	01/04/1979	United States	Discus (w)	0
José	Leyver	12/11/1985	Mexico	50km Walk (m)	0
Jianbo	Li	14/11/1986	China	50km Walk (m)	09
Ling	Li	07/02/1985	China	Shot Put (w)	07
Ling	Li	06/07/1989	China	Pole Vault (w)	09
Yanfeng	Li	15/05/1979	China	Discus (w)	0
Yanmei	Li	06/02/1990	China	Triple Jump (w)	0
Yanxi	Li	26/06/1983	China	Triple Jump (m)	05 07 09
Zhilong	Li	09/03/1988	China	400m Hurdles (m)	0
Zicheng	Li	10/04/1990	China	Marathon (m)	0
Jiahong	Liang	06/03/1988	China	4x100m (m)	0
Qiuping	Liang	11/03/1988	China	4x100m (w)	0
Ching-Hsien	Liao	22/06/1994	Chinese Taipei	100m (w)	0
Hanna	Liapeshka	18/07/1985	Belarus	4x100m (w)	0
Agnieszka	Ligieza	19/03/1986	Poland	4x100m (w)	0
Feyisa	Lilesa	01/02/1990	Ethiopia	Marathon (m)	0
Chanho	Lim	11/03/1992	South Korea	4x400m (m)	0
Hee-nam	Lim	29/05/1984	South Korea	4x100m (m)	0
Ching-Hsuan	Lin	14/05/1992	Chinese Taipei	Long Jump (m)	0
Janin	Lindenberg	20/01/1987	Germany	4x400m (w)	0
Christopher	Linke	24/10/1988	Germany	20km Walk (m), 50km Walk (m)	0
Sergej	Litvinov	27/01/1986	Russia	Hammer (m)	09
Lyudmila	Litvinova	08/06/1985	Russia	4x400m (w)	09
Chunhua	Liu	01/10/1986	China	Javelin (w)	0
Hong	Liu	12/05/1987	China	20km Walk (w)	07 09
Tingting	Liu	29/10/1990	China	Hammer (w)	0

143

Forenames	Surname	Born	Country	Events	Prev Apps
Xiang	Liu	13/07/1983	China	110m Hurdles (m)	01 03 05 07
Xiangrong	Liu	06/06/1988	China	Shot Put (w)	09
Yuan-Kai	Liu	02/12/1981	Chinese Taipei	4x100m (m)	0
Shereefa	Lloyd	02/09/1982	Jamaica	4x400m (w)	07 09
Diana	Lobacevske	07/08/1980	Lithuania	Marathon (w)	0
Liliya	Lobanova	14/10/1985	Ukraine	800m (w)	0
Marcel	Lomnický	06/07/1987	Slovakia	Hammer (m)	0
Thomas Pkemei	Longosiwa	14/01/1982	Kenya	5000m (m)	0
Kevin	López	12/06/1990	Spain	800m (m)	0
Luis Fernando	López	03/06/1979	Colombia	20km Walk (m)	05 07 09
Miguel	López	09/04/1990	Puerto Rico	4x100m (m)	0
Miguel Ángel	López	03/07/1988	Spain	20km Walk (m)	0
Olive	Loughnane	14/01/1976	Ireland	20km Walk (w)	01 03 05 07 09
Joanne Pricilla	Loutoy	31/12/1992	Seychelles	100m (w)	0
Ion	Luchianov	31/01/1981	Moldova	3000m SC (m)	05 09
Joseph Andy	Lui	07/01/1992	Tonga	100m (m)	0
Tintu	Luka	26/04/1989	India	800m (w)	0
Evgeniy	Lukyanenko	23/01/1985	Russia	Pole Vault (m)	07
Marcela	Lustigová	11/11/1982	Czech Republic	3000m SC (w)	0
Tatyana	Lysenko	09/10/1983	Russia	Hammer (w)	05 09
Pavel	Lyzhyn	24/03/1981	Belarus	Shot Put (m)	03 05 07 09
Xuejun	Ma	26/03/1985	China	Discus (w)	07 09
Julia	Mächtig	01/11/1986	Germany	Heptathlon	09
Isabel	Macías	11/08/1984	Spain	1500m (w)	0
Viktória	Madarász	12/05/1985	Hungary	20km Walk (w)	0
Moleboheng	Mafata	03/03/1985	Lesotho	Marathon (w)	0
Simon	Magakwe	25/05/1985	South Africa	100m (m)	09
Maurren Higa	Maggi	25/06/1976	Brazil	Long Jump (w)	99 01 07 09
Maris	Mägi	11/08/1987	Estonia	400m (w)	0
Fantu	Magiso	09/06/1992	Ethiopia	400m (w), 800m (w)	0
Ali Hasan	Mahbood	31/12/1981	Brunei	10000m (m)	07 09
Renjith	Maheshwary	30/01/1986	India	Triple Jump (m)	07
Michael	Mai	27/09/1977	United States	Hammer (m)	09
Edi	Maia	10/11/1987	Portugal	Pole Vault (m)	0
Tomasz	Majewski	30/08/1981	Poland	Shot Put (m)	05 07 09
Maguy Safi	Makanda	30/04/1992	Democratic Republic of Cc	100m (w)	0
Sergey	Makarov	19/03/1973	Russia	Javelin (m)	99 01 03 05 07 09
Taoufik	Makhloufi	29/04/1988	Algeria	1500m (m)	09
Ngonidzashe	Makusha	11/03/1987	Zimbabwe	100m (m), Long Jump (m)	09
Piotr	Malachowski	07/06/1983	Poland	Discus (m)	07 09
Christian	Malcolm	03/06/1979	Great Britain	200m (m), 4x100m (m)	01 03 05
Chantel	Malone	06/04/1977	British Virgin Islands	Long Jump (w)	03 05 09
Hugo	Mamba-Schlick	01/02/1982	Cameroon	Triple Jump (m)	07 09
Patricia	Mamona	21/11/1988	Portugal	Triple Jump (w)	0
Pascal	Mancini	18/04/1989	Switzerland	4x100m (m)	09
Derek	Mandell	18/09/1986	Guam	800m (m)	0
Véronique	Mang	15/12/1984	France	4x100m (w)	0
Francis	Manioru	17/09/1981	Solomon Islands	100m (m)	0
Ari	Mannio	23/07/1987	Finland	Javelin (m)	09
Asenate	Manoa	23/05/1992	Tuvalu	100m (w)	09
Luvo	Manyonga	06/03/1985	South Africa	Long Jump (m)	05 07 09
Leonel	Manzano	12/09/1984	United States	1500m (m)	07 09
Jan	Marcell	04/06/1985	Czech Republic	Discus (m), Shot Put (m)	0
Marcin	Marciniszyn	07/09/1982	Poland	400m (m), 4x400m (m)	05 07 09
Luis Alberto	Marco	20/08/1986	Spain	800m (m)	09
Ida	Marcussen	01/11/1987	Norway	Heptathlon	07 09
Marina	Marghieva	28/06/1986	Moldova	Hammer (w)	09
Zalina	Marghieva	05/02/1988	Moldova	Hammer (w)	09
Brian	Mariano	22/01/1985	Netherlands	4x100m (m)	0
Martin	Maric	19/04/1984	Croatia	Discus (m)	0
Dzmitry	Marshin	15/09/1972	Azerbaijan	Hammer (m)	0
Jenna	Martin	31/03/1988	Canada	4x400m (w)	09
Diana	Martín	05/11/1973	Spain	3000m SC (w)	99 01 03 05 07 09
Churandy	Martina	03/07/1984	Netherlands	100m (m), 200m (m)	03 05 07 09
Kaina	Martinez	02/02/1986	Belize	100m (w)	0
Aymeé	Martínez	17/11/1988	Cuba	400m (w), 4x400m (w)	07

Forenames	Surname	Born	Country	Events	Prev Apps
Guillermo	Martínez	28/06/1981	Cuba	Javelin (m)	05 07 09
José Manuel	Martínez	22/10/1971	Spain	Marathon (m)	01 03 05 07 09
Plácida	Martínez	14/05/1985	Spain	4x100m (w)	0
Yarianna	Martínez	20/09/1984	Cuba	Triple Jump (w)	07 09
Graciela	Martins	05/04/1987	Guinea-Bissau	400m (w)	0
Geoffrey	Martinson	26/03/1986	Canada	1500m (m)	0
Anita	Márton	15/01/1989	Hungary	Shot Put (w)	09
Ekaterina	Martynova	06/08/1986	Russia	1500m (w)	0
Linet Chepkwemoi	Masai	01/06/1986	Kenya	5000m (w), 10000m (w)	09
Pavel	Maslák	21/02/1991	Czech Republic	200m (m)	0
Marina	Maslenko	03/07/1982	Kazakhstan	4x400m (w)	09
Jamele	Mason	19/10/1989	Puerto Rico	400m Hurdles (m)	0
Yousef Ahmed	Masrahi	31/12/1987	Saudi Arabia	4x400m (m)	09
Richard Kipkemboi	Mateelong	14/10/1983	Kenya	3000m SC (m)	07 09
Martin Irungu	Mathathi	25/12/1985	Kenya	10000m (m)	05 07
Michael	Mathieu	24/06/1984	Bahamas	200m (m)	09
Willi	Mathiszik	17/06/1984	Germany	110m Hurdles (m)	0
Alena	Matoshka	23/06/1982	Belarus	Hammer (w)	0
Sibusiso	Matsenjwa	02/05/1988	Swaziland	200m (m)	09
Margarita	Matsko	04/01/1986	Kazakhstan	800m (w)	0
Radoslava	Mavrodieva	13/03/1987	Bulgaria	Shot Put (w)	0
Tanith	Maxwell	02/06/1976	South Africa	Marathon (w)	07 09
Gerhard	Mayer	20/05/1980	Austria	Discus (m)	09
Jeneva	McCall	28/10/1989	United States	Hammer (w)	0
Lee	McConnell	09/10/1978	Great Britain	400m (w), 4x400m (w)	03 05 07 09
Francena	McCorory	20/10/1988	United States	400m (w), 4x400m (w)	0
Jorge	McFarlane	14/06/1972	Peru	Long Jump (m)	99 01 03 05 07 09
Alisa	McKaig	21/02/1986	United States	Marathon (w)	0
Kaila	McKnight	05/05/1986	Australia	1500m (w)	0
Inika	McPherson	29/09/1986	United States	High Jump (w)	0
Tony	McQuay	16/04/1990	United States	400m (m)	0
Jennifer	Meadows	17/04/1981	Great Britain	800m (w)	07 09
Teklemariam	Medhin	24/06/1989	Eritrea	10000m (m)	09
Kenneth	Medwood	14/12/1987	Belize	400m Hurdles (m)	0
Jirapong	Meenapra	05/11/1993	Thailand	4x100m (m)	0
Ben Youssef	Meité	11/11/1986	Ivory Coast	100m (m), 200m (m)	09
Mahiedine	Mekhissi-Benabbad	15/03/1985	France	3000m SC (m)	07 09
Deresse	Mekonnen	20/10/1987	Ethiopia	1500m (m)	07 09
Melanie	Melfort	08/11/1982	France	High Jump (w)	05 07 09
Karin Mey	Melis	31/05/1983	Turkey	Long Jump (w)	09
Luis Felipe	Méliz	11/08/1979	Spain	Long Jump (m)	99 01 03 09
Meselech	Melkamu	27/04/1985	Ethiopia	10000m (w)	05 07 09
Stanislav	Melnykov	26/02/1987	Ukraine	400m Hurdles (m)	09
Aleksandr	Menkov	07/12/1990	Russia	Long Jump (m)	09
Imane	Merga	15/10/1988	Ethiopia	5000m (m), 10000m (m)	09
Aselefech	Mergia	23/01/1985	Ethiopia	Marathon (w)	09
Brigitte	Merlano	29/04/1982	Colombia	100m Hurdles (w)	05 07 09
Lee	Merrien	24/04/1978	Great Britain	Marathon (m)	0
Christine	Merrill	20/08/1987	Sri Lanka	400m Hurdles (w)	0
Aries	Merritt	24/07/1985	United States	110m Hurdles (m)	09
LaShawn	Merritt	27/06/1986	United States	400m (m), 4x400m (m)	05 07 09
Amanuel	Mesel	29/12/1990	Eritrea	5000m (m)	0
Nahom	Mesfin	24/11/1974	Ethiopia	3000m SC (m)	09
Romain	Mesnil	13/06/1977	France	Pole Vault (m)	99 01 03 07 09
Daniele	Meucci	07/10/1985	Italy	5000m (m), 10000m (m)	09
Lukasz	Michalski	02/08/1988	Poland	Pole Vault (m)	09
Maria	Michta	23/06/1986	United States	20km Walk (w)	0
Kimberley	Mickle	28/12/1984	Australia	Javelin (w)	09
Andrei	Mikhnevich	12/07/1976	Belarus	Shot Put (m)	01 03 05 07 09
Natallia	Mikhnevich	25/05/1982	Belarus	Shot Put (w)	05 09
Marta	Milani	09/03/1987	Italy	400m (w), 4x400m (w)	09
Derek	Miles	28/09/1972	United States	Pole Vault (m)	03 09
Ramon	Miller	13/03/1982	Bahamas	400m (m), 4x400m (m)	09
Tatiana	Mineeva	10/08/1990	Russia	20km Walk (w)	0
Gülcan	Mingir	21/05/1989	Turkey	3000m SC (w)	0
Mounir	Miout	14/09/1984	Algeria	5000m (m)	0

Forenames	Surname	Born	Country	Events	Prev Apps
Nastassia	Mironchyk-Ivanova	13/04/1989	Belarus	Long Jump (w)	09
Jemena	Misayauri	11/12/1978	Peru	Marathon (w)	0
Anna	Mishchenko	25/08/1983	Ukraine	1500m (w)	09
Maurice	Mitchell	22/12/1989	United States	4x100m (m)	0
Risa	Miyashita	26/04/1984	Japan	Javelin (w)	0
Lebogang	Moeng	01/01/1989	South Africa	200m (w)	0
Ofentse	Mogawane	20/02/1982	South Africa	4x100m (m), 4x400m (m)	09
Sostene	Moguenara	17/10/1989	Germany	Long Jump (w)	0
Modike Lucky	Mohale	21/08/1985	South Africa	Marathon (m)	0
Shifaz	Mohamed	01/03/1979	Maldives	800m (m)	03 05 07 09
Alia Saeed	Mohammed	18/05/1991	United Arab Emirates	5000m (w)	0
Malte	Mohr	27/06/1986	Germany	Pole Vault (m)	09
Godfrey Khotso	Mokoena	06/03/1985	South Africa	Long Jump (m)	05 07 09
Stephen	Mokoka	31/01/1985	South Africa	10000m (m)	0
Kathrina	Molitor	08/11/1983	Germany	Javelin (w)	09
Anders	Møller	05/09/1977	Denmark	Triple Jump (m)	05 07
Anne	Möllinger	27/09/1985	Germany	4x100m (w)	09
Avard	Moncur	02/11/1978	Bahamas	4x400m (m)	03 07 09
Roudy	Monrose	26/04/1978	Haiti	200m (m)	0
Concepción	Montaner	14/01/1981	Spain	Long Jump (w), 4x100m (w)	03 05 07
Alysia Johnson	Montano	23/04/1986	United States	800m (w)	07
Ricardo	Monteiro	18/05/1980	Portugal	4x100m (m)	05 09
Amantle	Montsho	04/07/1983	Botswana	400m (w)	05 07 09
Tera	Moody	18/12/1980	United States	Marathon (w)	09
Sajad	Moradi	30/03/1983	Iran	800m (m)	05 07 09
Sara	Moreira	28/09/1983	Portugal	3000m SC (w)	07 09
Yipsi	Moreno	15/04/1985	Cuba	Hammer (w)	09
Jason	Morgan	06/10/1982	Jamaica	Discus (m)	07
Mike	Morgan	20/02/1980	United States	Marathon (m)	07
Koichiro	Morioka	02/04/1985	Japan	50km Walk (m)	05 07 09
Sergey	Morozov	21/03/1988	Russia	20km Walk (m)	0
Brett	Morse	11/02/1989	Great Britain	Discus (m)	0
Craig	Mottram	18/06/1980	Australia	5000m (m)	01 05 07
Bertrand	Moulinet	06/01/1987	France	50km Walk (m)	0
Kaveh Sadegh	Mousavi	27/05/1985	Iran	Hammer (m)	0
Mohamed	Moustaoui	02/04/1985	Morocco	1500m (m)	07 09
Víctor	Moya	24/10/1982	Cuba	High Jump (m)	05 07
Thuso	Mpuang	01/03/1985	South Africa	200m (m), 4x100m (m)	09
Zakia	Mrisho	19/02/1984	Tanzania	5000m (w)	05 07 09
Nadine	Müller	07/08/1985	Germany	Discus (w)	07 09
Ángel	Mullera	20/04/1984	Spain	3000m SC (m)	09
Prince	Mumba	28/09/1984	Zambia	800m (m)	01 05 09
Markus	Münch	13/06/1986	Germany	Discus (m)	09
Yukifumi	Murakami	23/12/1979	Japan	Javelin (m)	05 07 09
Fabiana	Murer	16/03/1981	Brazil	Pole Vault (w)	05 07 09
María	Murillo	05/05/1991	Colombia	Javelin (w)	0
Koji	Murofushi	08/10/1974	Japan	Hammer (m)	01 03 05 07 09
Mark Kiprotich	Mutai	12/10/1984	Kenya	4x400m (m)	09
Anderson Mureta	Mutegi	01/05/1987	Kenya	4x400m (m)	0
Julius	Mutekanga	01/12/1987	Uganda	800m (m)	0
Semiha	Mutlu	15/03/1987	Turkey	20km Walk (w)	0
Gabriel	Mvumvure	23/02/1988	Zimbabwe	100m (m), 200m (m)	09
Marshevet	Myers	25/09/1984	United States	4x100m (w)	09
Carl	Myerscough	21/10/1979	Great Britain	Discus (m)	03 05 09
Povilas	Mykolaitis	23/02/1983	Lithuania	Long Jump (m)	05
Racheal	Nachula	14/01/1990	Zambia	400m (w)	09
Kentaro	Nakamoto	07/12/1982	Japan	Marathon (m)	0
Remi	Nakazato	24/06/1988	Japan	Marathon (w)	0
Sarah	Nambawa	23/09/1984	Uganda	Triple Jump (w)	0
Yazalde	Nascimento	17/04/1986	Portugal	4x100m (m)	05
Horacio	Nava	15/04/1981	Mexico	20km Walk (m)	09
Dilshod	Nazarov	06/05/1982	Tajikistan	Hammer (m)	05 07 09
Hinikissia Albertine	Ndikert	15/09/1992	Chad	200m (w)	0
Jaysuma Saidy	Ndure	01/07/1984	Norway	100m (m), 200m (m)	03 05 09
Phumlile	Ndzinisa	21/08/1992	Swaziland	200m (w)	0
Annet	Negesa	24/04/1992	Uganda	800m (w)	0

Forenames	Surname	Born	Country	Events	Prev Apps
Adam	Nelson	07/07/1975	United States	Shot Put (m)	01 03 05 07 09
William	Nelson	11/09/1984	United States	3000m SC (m)	0
Kristóf	Németh	17/09/1987	Hungary	Hammer (m)	0
Alena	Neumiarzhitskaya	27/07/1980	Belarus	4x100m (w)	0
Kathy	Newberry	31/08/1978	United States	Marathon (w)	0
Brent	Newdick	31/01/1985	New Zealand	Decathlon	09
David	Ngakane	12/03/1980	South Africa	Marathon (m)	0
Coolboy	Ngamole	21/06/1977	South Africa	Marathon (m)	09
Daniel	Nghipandulwa	08/06/1989	Namibia	800m (m)	0
Christian	Ngningba	30/12/1984	Gabon	5000m (m)	0
Marek	Niit	09/08/1987	Estonia	100m (m), 200m (m)	07 09
Hitomi	Niiya	26/02/1988	Japan	5000m (w)	0
Amin	Nikfar	02/01/1981	Iran	Shot Put (m)	0
Minna	Nikkanen	09/04/1988	Finland	Pole Vault (w)	07 09
Viktor	Ninov	19/06/1988	Bulgaria	High Jump (m)	0
Greg	Nixon	12/09/1981	United States	400m (m), 4x400m (m)	0
Pauline	Niyongere	21/10/1988	Burundi	5000m (w)	09
Denis	Nizhegorodov	26/07/1980	Russia	50km Walk (m)	03 07 09
Mercy Wanjiku	Njoroge	10/06/1986	Kenya	3000m SC (w)	0
Grace Wanjiru	Njue	10/10/1979	Kenya	20km Walk (w)	0
Jean-Jacques	Nkouloukidi	15/04/1982	Italy	50km Walk (m)	09
Azusa	Nojiri	06/06/1982	Japan	Marathon (w)	0
Isaac	Ntiamoah	27/10/1982	Australia	4x100m (m)	0
Cuthbert	Nyasango	17/09/1982	Zimbabwe	Marathon (m)	0
Tandiwe	Nyathi	26/05/1992	Zimbabwe	1500m (w)	0
Epiphanie	Nyirabarame	15/12/1981	Rwanda	Marathon (w)	03 05 09
Trond	Nymark	28/12/1976	Norway	50km Walk (m)	99 01 03 05 07 09
Christina	Obergföll	22/08/1981	Germany	Javelin (w)	05 07 09
Hellen Onsando	Obiri	13/12/1989	Kenya	1500m (w)	0
Darlenis	Obregón	21/02/1986	Colombia	4x100m (w)	09
Yoshinori	Oda	05/12/1980	Japan	Marathon (m)	0
Mikel	Odriozola	25/05/1973	Spain	50km Walk (m)	99 01 03 05 07 09
Muizat Ajoke	Odumosu	27/10/1987	Nigeria	400m Hurdles (w), 4x400m (w)	07 09
Jennifer	Oeser	29/11/1983	Germany	Heptathlon	07 09
Ben	Offereins	12/03/1986	Australia	4x400m (m)	09
Femi	Ogunode	15/05/1991	Qatar	200m (m), 400m (m)	0
Se-Ra	Oh	30/08/1987	South Korea	4x400m (w)	0
Christine	Ohuruogu	17/05/1984	Great Britain	400m (w), 4x400m (w)	05 07 09
Nao	Okabe	28/08/1988	Japan	4x100m (w)	0
Blessing	Okagbare	09/10/1988	Nigeria	200m (w), Long Jump (w), 4x100m (w)	09
Tosin	Oke	01/10/1980	Nigeria	Triple Jump (m)	09
Marilyn	Okoro	23/09/1984	Great Britain	800m (w)	07 09
Oksana	Okuneva	14/03/1990	Ukraine	High Jump (w)	0
Ercüment	Olgundeniz	07/07/1976	Turkey	Discus (m)	99 07 09
Ciaran	O'Lionaird	11/04/1988	Ireland	1500m (m)	0
David	Oliver	24/04/1982	United States	110m Hurdles (m)	07
Manuel	Olmedo	17/05/1983	Spain	1500m (m)	03 05 07 09
Christian	Olsson	25/01/1980	Sweden	Triple Jump (m)	01 03 07
Anna	Omarova	03/10/1981	Russia	Shot Put (w)	07
Omolara	Omotosho	25/05/1993	Nigeria	4x400m (w)	0
Eike	Onnen	03/08/1982	Germany	High Jump (m)	07
Anyika	Onuora	28/10/1984	Great Britain	200m (w), 4x100m (w)	0
John Robert	Oosthuizen	23/01/1987	South Africa	Javelin (m)	07 09
Marian	Oprea	06/06/1982	Romania	Triple Jump (m)	01 03 05 07
Éva	Orbán	29/11/1984	Hungary	Hammer (w)	05 09
Arabelly	Orjuela	24/07/1988	Colombia	20km Walk (w)	0
Derval	O'Rourke	28/05/1981	Ireland	100m Hurdles (w)	03 05 07 09
Andrew	Osagie	19/02/1988	Great Britain	800m (m)	0
Oludamola	Osayomi	26/06/1986	Nigeria	4x100m (w)	07 09
Agnes	Osazuwa	26/06/1989	Nigeria	4x100m (w)	0
Nadzeya	Ostapchuk	28/10/1980	Belarus	Shot Put (w)	01 03 05 07
Luvsanlundeg	Otgonbayar	13/07/1982	Mongolia	Marathon (w)	07 09
Kumi	Otoshi	29/07/1985	Japan	20km Walk (w)	09
Elodie	Ouédraogo	27/02/1981	Belgium	400m Hurdles (w)	07 09
Hanane	Ouhaddou	01/01/1982	Morocco	3000m SC (w)	07 09
Aziz	Ouhadi	24/07/1984	Morocco	100m (m)	09

147

Forenames	Surname	Born	Country	Events	Prev Apps
Vladislava	Ovcharenko	18/12/1986	Tajikistan	100m (w)	03
Yoshimi	Ozaki	01/07/1981	Japan	Marathon (w)	09
Sinta	Ozolina-Kovala	26/02/1988	Latvia	Javelin (w)	0
Travis	Padgett	13/12/1986	United States	4x100m (m)	0
Lutmar	Paes	12/12/1988	Brazil	800m (m)	0
Mikk	Pahapill	18/07/1983	Estonia	Decathlon	05 09
Rolando	Palacios	03/05/1987	Honduras	200m (m)	05 09
Madara	Palameika	18/06/1987	Latvia	Javelin (w)	09
Nicolau	Palanca	15/11/1988	Angola	400m (m)	07
Níki	Panéta	21/04/1986	Greece	Triple Jump (w)	0
Babubhai Kesharabhai	Panucha	10/08/1978	India	20km Walk (m)	09
Paraskeví	Papahrístou	17/04/1989	Greece	Triple Jump (w)	09
Alexándra	Papayeoryíou	17/12/1980	Greece	Hammer (w)	03 07 09
Krisztina	Papp	17/12/1982	Hungary	10000m (w)	09
Bonggo	Park	08/05/1991	South Korea	400m (m), 4x400m (m)	0
Chil-sung	Park	08/07/1982	South Korea	20km Walk (m), 50km Walk (m)	07 09
Jun-Sook	Park	25/03/1980	South Korea	Marathon (w)	0
Seongmyun	Park	13/06/1995	South Korea	4x400m (w)	0
So-Yeun	Park	03/06/1987	South Korea	4x100m (w)	0
Tae-kyong	Park	30/07/1980	South Korea	110m Hurdles (m)	09
Barbara	Parker	08/11/1982	Great Britain	3000m SC (w)	0
Krisztián	Pars	18/02/1982	Hungary	Hammer (m)	05 07 09
Tom	Parsons	05/05/1984	Great Britain	High Jump (m)	07
Lukasz	Parszczynski	04/05/1985	Poland	3000m SC (m)	0
Susan	Partridge	04/01/1980	Great Britain	Marathon (w)	0
Beatriz	Pascual	09/05/1982	Spain	20km Walk (w)	07 09
Agnese	Pastare	27/10/1988	Latvia	20km Walk (w)	0
Kara	Patterson	10/02/1985	United States	Javelin (w)	09
Darvis	Patton	04/12/1977	United States	200m (m), 4x100m (m)	03 09
Jorge	Paula	08/10/1984	Portugal	400m Hurdles (m)	0
Alberto	Paulo	03/10/1985	Portugal	3000m SC (m)	09
Alda	Paulo	10/07/1991	Angola	100m (w)	0
Sally	Pearson	19/09/1986	Australia	100m Hurdles (w), 4x100m (w)	07 09
Arismendy	Peguero	02/08/1980	Dominican Republic	400m (m)	05 07 09
Lucie	Pelantová	07/05/1986	Czech Republic	20km Walk (w)	0
Tori	Pena	30/07/1987	Ireland	Pole Vault (w)	0
Diosmely	Peña	12/06/1985	Cuba	4x400m (w)	09
Bianca	Perie	01/06/1990	Romania	Hammer (w)	07 09
Ruggero	Pertile	08/08/1974	Italy	Marathon (m)	03 05 09
Mario	Pestano	08/04/1978	Spain	Discus (m)	99 01 03 05 07 09
Allison	Peter	04/07/1992	US Virgin Islands	200m (w)	0
Sara	Petersen	09/04/1987	Denmark	400m Hurdles (w)	09
Tetiana	Petlyuk	22/02/1982	Ukraine	800m (w)	05 07 09
Esthera	Petre	13/05/1990	Romania	High Jump (w)	0
Orrin Ogumoro	Pharmin	06/12/1986	Northern Mariana Islands	100m (m)	0
Weerawat	Pharueang	11/03/1991	Thailand	4x100m (m)	0
Dwight	Phillips	26/01/1983	United States	Long Jump (m)	01 03 05 07 09
Isa	Phillips	22/04/1984	Jamaica	400m Hurdles (m)	07 09
Richard	Phillips	26/01/1983	Jamaica	110m Hurdles (m)	09
Gerald	Phiri	06/10/1988	Zambia	100m (m)	09
Craig	Pickering	16/10/1986	Great Britain	4x100m (m)	07
Bayron	Piedra	19/08/1982	Ecuador	10000m (m)	07 09
Demetrius	Pinder	13/02/1989	Bahamas	400m (m)	0
George	Pine	20/01/1991	Kiribati	100m (m)	0
Ana	Pinero	15/01/1986	Spain	Pole Vault (w)	0
Darya	Pishchalnikova	19/07/1985	Russia	Discus (w)	05
Oscar	Pistorius	22/11/1986	South Africa	400m (m), 4x400m (m)	0
Tero	Pitkämäki	19/12/1982	Finland	Javelin (m)	05 07 09
Margarita	Plaksina	01/10/1977	Russia	Marathon (w)	0
Jonas	Plass	01/08/1986	Germany	4x400m (m)	0
Renata	Plis	05/02/1985	Poland	1500m (w)	0
Nataliya	Pohrebnyak	19/12/1988	Ukraine	4x100m (w)	07 09
Viktoriia	Poliudina	29/06/1989	Kyrgyzstan	5000m (w)	09
Tori	Polk	21/09/1983	United States	Long Jump (w)	0
Marie	Polli	28/11/1980	Switzerland	20km Walk (w)	07 09
Aliann	Pompey	09/03/1978	Guyana	400m (w)	01 03 05 07 09

Forenames	Surname	Born	Country	Events	Prev Apps
Pak Yan	Poon	03/09/1986	Hong Kong	100m Hurdles (w)	05 07 09
Marika	Popowicz	28/04/1988	Poland	4x100m (w)	0
Tiffany	Porter	13/11/1987	Great Britain	100m Hurdles (w), 4x100m (w)	09
Vera	Pospíšilová-Cechlová	19/11/1978	Czech Republic	Discus (w)	01 03 05 07 09
María José	Poves	16/03/1978	Spain	20km Walk (w)	05 07
Olesya	Povh	18/10/1987	Ukraine	4x100m (w)	0
Adrienne	Power	11/12/1981	Canada	4x400m (w)	09
Dipna Lim	Prasad	07/06/1991	Singapore	100m Hurdles (w)	0
Davita	Prendergast	16/12/1984	Jamaica	4x400m (w)	0
Martina	Pretelli	28/12/1988	San Marino	100m (w)	09
Rožle	Prezelj	26/09/1979	Slovenia	High Jump (m)	03 05 07
Shara	Proctor	16/09/1988	Great Britain	Long Jump (w)	07 09
Shinelle	Proctor	27/06/1991	Anguilla	100m (w)	0
Andriy	Protsenko	20/05/1988	Ukraine	High Jump (m)	09
Jirina	Ptácniková	20/05/1986	Czech Republic	Pole Vault (w)	09
Irene	Pusterla	21/06/1988	Switzerland	Long Jump (w)	0
Oleksandr	Pyatnytsya	14/07/1985	Ukraine	Javelin (m)	09
Nataliya	Pyhyda	31/01/1981	Ukraine	400m (w), 4x400m (w)	0
Monika	Pyrek	11/08/1980	Poland	Pole Vault (w)	01 03 05 07 09
Shenjie	Qieyang	11/11/1990	China	20km Walk (w)	0
Trevell	Quinley	16/01/1983	United States	Long Jump (m)	07
Ronal	Quispe	05/03/1989	Bolivia	20km Walk (m)	0
Anatercia	Quive	14/03/1987	Mozambique	100m (w)	0
Renny	Quow	25/08/1987	Trinidad & Tobago	400m (m), 4x400m (m)	07 09
Anastasiya	Rabchenyuk	14/09/1983	Ukraine	400m Hurdles (w), 4x400m (w)	07 09
Ineta	Radevica	13/07/1981	Latvia	Long Jump (w)	05
Svetlana	Radzivil	17/01/1987	Uzbekistan	High Jump (w)	09
Eriks	Rags	01/06/1975	Latvia	Javelin (m)	99 01 03 05 07 09
Khalilur	Rahman	01/02/1990	Bangladesh	200m (m)	0
Baya	Rahouli	27/07/1979	Algeria	Triple Jump (w)	03 05
Andres	Raja	02/06/1982	Estonia	Decathlon	07 09
Luka	Rakic	02/08/1991	Montenegro	200m (m)	0
Ruben	Ramolefi	17/07/2008	South Africa	3000m SC (m)	05 07 09
Beverly	Ramos	24/08/1987	Puerto Rico	3000m SC (w)	0
Martina	Ratej	02/11/1981	Slovenia	Javelin (w)	09
Hanitrasoa Olga	Razanamalala	08/09/1988	Madagascar	400m Hurdles (w)	0
Vira	Rebryk	25/02/1989	Ukraine	Javelin (w)	09
Janelle	Redhead	03/07/1986	Grenada	200m (w)	09
Meliz	Redif	26/03/1989	Turkey	4x400m (w)	0
Brittney	Reese	09/09/1986	United States	Long Jump (w)	07 09
Dejene	Regassa	18/04/1989	Brunei	5000m (m)	0
Christian	Reif	24/10/1984	Germany	Long Jump (m)	07
Stephanie	Reilly	23/02/1978	Ireland	3000m SC (w)	0
Antonio Manuel	Reina	15/05/1981	Spain	800m (m)	07 09
Maysa	Rejepova	04/01/1993	Turkmenistan	100m (w)	0
James	Rendón	07/04/1985	Colombia	20km Walk (m)	0
Gustavo	Restrepo	27/07/1982	Colombia	20km Walk (m)	07
Clélia	Reuse	01/08/1988	Switzerland	4x100m (w)	0
Quentin	Rew	16/07/1984	New Zealand	50km Walk (m)	0
Sergio	Reyes	25/10/1981	United States	Marathon (m)	0
Jennifer	Rhines	01/07/1974	United States	10000m (w)	01 05 07 09
Jason	Richardson	04/04/1986	United States	110m Hurdles (m)	0
Sanya	Richards-Ross	26/02/1985	United States	400m (w), 4x400m (w)	03 05 07 09
Miguel	Rigau	22/07/1985	Germany	4x400m (m)	0
Elisa	Rigaudo	17/06/1980	Italy	20km Walk (w)	03 05 07 09
Andrew	Riley	09/06/1988	Jamaica	110m Hurdles (m)	0
Michael	Rimmer	03/12/1986	Great Britain	800m (m)	07 09
Jeffrey	Riseley	11/11/1986	Australia	1500m (m)	07 09
Edgar	Rivera	13/02/1991	Mexico	High Jump (m)	0
Justine	Robbeson	15/05/1985	South Africa	Javelin (w)	0
Jake	Robertson	14/11/1989	New Zealand	5000m (m)	0
Josef	Robertson	14/05/1987	Jamaica	400m Hurdles (m)	09
Khadevis	Robinson	19/07/1976	United States	800m (m)	99 01 03 05 07 09
Dayron	Robles	19/11/1986	Cuba	110m Hurdles (m)	05 07 09
Ángel David	Rodríguez	25/04/1980	Spain	100m (m)	07 09
Carlos	Rodríguez	02/07/1992	Puerto Rico	4x100m (m)	0

Forenames	Surname	Born	Country	Events	Prev Apps
Déborah	Rodríguez	02/12/1992	Uruguay	400m Hurdles (w)	09
Natalia	Rodríguez	02/06/1979	Spain	1500m (w)	01 03 05 09
Rafith	Rodríguez	01/06/1989	Colombia	800m (m)	0
Jason	Rogers	31/08/1991	St Kitts & Nevis	4x100m (m)	0
Keiron	Rogers	08/09/1988	Anguilla	100m (m)	07
Anna	Rogowska	21/05/1981	Poland	Pole Vault (w)	03 05 07 09
Marielys	Rojas	30/04/1986	Venezuela	High Jump (w)	0
Cindy	Roleder	21/08/1989	Germany	100m Hurdles (w)	0
Jarred	Rome	21/12/1976	United States	Discus (m)	01 03 05 07 09
Kabotaake	Romeri	05/08/1995	Kiribati	100m (w)	0
Juan Carlos	Romero	15/12/1977	Mexico	10000m (m)	09
Martyn	Rooney	03/04/1987	Great Britain	400m (m), 4x400m (m)	07 09
Chiara	Rosa	28/01/1983	Italy	Shot Put (w)	05 07 09
Milángela	Rosales	21/02/1987	Venezuela	20km Walk (w)	0
Ak. Hafiy Tajuddin	Rositi	04/07/1991	Brunei	400m (m)	0
Denisa	Rosolová	21/08/1986	Czech Republic	400m (w), 4x400m (w)	07
Caroline	Rotich	13/05/1984	Kenya	Marathon (w)	0
David Kimutai	Rotich	19/05/1969	Kenya	20km Walk (m)	09
Lydia Chebet	Rotich	08/08/1988	Kenya	3000m SC (w)	0
Aaron	Rouge-Serret	21/01/1988	Australia	4x100m (m)	09
Shannon	Rowbury	19/09/1984	United States	1500m (w)	09
Ivana	Rožhman	14/07/1989	FYR Macedonia	100m (w)	09
Yuliya	Ruban	06/10/1983	Ukraine	Marathon (w)	0
Anneliese	Rubie	22/04/1992	Australia	4x400m (w)	0
Giorgio	Rubino	15/04/1986	Italy	20km Walk (m)	07 09
David Lekuta	Rudisha	17/12/1988	Kenya	800m (m)	09
Diego	Ruiz	05/02/1982	Spain	1500m (m)	09
Sylvain	Rukundo	20/12/1988	Rwanda	5000m (m)	0
Galen	Rupp	08/05/1986	United States	5000m (m), 10000m (m)	07 09
Natalia	Rusakova	12/12/1979	Russia	4x100m (w)	07 09
Yuliya	Rusanova	03/07/1986	Russia	800m (w)	0
Scott	Russell	16/01/1979	Canada	Javelin (m)	01 03 05 07
Greg	Rutherford	17/11/1986	Great Britain	Long Jump (m)	07 09
Adam	Rutter	24/12/1986	Australia	20km Walk (m)	09
Antti	Ruuskanen	21/02/1984	Finland	Javelin (m)	07 09
Deirdre	Ryan	01/06/1982	Ireland	High Jump (w)	09
Viktoriya	Rybalko	26/10/1982	Ukraine	Long Jump (w)	07 09
Mariya	Ryemyen	02/08/1987	Ukraine	200m (w), 4x100m (w)	09
Olga	Rypakova	30/11/1984	Kazakhstan	Triple Jump (w)	07 09
Jefferson	Sabino	04/11/1982	Brazil	Triple Jump (m)	07 09
Grit	Šadeiko	29/07/1989	Estonia	Heptathlon	0
Hitoshi	Saito	09/10/1986	Japan	200m (m), 4x100m (m)	09
Pinar	Saka	05/11/1985	Turkey	400m (w), 4x400m (w)	0
Rytis	Sakalauskas	27/06/1987	Lithuania	100m (m)	0
Irving	Saladino	23/01/1983	Panama	Long Jump (m)	05 07 09
Olha	Saladuha	04/06/1983	Ukraine	Triple Jump (w)	07
Silvia	Salis	17/09/1985	Italy	Hammer (w)	09
Kristina	Saltanovic	20/02/1975	Lithuania	20km Walk (w)	99 03 05 09
Mohammad	Samimi	29/03/1987	Iran	Discus (m)	0
Abdou Razack Rabo	Samma	07/09/1983	Niger	400m (m)	0
Jamile	Samuel	24/04/1992	Netherlands	4x100m (w)	0
Dani	Samuels	26/05/1988	Australia	Discus (w)	07 09
Jessica	Samuelsson	14/03/1985	Sweden	Heptathlon	07 09
Ruben	Sanca	13/12/1986	Cape Verde	Marathon (m)	0
Eder	Sánchez	21/05/1986	Mexico	20km Walk (m)	05 07 09
Felix	Sánchez	30/08/1977	Dominica	400m Hurdles (m)	01 03 05 07 09
Maria Guadalupe	Sánchez	03/01/1977	Mexico	20km Walk (w)	01
Nicola	Sanders	23/06/1982	Great Britain	400m (w), 4x400m (w)	05 07 09
Leevan	Sands	30/04/1985	Bahamas	Triple Jump (m)	07 09
Suwaibou	Sanneh	30/10/1990	Gambia	100m (m)	09
Rosângela	Santos	03/12/1981	Brazil	4x100m (w)	03 05 07 09
Evodie-Lydie	Saramandji	03/08/1983	Central African Republic	400m (w)	09
Caitlin	Sargent	14/06/1992	Australia	4x400m (w)	0
Patricia	Sarrapio	16/11/1982	Spain	Triple Jump (w)	07
Yuki	Sato	14/09/1982	Japan	10000m (m)	09
Yargeris	Savigne	13/11/1984	Cuba	Triple Jump (w)	05 07 09

Forenames	Surname	Born	Country	Events	Prev Apps
Mariya	Savinova	13/08/1985	Russia	800m (w)	09
Elizabeta	Savlinis	08/04/1987	Russia	200m (w), 4x100m (w)	0
Daichi	Sawano	16/09/1980	Japan	Pole Vault (m)	03 05 07 09
Mike	Sayenko	12/07/1984	United States	Marathon (m)	0
Goldie	Sayers	16/07/1982	Great Britain	Javelin (w)	05 07 09
Alex	Schaf	28/04/1987	Germany	4x100m (m)	0
Fabrizio	Schembri	27/01/1981	Italy	Triple Jump (m)	09
Reto	Schenkel	28/04/1988	Switzerland	200m (m), 4x100m (m)	09
Zuzana	Schindlerová	25/04/1987	Czech Republic	20km Walk (w)	09
Dafne	Schippers	15/06/1992	Netherlands	200m (w), 4x100m (w)	0
Anna Katharina	Schmid	02/12/1989	Switzerland	Pole Vault (w)	07
Alice	Schmidt	03/10/1981	United States	800m (w)	05 07
Lena	Schmidt	04/08/1989	Germany	4x400m (w)	0
Marco	Schmidt	05/09/1983	Germany	Shot Put (m)	09
Marc	Schneeberger	05/07/1981	Switzerland	200m (m), 4x100m (m)	07 09
Thomas	Schneider	07/11/1988	Germany	4x400m (m)	0
Beate	Schrott	15/04/1988	Austria	100m Hurdles (w)	0
Christina	Schwanitz	24/12/1985	Germany	Shot Put (w)	05 09
Jillian	Schwartz	19/09/1979	Israel	Pole Vault (w)	03 05 07 09
Lilli	Schwarzkopf	28/08/1983	Germany	Heptathlon	05 07 09
Alex	Schwazer	26/12/1984	Italy	20km Walk (m)	05 07 09
Jeremy	Scott	01/05/1981	United States	Pole Vault (m)	09
Sharolyn	Scott	27/10/1983	Costa Rica	400m Hurdles (w)	09
Salim	Sdiri	26/10/1978	France	Long Jump (m)	03 05 09
Rachel Lavallée	Seaman	14/01/1986	Canada	20km Walk (w)	09
Hassanine	Sebei	21/01/1984	Tunisia	20km Walk (m)	07 09
Roman	Šebrle	26/11/1974	Czech Republic	Decathlon	99 01 03 05 07 09
Melanie	Seeger	08/01/1977	Germany	20km Walk (w)	01 03 05 07
Kai	Selvon	13/04/1992	Trinidad & Tobago	200m (w), 4x100m (w)	0
Yevhen	Semenenko	17/07/1984	Ukraine	Triple Jump (m)	09
Andriy	Semenov	27/06/1982	Ukraine	Shot Put (m)	09
Caster	Semenya	07/01/1991	South Africa	800m (w)	09
Zinaida	Sendriute	20/12/1984	Lithuania	Discus (w)	09
Amy	Séné	06/04/1986	Senegal	Hammer (w)	0
Hyeokje	Seong	09/10/1990	South Korea	4x400m (m)	0
Amr Ibrahim Mostafa	Seoud	10/06/1986	Egypt	200m (m)	07 09
Hadi	Sepehrzad	19/01/1983	Iran	Decathlon	0
Pako	Seribe	07/04/1991	Botswana	400m (m)	0
Ola	Sesay	30/05/1979	Sierra Leone	Long Jump (w)	09
Marija	Šestak	17/04/1979	Slovenia	Triple Jump (w)	07 09
Perri	Shakes-Drayton	21/12/1988	Great Britain	400m Hurdles (w), 4x400m (w)	09
James	Shane	18/12/1989	Great Britain	1500m (m)	0
William	Sharman	12/09/1984	Great Britain	110m Hurdles (m)	09
Amailya	Sharoyan	19/06/1988	Armenia	400m Hurdles (w)	0
Mohammed	Shaween	15/02/1986	Saudi Arabia	1500m (m)	07 09
Yury	Shayunou	22/10/1987	Belarus	Hammer (m)	09
Anzhelika	Shevchenko	29/10/1987	Ukraine	1500m (w)	0
Dongpeng	Shi	06/01/1982	China	110m Hurdles (m)	03 05 07 09
Svetlana	Shkolina	09/03/1986	Russia	High Jump (w)	09
Svitlana	Shmidt	20/03/1990	Ukraine	3000m SC (w)	0
Fanny	Shonobi	08/04/1987	Gambia	200m (w)	0
Sergey	Shubenkov	10/10/1990	Russia	110m Hurdles (m)	0
Bilisuma	Shugi	19/07/1989	Brunei	5000m (m)	0
Genzeb	Shumi	29/01/1991	Brunei	1500m (w)	0
Olena	Shumkina	24/01/1988	Ukraine	20km Walk (w)	0
Aleksandr	Shustov	29/06/1984	Russia	High Jump (m)	0
Veronika	Shutkova	26/05/1986	Belarus	Long Jump (w)	0
Anastasiya	Shvedova	03/05/1979	Belarus	Pole Vault (w)	0
Tianfeng	Si	17/06/1984	China	50km Walk (m)	0
Maksim	Sidorov	13/05/1986	Russia	Shot Put (m)	09
Sileshi	Sihine	09/05/1983	Ethiopia	10000m (m)	03 05 07 09
Rafal	Sikora	17/02/1987	Poland	50km Walk (m)	0
Ana Claudia	Silva	06/11/1988	Brazil	200m (w), 4x100m (w)	0
Andrés	Silva	27/03/1986	Uruguay	400m Hurdles (w)	07 09
Rui	Silva	03/08/1977	Portugal	5000m (m), 10000m (m)	01 03 05 07 09
Vânia	Silva	08/06/1980	Portugal	Hammer (w)	01 03 07 09

Forenames	Surname	Born	Country	Events	Prev Apps
Yarisley	Silva	01/06/1987	Cuba	Pole Vault (w)	0
Jennifer	Simpson	10/02/1984	United States	1500m (w)	07 09
Margaret	Simpson	10/02/1984	Ghana	Heptathlon	01 03 05 07
Sherone	Simpson	10/02/1984	Jamaica	200m (w), 4x100m (w)	05
Ambwene	Simukonda	23/03/1984	Malawi	400m (w)	0
Sang-Min	Sin	27/06/1986	South Korea	1500m (m)	0
Kenia	Sinclair	14/07/1980	Jamaica	800m (w)	05 07 09
Gurmeet	Singh	01/07/1985	India	20km Walk (m)	0
Om Prakash	Singh	11/01/1987	India	Shot Put (m)	0
Eelco	Sintnicolaas	07/04/1987	Netherlands	Decathlon	09
Zigismunds	Sirmais	06/05/1992	Latvia	Javelin (m)	0
Lucie	Škrobáková	04/01/1982	Czech Republic	100m Hurdles (w)	05 09
Austra	Skujyte	12/08/1979	Lithuania	Heptathlon	01 03 05 07 09
Elena	Slesarenko	28/02/1982	Russia	High Jump (w)	05 07 09
Gavin	Smellie	26/06/1986	Canada	4x100m (m)	09
Maurice	Smith	28/09/1980	Jamaica	Decathlon	05 07 09
Nivea	Smith	18/02/1990	Bahamas	200m (w), 4x100m (w)	0
Rutger	Smith	09/07/1981	Netherlands	Discus (m)	03 05 07
Tyrone	Smith	07/08/1984	Bermuda	Long Jump (m)	09
Amanda	Smock	27/04/1982	United States	Triple Jump (w)	0
Jason	Smyth	04/07/1987	Ireland	100m (m)	0
Aleksey	Sokolov	14/11/1979	Russia	Marathon (m)	0
Vera	Sokolova	08/06/1987	Russia	20km Walk (w)	09
Igors	Sokolovs	17/08/1974	Latvia	Hammer (m)	07 09
Olexiy	Sokyrskiyy	16/03/1985	Ukraine	Hammer (m)	09
Jarrin	Solomon	11/01/1986	Trinidad & Tobago	4x400m (m)	0
Shalonda	Solomon	19/12/1985	United States	200m (w), 4x100m (w)	0
Steven	Solomon	16/05/1993	Australia	4x400m (m)	0
Bram	Som	20/12/1980	Netherlands	800m (m)	01 03 07 09
Kyeong-Mi	Son	09/02/1990	South Korea	400m Hurdles (w)	0
Anastasiya	Soprunova	14/01/1986	Kazakhstan	100m Hurdles (w)	0
Arnold	Sorina	06/01/1988	Vanuatu	400m (m)	09
Rondel	Sorrillo	21/01/1986	Trinidad & Tobago	200m (m)	09
Nafissa	Souleymane	18/11/1992	Niger	100m (w)	0
Ndeye Fatou	Soumah	06/04/1986	Senegal	400m (w)	0
Myriam	Soumaré	29/10/1986	France	200m (w), 4x100m (w)	09
Joelma	Sousa	13/07/1984	Brazil	4x400m (w)	0
Maria Enrica	Spacca	20/03/1986	Italy	4x400m (w)	09
Raul	Spank	13/07/1988	Germany	High Jump (m)	09
Ivana	Španovic	10/05/1990	Serbia	Long Jump (w)	0
Indira	Spence	08/09/1986	Jamaica	100m Hurdles (w)	0
Lansford	Spence	15/12/1982	Jamaica	4x400m (m)	05
Kaliese	Spencer	06/05/1987	Jamaica	400m Hurdles (w)	07 09
Levern	Spencer	23/06/1984	St Lucia	High Jump (w)	05 07 09
Silke	Spiegelburg	17/03/1986	Germany	Pole Vault (w)	07 09
Barbora	Špotáková	30/06/1981	Czech Republic	Javelin (w)	05 07 09
Ellen	Sprunger	05/08/1986	Switzerland	4x100m (w)	0
Léa	Sprunger	05/03/1990	Switzerland	4x100m (w)	0
Ben	St.Lawrence	07/11/1981	Australia	5000m (m)	0
Linda	Stahl	02/10/1985	Germany	Javelin (w)	07 09
Vania	Stambolova	28/11/1983	Bulgaria	400m Hurdles (w)	05 09
Augusto	Stanley	03/08/1987	Paraguay	400m (m)	0
Raivydas	Stanys	03/02/1987	Lithuania	High Jump (m)	0
Dmitry	Starodubtsev	03/01/1986	Russia	Pole Vault (m)	0
Heather	Steacy	14/04/1988	Canada	Hammer (w)	0
James	Steacy	29/05/1984	Canada	Hammer (m)	07
Claudia	Stef	25/02/1978	Romania	20km Walk (w)	99 03 05 07 09
Pawel	Stempel	06/08/1987	Poland	4x100m (m)	0
Kateryna	Stetsenko	22/01/1982	Ukraine	Marathon (w)	0
Sarah	Stevens-Walker	02/04/1986	United States	Shot Put (w)	07
Kerron	Stewart	16/04/1984	Jamaica	200m (w), 4x100m (w)	07 09
Nelson	Stone	02/06/1984	Papua New Guinea	400m (m)	09
David	Storl	27/07/1990	Germany	Shot Put (m)	09
Anthonique	Strachan	22/08/1993	Bahamas	200m (w), 4x100m (w)	0
Anthonique	Strachan	22/08/1993	Bahamas	200m (w)	0
Richard	Strachan	18/11/1986	Great Britain	4x400m (m)	0

Forenames	Surname	Born	Country	Events	Prev Apps
Martina	Strutz	04/11/1981	Germany	Pole Vault (w)	0
Bianca	Stuart	17/05/1988	Bahamas	Long Jump (w)	0
Lisa Christina	Stublic	18/05/1984	Croatia	Marathon (w)	0
Hrystyna	Stuy	03/02/1988	Ukraine	200m (w), 4x100m (w)	09
Vita	Styopina	21/02/1976	Ukraine	High Jump (w)	03 05
Bingtian	Su	29/08/1989	China	4x100m (m)	0
Xiongfeng	Su	21/03/1987	China	Long Jump (m)	0
Leonel	Suárez	01/09/1987	Cuba	Decathlon	09
Grzegorz	Sudol	28/08/1978	Poland	50km Walk (m)	03 05 07 09
Kayo	Sugihara	24/02/1983	Japan	5000m (w), 10000m (w)	07
Mahau	Suguimati	13/11/1984	Brazil	400m Hurdles (m)	0
Jennifer	Suhr	05/02/1982	United States	Pole Vault (w)	07 09
Eunice Jepkoech	Sum	10/04/1988	Kenya	800m (w)	0
Yawei	Sun	13/01/1985	China	100m Hurdles (w)	07 09
Tadas	Šuškevicius	22/05/1985	Lithuania	50km Walk (m)	09
Jana	Sussmann	12/10/1990	Germany	3000m SC (w)	0
Tina	Šutej	07/11/1988	Slovenia	Pole Vault (w)	0
Sompote	Suwannarangsri	01/06/1985	Thailand	4x100m (m)	0
Yusuke	Suzuki	02/01/1988	Japan	20km Walk (m)	09
Konstantin	Svechkar	17/07/1984	Russia	4x400m (m)	09
Valeriy	Sviatokha	20/07/1981	Belarus	Hammer (m)	0
Nick	Symmonds	30/12/1983	United States	800m (m)	07 09
Olesya	Syreva	25/11/1983	Russia	1500m (w)	0
Zersenay	Tadese	08/02/1982	Eritrea	10000m (m)	03 05 07 09
Patricia	Taea	25/05/1993	Cook Islands	100m (w)	0
Bouabdellah	Tahri	20/12/1978	France	3000m SC (m)	99 01 03 05 07 09
Tomás	Tajadura	25/06/1985	Spain	3000m SC (m)	0
Momoko	Takahashi	16/11/1988	Japan	4x100m (w)	07 09
Shinji	Takahira	18/07/1984	Japan	200m (m), 4x100m (m)	05 07 09
Kei	Takase	25/11/1988	Japan	4x400m (m)	0
Belinda	Talakai	16/03/1994	Tonga	100m (w)	0
Mohamed Ghossem	Taled	31/12/1992	Mauritania	100m (m)	0
Claire	Tallent	06/07/1981	Australia	20km Walk (w)	09
Jared	Tallent	17/10/1984	Australia	20km Walk (m), 50km Walk (m)	05 07 09
Susan	Tama	22/01/1984	Vanuatu	100m (w)	03
Sonata	Tamošaityte	28/06/1987	Lithuania	100m Hurdles (w)	09
Jian	Tan	20/01/1988	China	Discus (w)	0
Xiaoyin	Tang	29/04/1985	China	4x400m (w)	0
Takayuki	Tanii	14/02/1983	Japan	50km Walk (m)	05 07 09
Paul Kipngetich	Tanui	22/12/1990	Kenya	10000m (m)	0
Yujia	Tao	16/02/1987	China	4x100m (w)	0
Dmitri	Tarabin	29/10/1991	Russia	Javelin (m)	0
Yuliya	Tarasova	13/03/1986	Uzbekistan	Long Jump (w)	09
Jeneba	Tarmoh	27/09/1989	United States	200m (w)	0
Rinat	Tarzumanov	26/03/1984	Uzbekistan	Javelin (m)	0
Hanna	Tashpulatava	21/10/1987	Belarus	4x400m (w)	0
Joycelyn	Taurikeni	26/01/1988	Solomon Islands	100m (w)	0
Maria Eleonor	Tavares	21/03/1986	Portugal	Pole Vault (w)	09
Angelo	Taylor	29/12/1978	United States	400m Hurdles (m), 4x400m (m)	01 07 09
Christian	Taylor	18/06/1990	United States	Triple Jump (m)	0
Mike	Tebulo	05/06/1985	Malawi	Marathon (m)	0
Matthew	Tegenkamp	19/01/1982	United States	10000m (m)	07 09
Rodman	Teltull	29/01/1994	Palau	100m (m)	0
Sief El Islem	Temacini	05/03/1988	Algeria	Triple Jump (m)	0
Hédi	Teraoui	10/11/1989	Tunisia	20km Walk (m)	0
Josephine	Terlecki	17/02/1986	Germany	Shot Put (w)	0
Michael	Tesfay	23/09/1976	Eritrea	Marathon (m)	0
Tumelo	Thagane	03/07/1984	South Africa	Triple Jump (m)	0
Chandra Kala	Thapa	02/09/1980	Nepal	100m (w)	03
Tilak Ram	Tharu	10/04/1993	Nepal	100m (m)	0
Jurgen	Themen	26/10/1985	Surinam	100m (m)	07 09
Wenda	Theron	06/04/1988	South Africa	400m Hurdles (w)	0
Zaw Win	Thet	01/03/1991	Myanmar	800m (m)	09
Sandrine	Thiébaud-Kangni	21/04/1976	Togo	400m (w)	01 03 05 07
Donald	Thomas	01/07/1984	Bahamas	High Jump (m)	07 09
Dwight	Thomas	23/09/1980	Jamaica	110m Hurdles (m)	01 03 05 09

Forenames	Surname	Born	Country	Events	Prev Apps
Tristan	Thomas	23/05/1986	Australia	4x400m (m)	09
Richard	Thompson	07/06/1985	Trinidad & Tobago	100m (m), 4x100m (m)	07 09
Andreas	Thorkildsen	01/04/1982	Norway	Javelin (m)	01 03 05 07 09
Aretha	Thurmond	14/08/1976	United States	Discus (w)	99 03 05 09
Okilani	Tinilau	02/01/1989	Tuvalu	100m (m)	09
Teddy	Tinmar	30/05/1987	France	4x100m (m)	0
Hanna	Titimets	05/03/1989	Ukraine	400m Hurdles (w)	09
Nataliya	Tobias	22/11/1980	Ukraine	1500m (w)	0
Dragana	Tomaševic	04/06/1982	Serbia	Discus (w)	05 07 09
Stine Meland	Tomb	27/06/1986	Norway	400m Hurdles (w)	0
Marina	Tomic	30/04/1983	Slovenia	100m Hurdles (w)	0
Christopher	Tomlinson	15/09/1981	Great Britain	Long Jump (m)	03 05 07 09
Maryam	Toosi	05/12/1988	Iran	200m (w)	0
Biljana	Topic	12/03/1971	Serbia	Triple Jump (w)	99 03 05 07 09
Kristinn	Torfason	31/08/1984	Iceland	Long Jump (m)	0
Judith	Toribio	09/01/1982	Peru	Marathon (w)	0
Michel	Tornéus	26/05/1986	Sweden	Long Jump (m)	09
Jamaal	Torrance	20/07/1983	United States	400m (m), 4x400m (m)	0
Marestella	Torres	20/02/1981	Philippines	Long Jump (m)	05 07 09
Osku	Torro	21/08/1979	Finland	High Jump (m)	0
Matej	Tóth	10/02/1983	Slovakia	20km Walk (m), 50km Walk (m)	05 07 09
Moudjib	Toyb	14/10/1988	Comoros	100m (m)	0
Chaima	Trabelsi	11/03/1982	Tunisia	20km Walk (w)	09
Ristananna	Tracey	09/05/1992	Jamaica	400m Hurdles (w)	0
Stephanie Brown	Trafton	01/12/1979	United States	Discus (w)	07 09
Emma Green	Tregaro	08/12/1984	Sweden	High Jump (w)	05 07 09
Pavel	Trenikhin	24/03/1986	Russia	400m (m), 4x400m (m)	0
Meng-Lin	Tsai	21/03/1978	Chinese Taipei	4x100m (m)	0
Loúis	Tsátoumas	12/02/1982	Greece	Long Jump (m)	03 05 09
Cathleen	Tschirch	23/07/1979	Germany	4x100m (w)	07 09
Chi Ho	Tsui	17/02/1990	Hong Kong	100m (m)	09
Ruslana	Tsykhotska	23/03/1986	Ukraine	Triple Jump (w)	0
Michael	Tumi	12/02/1990	Italy	4x100m (m)	0
David Barmasai	Tumo	01/01/1989	Kenya	Marathon (m)	0
Dire	Tune	19/06/1985	Ethiopia	Marathon (w)	05 07 09
Andrew	Turner	19/09/1980	Great Britain	110m Hurdles (m)	07 09
Laura	Turner	12/08/1982	Great Britain	4x100m (w)	07
Sogelau	Tuvalu	05/06/1994	American Samoa	100m (m)	0
Karolina	Tyminska	04/10/1984	Poland	Heptathlon	07 09
Morgan	Uceny	10/03/1985	United States	1500m (w)	0
Ivan	Ukhov	04/04/1986	Russia	High Jump (m)	09
Steffen	Uliczka	17/07/1984	Germany	3000m SC (m)	09
Tobias	Unger	10/07/1979	Germany	4x100m (m)	01 03 05 09
Lisa	Urech	27/07/1989	Switzerland	100m Hurdles (w)	09
Keisuke	Ushiro	24/07/1986	Japan	Decathlon	0
Binnaz	Uslu	12/03/1985	Turkey	3000m SC (w)	05
Ilona	Usovich	14/11/1982	Belarus	4x400m (w)	05 07
Sviatlana	Usovich	14/10/1980	Belarus	800m (w), 4x400m (w)	03 05 07
Jakub	Vadlejch	10/10/1990	Czech Republic	Javelin (m)	0
Thomas	van der Plaetsen	24/12/1990	Belgium	Decathlon	0
Ramona	van der Vloot	31/12/1994	Surinam	200m (w)	0
Patrick	van Luijk	17/09/1984	Netherlands	4x100m (m)	09
Annerien	van Schalkwyk	06/02/1979	South Africa	Marathon (w)	0
Charlotte	Van Veenendaal	18/06/1988	Australia	4x100m (w)	0
Louis	van Zyl	20/07/1985	South Africa	400m Hurdles (m), 4x100m (m)	05 07 09
Thomas	Vandy	29/04/1989	Sierra Leone	800m (m)	0
Roland	Varga	22/10/1977	Croatia	Discus (m)	01 03 05
Mailín	Vargas	12/07/1977	Cuba	Shot Put (w)	05 07 09
María	Vasco	26/12/1975	Spain	20km Walk (w)	99 01 03 05 07 09
Vadims	Vasilevskis	05/01/1982	Latvia	Javelin (m)	05 07 09
Kadene	Vassell	29/01/1989	Netherlands	4x100m (w)	0
Kseniya	Vdovina	19/04/1987	Russia	4x400m (w)	0
Dana	Veldáková	03/06/1981	Slovakia	Triple Jump (w)	07 09
Carlos	Véliz	12/08/1987	Cuba	Shot Put (m)	09
Teddy	Venel	16/03/1985	France	4x400m (m)	09
Venelina	Veneva-Mateeva	13/06/1974	Bulgaria	High Jump (w)	99 01 03 05 09

Forenames	Surname	Born	Country	Events	Prev Apps
Vítezslav	Veselý	27/02/1983	Czech Republic	Javelin (m)	09
Maggie	Vessey	23/12/1981	United States	800m (w)	09
Sandro	Viana	26/03/1977	Brazil	200m (m), 4x100m (m)	07 09
Jimmy	Vicaut	27/02/1992	France	100m (m), 4x100m (m)	0
Shane	Victor	29/12/1988	South Africa	4x400m (m)	0
Jean Antonio	Vieillesse	24/01/1986	Mauritius	400m Hurdles (m)	0
João	Vieira	20/02/1976	Portugal	20km Walk (m)	07 09
Sunette	Viljoen	06/10/1983	South Africa	Javelin (w)	03 09
Pablo	Villalobos	20/04/1987	Spain	Marathon (m)	09
Eduar	Villanueva	29/12/1984	Venezuela	1500m (m)	07 09
Paulo	Villar	28/07/1978	Colombia	110m Hurdles (m)	01 05 09
Mary Jane	Vincent	25/01/1988	Mauritius	200m (w)	0
Brigita	Virbalyté	01/02/1985	Lithuania	20km Walk (w)	09
Borja	Vivas	26/05/1984	Spain	Shot Put (m)	09
Nicola	Vizzoni	04/11/1973	Italy	Hammer (m)	99 01 03 05 07 09
Blanka	Vlašic	08/11/1983	Croatia	High Jump (w)	01 03 05 07 09
Andreas	Vojta	09/06/1989	Austria	1500m (m)	0
Boudsadee	Vongdala	19/01/1994	Laos	100m (w)	0
Ingmar	Vos	28/05/1986	Netherlands	Decathlon	09
Marija	Vukovic	21/01/1992	Montenegro	High Jump (w)	0
Marion	Wagner	01/02/1978	Germany	4x100m (w)	99 01 09
Melaine	Walker	01/03/1983	Jamaica	400m Hurdles (w)	01 05 07 09
Wilbert	Walker	07/01/1985	Jamaica	Triple Jump (m)	0
Gabriel	Wallin	14/10/1981	Sweden	Javelin (m)	05 07
Hao	Wang	16/08/1989	China	20km Walk (m)	09
Jiali	Wang	01/02/1986	China	Marathon (w)	09
Wen-Tang	Wang	11/07/1987	Chinese Taipei	4x100m (m)	0
Xuequin	Wang	01/01/1991	China	Marathon (w)	0
Zhen	Wang	24/08/1991	China	20km Walk (m)	0
Sangay	Wangchuk	01/01/1983	Bhutan	Marathon (m)	09
Damian	Warner	04/10/1989	Canada	Decathlon	0
Justyn	Warner	28/06/1987	Canada	4x100m (m)	0
Justyn	Warner	28/06/1987	Canada	100m (m)	0
Kazuya	Watanabe	06/06/1983	Japan	5000m (m)	09
Mitchell	Watt	25/03/1988	Australia	Long Jump (m)	09
David	Webb	03/10/1976	Great Britain	Marathon (m)	05 09
Yongli	Wei	11/10/1991	China	4x100m (w)	0
Eloise	Wellings	09/11/1982	Australia	10000m (w)	0
Kellie	Wells	16/07/1982	United States	100m Hurdles (w)	0
Eshetu	Wendimu	03/10/1986	Ethiopia	Marathon (m)	0
Mihter	Wendolin	03/02/1987	Federated States of Micror	100m (w)	0
Megan	West	24/08/1994	American Samoa	100m (w)	0
Andrew	Wheating	21/11/1987	United States	1500m (m)	0
Ryan	Whiting	24/11/1986	United States	Shot Put (m)	0
Rosemarie	Whyte	22/05/1980	Jamaica	400m (w), 4x400m (w)	01 03 05 07 09
Piotr	Wiaderek	05/02/1984	Poland	4x400m (m)	0
Martin	Wierig	10/06/1987	Germany	Discus (m)	0
Chaminda Indika	Wijekoon	15/09/1981	Sri Lanka	1500m (m)	0
Andrae	Williams	12/07/1983	Bahamas	4x400m (m)	05 07
Jesse	Williams	27/12/1983	United States	High Jump (m)	05 07 09
Kimberly	Williams	03/11/1988	Jamaica	Triple Jump (w)	09
LaToy	Williams	28/05/1988	Bahamas	4x400m (m)	0
Shericka	Williams	17/09/1985	Jamaica	400m (w), 4x400m (w)	05 07 09
Novlene	Williams-Mills	26/04/1982	Jamaica	400m (w), 4x400m (w)	05 07 09
Nicholas	Willis	25/04/1983	New Zealand	1500m (m)	05 07
Caitlin	Willis-Pincott	18/12/1982	Australia	4x400m (w)	09
Alex	Wilson	28/07/1986	Switzerland	4x100m (m)	0
Alex	Wilson	19/09/1990	Switzerland	200m (m)	0
Nickiesha	Wilson	28/07/1986	Jamaica	400m Hurdles (w)	07 09
Wassana	Winatho	30/06/1980	Thailand	Heptathlon	0
Shariska	Winterdal	04/08/1977	Aruba	Marathon (w)	0
Anita	Wlodarczyk	08/08/1985	Poland	Hammer (w)	09
Pawel	Wojciechowski	06/06/1989	Poland	Pole Vault (m)	0
Yu-jin	Woo	17/10/1993	South Korea	4x400m (w)	0
Nathan	Woodward	17/10/1989	Great Britain	400m Hurdles (m)	0
Bazu	Worku	15/09/1990	Ethiopia	Marathon (m)	0

Forenames	Surname	Born	Country	Events	Prev Apps
Sean	Wroe	18/03/1985	Australia	4x400m (m)	07 09
Jian	Wu	25/05/1986	China	Discus (m)	0
Sha	Wu	21/10/1987	China	Pole Vault (w)	0
Shiwei	Wu	11/02/1986	China	Marathon (m)	0
Limei	Xie	27/06/1986	China	Triple Jump (w)	07 09
Faguang	Xu	17/05/1987	China	50km Walk (m)	09
Viktoriya	Yalovtseva	04/11/1977	Kazakhstan	4x400m (w)	0
Nevin	Yanit	16/02/1986	Turkey	100m Hurdles (w)	07 09
Hanna	Yaroshchuk	24/11/1989	Ukraine	400m Hurdles (w), 4x400m (w)	0
Khalid Kamal	Yaseen	10/10/1982	Brunei	Marathon (m)	07 09
Nastassia	Yatsevich	18/01/1985	Belarus	20km Walk (w)	0
Antonina	Yefremova	19/07/1981	Ukraine	400m (w), 4x400m (w)	03 05 09
Alfred Kirwa	Yego	28/11/1986	Kenya	800m (m)	05 07 09
Foo Ee	Yeo	30/08/1986	Singapore	100m (m)	0
Ho-suah	Yeo	05/04/1987	South Korea	4x100m (m)	0
Wei-Chen	Yi	28/08/1988	Chinese Taipei	4x100m (m)	0
Junghyun	Yim	08/09/1987	South Korea	50km Walk (m)	0
Masato	Yokota	19/11/1987	Japan	800m (m)	07
Hikari	Yoshimoto	14/01/1990	Japan	10000m (w)	0
Lyudmyla	Yosypenko	24/09/1984	Ukraine	Heptathlon	09
Jason	Young	25/07/1979	United States	Discus (m)	09
Rabah	Yousif	11/12/1986	Sudan	400m (m)	09
Ye-Hwan	Yun	28/05/1972	South Korea	High Jump (m)	01 09
Denys	Yurchenko	27/01/1978	Ukraine	Pole Vault (m)	03 05 07
Rachel	Yurkovich	10/10/1986	United States	Javelin (w)	09
Yulyana	Yushchanka	14/08/1984	Belarus	4x400m (w)	0
Ksenia	Zadorina	02/03/1987	Russia	4x400m (w)	0
Yelena	Zadorozhnaya	03/12/1977	Russia	5000m (w)	01 03 05
Anne	Zagre	13/03/1990	Belgium	100m Hurdles (w)	09
Aziz	Zakari	02/09/1976	Ghana	100m (m), 4x100m (m)	01 03 05 09
Yuliya	Zaripova	26/04/1986	Russia	3000m SC (w)	09
Olha	Zavhorodnya	06/01/1983	Ukraine	4x400m (w)	0
Olga	Zaytseva	10/11/1984	Russia	Long Jump (w)	09
Jessica	Zelinka	03/09/1981	Canada	Heptathlon	05
Zohar	Zemiro	01/01/1977	Israel	Marathon (m)	0
Omar	Zepeda	08/06/1977	Mexico	50km Walk (m)	01 05 07 09
Guowei	Zhang	04/06/1991	China	High Jump (m)	0
Wenxiu	Zhang	22/03/1986	China	Hammer (w)	01 03 05 07 09
Xingjuan	Zheng	20/03/1989	China	High Jump (w)	05 07
Zhihui	Zheng	20/09/1991	China	4x400m (w)	0
Xiaolin	Zhu	05/09/1988	China	Marathon (w)	09
Moacir	Zimmermann	30/12/1983	Brazil	20km Walk (m)	09
Szymon	Ziółkowski	01/07/1976	Poland	Hammer (m)	99 01 05 07 09
Nataliya	Zolotukhina	04/01/1985	Ukraine	Hammer (w)	05 07 09
Vincent	Zouaoui-Dandrieux	12/10/1980	France	3000m SC (m)	07 09
Viktoriya	Zyabkina	04/09/1992	Kazakhstan	200m (w)	0